£19.20

THE KANGAROO KEEPERS

THE
KANGAROO
KEEPERS

Edited by H.J. Lavery

University of Queensland Press

ST LUCIA • LONDON • NEW YORK

First published 1985 by University of Queensland Press
Box 42, St Lucia, Queensland, Australia

Typeset by University of Queensland Press
Designed by Paul Rendle
Printed in Australia by Globe Press, Melbourne

Distributed in the UK and Europe by University of Queensland Press
Dunhams Lane, Letchworth, Herts. SG6 1LF England

Distributed in the USA and Canada by University of Queensland Press
5 South Union Street, Lawrence, Mass. 01843 USA

Cataloguing in Publication Data

National Library of Australia

The Kangaroo keepers.

  Bibliography.
  Includes index.

  1. Kangaroos – Research – Queensland. 2. Wildlife
  conservation – Queensland. I. Lavery, H.J. (Hugh
John), 1935– .

599.2'09943

British Library (data available)

Library of Congress

The Kangaroo keepers.

  Bibliography: p.
  Includes index.
  1. Kangaroos. 2. Wildlife conservation – Australia.
  3. Mammals – Australia. I. Lavery, H.J.
  QL737.M35K36 1985 333.95'9 85-1426

ISBN 0 7022 1875 8

To McD

The Kangaroo

Kangaroo, Kangaroo!
Thou Spirit of Australia,
That redeems from utter failure,
From perfect desolation,
And warrants the creation
Of this fifth part of the Earth . . .

When sooty swans are once more rare,
And duck-moles the Museum's care,
Be still the glory of this land,
Happiest Work of finest Hand!

Barron Field (1819)

[Dr W. A. McDougall, D.Sc., Queensland Government Entomologist, 1949–71]

Contents

Preamble — exploitation of native faunas — wildlife management material available — historic interest in kangaroos — variety of macropodids — conservation — objectives of book

Origin of marsupials — fossil marsupials and fossil kangaroos — diversity of genera in the Family Macropodidae — list of species — conservation vs preservation — field identification including habits and habitat appearance — incipient species — hybrids and colour variants

Change and conservation priorities — pathways of national park management and wildlife management — extinction of species — saving the bridled nailtail-wallaby — history of the species — developing a management programme — singular attention demanded by bizarre species, "marginally distributed" species, "apparently extinct" species, isolated populations and little known species and zoo animals — the problems of selection

Illustrations

Figures

Tables

Contributors

Dr Hugh Lavery is assistant director, Queensland National Parks and Wildlife Service, Brisbane. He is a former president of the Royal Society of Queensland, Churchill Fellow, executive producer with the Australian Broadcasting Commission, and chairman of the State Zoo (QZOO) Study Team; he is presently also deputy chairman of the Raine Island Corporation and executive producer of a major documentary film and book on the place of the arts in nature conservation, funded by the Queensland Film Corporation and the Australian Film Commission.

Peter Amos, senior ranger, Queensland National Parks and Wildlife Service, has compiled over a number of years all of the statistics relating to the kangaroo industry. His research work has been devoted to the biology of the long-nosed potoroo.

Dr Martin Denny, formerly a zoologist with Queensland National Parks and Wildlife Service stationed in the far inland, has published extensively on the ecology, physiology and history of the kangaroos of the arid country. He is presently principal of Mount King Ecological Consultants, based in Sydney.

Peter Johnson is a chief ranger, Queensland National Parks and Wildlife Service. He has been concerned for many years with the life histories and the husbandry in captivity of the less well-known species of kangaroos, about which he has published many scientific articles.

Dr Tom Kirkpatrick is chief research officer, Queensland National Parks and Wildlife Service, and has devoted his professional career to the study of kangaroos about which he is a leading authority. He has been the long-term Queensland representative on the Australian Council of Nature Conservation Ministers' (CONCOM) working groups on kangaroo management and on endangered species.

Cathy Nance is a statistician employed by Queensland National Parks and Wildlife Service under continuing prestigious grants from the Reserve Bank of Australia (Rural Credits Development Fund) to plan, computerize and implement simulation models of kangaroo populations.

Peter Tierney, management officer, Queensland National Parks and Wildlife Service, has been employed as a management officer in central Queensland since "Taunton" was acquired to conserve the last habitat of the bridled nailtail-wallaby.

Photographer

Damian McGreevy is a chief ranger, Queensland National Parks and Wildlife Service; he has a wide interest in communication of natural history and its scientific study to the public, with particular emphasis on photography, and has trained at the BBC Natural History Unit in England for this.

Artist

Ruth Berry is a freelance artist who has worked on projects especially in inland Australia for Queensland National Parks and Wildlife Service, the Australian Broadcasting Commission, and the Queensland Education Department.

Forewords

1 An international view

In the eyes of the world, Australia is inseparable from the kangaroo. Some Australians may sometimes wish this weren't so — whoever does live in perfect comfort with a public image? — but in fact the country could hardly have done better. Usually animal symbols are chosen, as in arranged marriages, by some regime of the day with a particular theme to project and only a passing regard for natural appropriateness, so that we most often end up with forbidding predators — lions, bears, eagles . . .

But Australia got the kangaroo because it was there and nowhere else and, once heard of, was unforgettable. As a trademark, it is a public relations godsend — the engaging wild animal with its big eyes, its humanish stance and size, and its equally engaging joey perched in its pouch. It is on everyone's childhood list of animal favourites and, abstracted and stuffed, it is in all of the world's toy shops. Like it or not, the kangaroo is the first thing the mind's eye calls to view whenever this faraway, exotic, appealing island continent is mentioned.

Small wonder, then, that people in other countries are shocked and the Australian international image is shaken when word gets out that kangaroos are being killed in their millions and exported to us as shoes and dog food. To the world's press, it is an "ecology" scandal surpassed only by sealing and whaling, and is on a par, roughly, with the Japanese dolphin slaughter. People demonstrate to "save" the kangaroo. Legislators are flooded with demands for various kinds of trade bans and sanctions, and sometimes they comply.

Of course, all these other countries have their own agricultural pests — and each deals with them in its own peculiar unmerciful way — but by and large these are not also national symbols and nursery bywords. When animal lovers everywhere, even in Australian cities, are up in arms about a practice that the Australian farmer must see as necessary and routine, the public relations blessing probably begins to look more like a curse, and in defending themselves farmers might just be tempted to exaggerate the kangaroo menace, if only to make themselves heard above the outcry.

But *if* they are exaggerating, by how much? Are kangaroos – and here we are referring mainly to the three large species, the ones that are most commonly shot – in any real danger of extinction, or has the creation of so much pasture out of scrub actually benefited the animals more than the control programmes have harmed them? Has the fact that the kangaroos are used commercially – at first sight a simple matter of not wasting a resource – become a focus of vested interests whose concern may outweigh the farmer's? Should shooting be stopped in times of drought at least, or is drought only a natural control on both populations and shooting? How many kangaroos are there anyway, and where are they?

As usual in this kind of controversy, the two sides have dug in, and their arguments, which at best were never based on the soundest of facts (because they have not always been available), have hardened into lines. But the only honest answer to most of the above questions has been "no one knows", and the only way of finding out is through years of painstaking data gathering, in conditions and over terrain the difficulty and size of which most foreigners can only guess at.

Just how arduous this has been is evident in the following account. But it is heartening to know that the job is being done, and done correctly, and the reports here may represent the best picture we have of the status of kangaroos in the late twentieth century. The editor has also had the grace to put the problem in perspective, first with a history of kangaroo slaughter, not only of the species we know today but of some of their deceased relatives, including the ones that disappeared after the first wave of human immigrants – the Aborigines – and second, with a review of all of the species, not just the familiar ones in the headlines. Backing this up is a chapter on kangaroo biology, with a thorough description of the marsupial's extraordinary reproductive cycle.

This is the aspect of kangaroodom that is my own special interest. It derives from my first visit to Australia in 1962, when I was fortunate enough to see for myself some of the research being done by the CSIRO in Canberra by Dr Geoffrey Sharman (now Professor Sharman at Macquarie University). With his help and that of his colleagues, we were able to make the first complete film of the birth of a kangaroo for British television. Few events in my broadcasting career have been as exciting – the crew and I were like expectant fathers as we waited for the event to begin – and it has led to an abiding concern about the kangaroo problem. Because of the first-hand experience, this concern of mine is perhaps better informed than the average foreigner's, but it holds no less hope for a solution. And I believe the best chance of that is through fairness, understanding, humaneness and facts.

All four are contained within.

Christopher Parsons OBE
Head of Natural History Development
British Broadcasting Corporation

2   A local view

The great "kangaroo war" that stirred Queensland and indeed most of Australia in the late fifties and early sixties of this century was not fought between shooters and roos but opposing human factions – to wit, the man on the land and his opposite number in the street.

One side was necessarily concerned with the rigours of economic survival against a background of droughts, floods, fires, insect and rodent plagues, and of course grazing competition from those same hopping marsupials. The other side suffered from a nagging con-science apprehensive of further wildlife tragedies in a fast-changing world. Were we totally ignorant, for instance, of what befell the American buffalo, the passenger pigeon, the beaver, the Tasmanian "wolf", and what even then was taking place on the plains of Africa?

In those days, the welfare of Australia's natural heritage, or lack of it, rested largely on the actions of Queensland – for was this state not only the possessor of the greatest number and variety of faunal treasures but also the one lagging behind the rest of the Common-wealth in positive conservation action?

Many of us remembered only too well how koala open seasons as late as the twenties accounted for these innocent creatures by the million, though admittedly it was a tough era and durable hides brought hard-won currency to an impoverished community.

It is also important at this point to recall that each state conducts its fauna regulations independently of the other states. There was, and still is, no overall outlook and control.

As nature writer for Brisbane's *Courier-Mail* in those mid-century decades of controversy, I and others sought above all the regulated maintenance of various species of macropodids and vitally adequate controls in the new and fast-expanding marsupial meat industry.

Inevitably we caught a deal of flak and as one scrawled postal "gem" stuck in a scrap book to this day says explicitly, "Blokes of your type sitting in comfort on their _____ in cities would do far better to put up or shut up about matters on which they are not only b____ well ignorant but don't give a damn about the poor b___s in the bush anyway".

However the pros and cons expressed by the media, the spread of controversy far afield and the heat of printed and verbal exchange gave rise among other things to two allied and quite monumental moves.

One was the formation in Queensland – as an indication of a thoroughly aroused non-political outlook – of a Wildlife Preservation Society (1962), now firmly entrenched with its own regular high quality journal and membership branches flourishing exceedingly well in most main centres of the state.

Coincidentally, as a result of all-round concern reaching administrative levels, there arose a separate government department with the title of National Parks and Wildlife Service which set about amplifying *The Fauna Conservation Act of 1952*; this legislation initially involved the principle that no native fauna could be taken where survival of a species could be jeopardized.

Under the able and progressive directorship of Dr Graham Saunders, this newly created body was provided with a large staff of field officers and park rangers, many of whom were university graduates.

The new service also took over the inadequate sharing system where formerly the Entomology branch of the Primary Industries Department and the National Parks branch of the Forestry Department contained the responsible authorities for both fauna and flora and the environment.

Charles Roff, who for so many years courageously bore an exacting burden on his shoulders as sole fauna guardian for the huge state of Queensland, was at last able to find time to concentrate on his beloved bees. He admitted, without reservation, that turbulence arising from "the kangaroo war" had proved the catalyst in the government's final appropriate action.

So today, under the capable editorship of Dr Hugh Lavery, it has been possible to embody in this carefully researched matter a great many angles on an extremely complex subject. The book is an informative review of the impact of macropodids on our lifestyle and we on theirs. Grazing and agriculture, effects of hunting by both Aboriginal and white man, harvesting in modern days, extinction or threat thereof with some species, reproductive biology for management and conservation, the kangaroos of widely differing environments, bibliography, etc., all come under critical review.

Actually we are given an earnest view of the promising work being done by National Parks and Wildlife Service officers, notably the outstanding contributions of veteran roo authority Dr Tom Kirkpatrick. All concerned show by word and deed that Queensland's conservation laws are carefully administered and reasonably shaped and it would be less than appropriate for the title of this book to be anything other than "The Kangaroo Keepers".

David Fleay MBE AM
West Burleigh
Queensland

Acknowledgments

The Kangaroo Keepers is a Queensland National Parks and Wildlife Service publication that seeks to bring its responsibilities before a widespread audience in recorded, readable form.

No book covering so many zoological topics over such a large and unexplored area could have been compiled other than as a collaborative effort among concerned and experienced technical workers, some of whom are listed below. The result leans heavily on their published and unpublished studies, acknowledged in the Bibliography rather than as frequent interruptions throughout the text. The authors also have drawn freely on all published works on Macropodidae in Australia; again, references are in the Bibliography. The part played by officers of the National Parks and Wildlife Service is the consequence of the encouragement of the director of National Parks and Wildlife (Dr G. W. Saunders).

Dr T. H. Kirkpatrick, chief research officer of the National Parks and Wildlife Service, provided principal editorial support. Margaret McCaul, formerly of the same service, also substantially assisted production in all its aspects throughout the project. John Curtain, publishing consultant, Melbourne, gave sound advice and kind encouragement through all stages. Bronwyn Holm undertook the illustrative and design work and Joanne Shambler typed all drafts of the manuscript.

Others to whom credit also is due include: F. R. Allison, R. Atherton, S. Barker, P. Bayliss, J. G. Blackman, K. Buckley, David Butcher, T. Carey, Dr R. Close, D. Collins, M. J. Connolly, Dr D. Croft, Prof. T. J. Dawson, L. Dowling, H. M. Dunis, B. J. Egan, Graeme George, D. Gibson, Mr and Mrs J. E. Gleeson, Dr G. Gordon, A. T. Haffenden, S. Jones, N. Jonsen, B. C. Lawrie, L. Lim, Dr W. Low, J. S. McEvoy, J. P. McGahan, D. Marshall, J. H. D. Martin, Dr R. E. Molnar, A. J. Oliver, Messrs G. & L. Packer, M. Pople, Dr D. Priddell, D. Read,

G.J. Rees, D. Ritchie, the late C.R.R. Roff, Prof. G.B. Sharman, C. Sheehan, P. Sheehy, N.C. Shephert, Dr R. Sinclair, J.P. Stanton, G.J. Toop, R. Turnbull, G. Walsh, C.M. Weaver, C.G. Wilkinson, and Dr J.W. Winter.

Introduction

Man's history of exploitation of wild animals is not one that can be reviewed with much pride or satisfaction. Those species that have disappeared (and many have) were permitted to vanish with so little known about their lives that we can only wonder if it had to be that way, or whether a different and more prudent approach may have allowed both the animals and their uses to be with us still. Some few others — such as the northern elephant seal and the saiga — appear to have been restored to semblances of former numbers by recent actions.

One has only to look to the early 1500s to appreciate the extent of influence of trade particularly in fur-bearing animals. At the time, early French explorers returned to Europe with news of the vast numbers of furs available in North America. The European demand for furs at this time cannot be overemphasized; the European and Russian sources were depleted or extirpated over much of their ranges, and furs were basic and necessary winter garments in largely unheated houses. The French claimed possession of much of the northeastern North American coast and encouraged settlement in order to expand the fur trade and bolster the French economy; the Dutch and English quickly followed suit. The continent offered an apparently unlimited supply of furs and this served as a huge incentive to explore the continent westward and southward. North America was founded on its fur industry, and the first large fortune was made by a fur merchant (John Jacob Astor).

The sale of game each year is still a major source of income for landowners and of taxes for government, and such game species as red deer in Britain, wild boar in Belgium, and brown bear in Spain continue to survive despite the gross overpopulation by humans of the habitat in which these wild animals thrive. In South Africa, large areas of the Transvaal are being restored to bush from grain farms because the rearing and annual harvest of such wild species as impala, cape buffalo, and even predators such as lions and leopards provide more jobs, a better balance of payments, and more food for swelling human populations than the annual harvest of wheat or corn on the same sandy soil ever did.

Although native animals have been (and continue to be) of manifest interest throughout the world, the compilation over a long period of sound technical data for management purposes is rare, presumably because of lack of opportunity, motivation or overview. The result has been that any diminished populations are usually attributed directly to the effects of harvesting. This is not necessarily true and to continue in this belief without sound data is hardly a responsible approach to the vital task of conserving these resources.

Monographs that collate relevant matters of biology, ecology, husbandry, and economics — in long-term and suitably broad geographic scales and with management guidelines predicted — are the contribution that the field scientist must make to those who are responsible for the conservative use of native plants and animals — the wildlife managers. Such monographs are to be found mostly in relation to the fisheries, including those for oysters, fur seals, and whales. Yet there are terrestrial species that have attracted man's attention, for his own survival, for centuries — hares and rabbits, squirrels, beaver and some other rodents, wild dogs, bears, weasels, native cats, wild horses, and the numerous bovids including wild sheep, antelopes, buffalo, reedbuck, wildebeest and so on, feral pigs, and deer; remarkably few comprehensive reference books have been written on the management of these. Even then, such books almost never address the problems in view of modern technological means and opportunities.

Few animals have received more publicity in recent years than the kangaroos, particularly the largest three members of the family, the red and the eastern and the western grey kangaroos. Many unanswered questions must exist in the minds of those with more than a superficial interest in this native Australian fauna. Foremost among these must surely be how animals whose imminent extinction has been authoritatively predicted for more than a hundred years can still survive and in such numbers as to be regarded by the rural community generally as pests, and how reports of regular annual harvests, approaching the one million mark from one state (Queensland), can exist side by side with published complaints by travellers who describe trips of thousands of kilometres through the Australian outback without seeing a single kangaroo.

As recently as thirty years ago, anyone enquiring about either the biology or the welfare of these hunted species would not only have been given few (if any) accurate answers but also would have been considered unusual even for wanting to know. Kangaroos were, of course, as much a part of the Australian image as gum trees, but the great majority of Australians who had seen – or wanted to see – a kangaroo had done so in a zoo. The only real interest taken in the animals was by the graziers, who regarded them as vermin; and commercial kangaroo shooters were only too happy to help them because kangaroo skins were suitable for leather. There were, of course, some natural historians who wrote regretting the lack of biological knowledge of these unique animals, and some predicted their extinction from the thoughtless actions of the colonizing Europeans.

In the space of three decades, however, this state of affairs has changed dramatically. In the 1980s not only are kangaroos regarded with greater interest and affection by Australians, but the secrets of their lives are being unravelled and applied in what is now accepted universally as a vital matter – their conservation.

The kangaroo family, known as the family Macropodidae (see chapter 1 for definition and list of species), includes animals that range in size from the red and the grey kangaroos of the open forests and plains – whose largest males may exceed ninety kilograms – down to the relatively tiny musk rat-kangaroo of the tropical evergreen closed forests – of a weight little more than half a kilogram. Between these size extremes fit the many species of wallaroos, wallabies, tree-kangaroos, rock-wallabies, nailtail-wallabies, hare-wallabies, pademelons, potoroos and rat-kangaroos. Habitat requirements range from those of the grey kangaroos, for this group almost as widespread as the countryside (eucalypt forest and adjacent grassland habitat) to others that appear to be limited by some specific environmental need (rock-wallabies, for example, are never found far from cliff faces or rock-strewn hillsides).

For these species, time is still on their (and our) side. It is true that when serious biological study began at least one kangaroo, the toolache wallaby, seemed to have disappeared for ever; and there were perhaps a dozen other species (none of them exploited) which appeared to be hovering on the brink of extinction. But the species which gave the kangaroos their name – the red and the greys – were still present in abundance, and were still cursed by the grazier and preyed on by the commercial kangaroo shooter. They still are. But in those thirty years much has been learned and the new knowledge is being used in the formulation and application of management policies for their conservation.

In Queensland, where there are more species of the kangaroo family than elsewhere in the country and where the largest harvests of the species are taken, field studies to assist the administration of kangaroo conservation began in the 1950s with a study of the kangaroo industry. The stage was set for this research by an administration which established in 1954 the first act of Parliament dealing with native fauna that used the word "conservation" in its title. Under this act – *The Fauna Conservation Act of 1952* – the taking of native fauna including kangaroos was to be permitted only when the government was satisfied that such taking would not jeopardize survival of the species involved, a requirement that necessarily involved research into the biology, ecology and population dynamics of those species. Research has continued to the present day, and has served to provide the soundest available basis for the regulation of all the activities of man involving the kangaroos of Queensland, with the best interests of those animals in mind.

In this book is the story of that research. What has been found out, how it has been done, and above all, how it has been applied to ensure as far as possible the sound welfare of the kangaroos and those people involved with them – the graziers, the shooters, the general Australian public. It is not a book to justify these actions, nor does it set out to judge their value. This is for others to decide. The writers are merely those who have undertaken the work within the constraints of existing circumstances and whose studies have made them realize, among other things, how much must still be learnt about this unique natural resource if a full understanding of it is ever to be had.

The authors and their colleagues have worked throughout more than two million square kilometres of a countryside containing vast deserts at the one extreme and rainforest-clad mountains at the other. Millions of road and air kilometres have been covered. All except two of twenty-nine species have been studied in the wild and later at closer quarters in enclosures; one thought extinct has been rediscovered. More than seventy scientific papers and reports have been written not only about the species and their habitat types, but also about man's interactions with these. This experience is unprecedented. The scientists have been part of a process of learning that began with natural historians simply counting carcasses at remote chiller boxes and proceeded to sophisticated population simulation modelling by mathematicians on large computers.

Both public awareness and research effort have been concentrated on the larger species of commercial interest, particularly the eastern grey and the red kangaroos. The reasons are simple: public attention is attracted to the activities of commercial shooters by reports of numbers taken annually and the associated allegations of slaughter and cruelty, and the scientist finds large, abundant animals easier to study than smaller, more secretive and less abundant species. An industry, too, can be (and, in Queensland, is) of considerable assistance to research in the collection of the extensive samples needed for field studies.

It is frustrating to discover that relatively simple matters such as the determination of a gestation period or a breeding season continue to be matters of great public interest and even speculation long after their publication, whereas extremely difficult problems are regarded as matters that can be easily settled by anybody with a minimum of zoological knowledge and research effort! Measuring the effects of harvesting on wild populations, for example, may never be resolved to the satisfaction of zoologists.

This book has several purposes:

1. To leave a responsible record of the rationale by which a major harvest of one of the world's most unusual animals was permitted during a period when this was socially allowable, when it was extensive by any standards, and when it was measurable by technological methods not available in the places or times of earlier harvests of large native animals.

2. To establish a convenient and authoritative reference source for wildlife management personnel in the field, and to enable interim management conclusions to be expressed from a recorded experience and argument. This includes the opportunity so provided to set down the more general views of scientific staff who otherwise might not be inclined to hypothesize or speculate or to describe their personal experiences.

3. To provide material as a basis for closer collaboration between the conservation authority and a rural sector that relies at times on the natural resource. That is, to promote in the conservation authority a greater level of involvement in, and contact with, the rural community, so that an outlook for "rural" conservation can be developed beyond the device of the national park.

4. To justify to a broad audience the value of research and the usefulness of the field officers' contributions to kangaroo conservation.

5. To translate scientific jargon into forms more usable by interpretive staff for the interest of the general public.

Chapter 1

Family diversity among the kangaroos

Marsupials are a group of tropical origin. The current most acceptable hypothesis about marsupial biogeography is that the first significant radiation was in western North America at about 75 million years Before Present (B.P.) and that marsupials dispersed from there near the end of the Cretaceous period to South America and to eastern North America; later, one genus reached Europe. From South America they dispersed, probably by island hopping, across the Scotia arc and the archipelago of west Antarctica to east Antarctica and thus to Australia, arriving no later than 49 million years B.P.

The oldest known fossils of Australian marsupials were found at Geilston Bay in Tasmania from the late Oligocene epoch. The overlying basalt has been dated to a minimum age of 22 million years B.P. The oldest known fossil kangaroos were found in middle Miocene sediments – the Wipajiri fauna in the Etadunna formation near Lake Eyre; these are about 15 million years old. At that time Australia was much wetter than it is now, and large areas were covered with closed forest which is only a minor habitat for the family. When they first appeared as fossils, kangaroos were only a minor part of the fauna. As the climate and the vegetation changed, however, the family expanded and there are now as many fossil species of the family of kangaroos and wallabies as of all other Australian marsupials put together.

Their ancestors presumably came around the beginning of the Tertiary period and, once arrived in Australia, began the radiative development that resulted in the appearance of the marsupial equivalents of the placental mammals of other continents. Thus, the kangaroos occupy the place of the deer and antelopes, the rat-kangaroos the place of the hares and rabbits, and so on. As in other mammal groups elsewhere, species evolved and replaced one another throughout the Tertiary;in some of them there was a progressive increase in size culminating in the giant forms of the Pleistocene period. This gigantism was a feature of many lineages of marsupials, and there were many species of large Macropodidae. Some "wallabies" (*Protemnodon*) were bulkier than existing kangaroos and a "rat kangaroo" (*Propleopus oscillans*) was as large as a modern grey kangaroo. The largest kangaroos were members of the subfamily Sthenurinae; they were short-faced, heavily built, browsing forms, an adaptive type absent from the modern fauna. The greatest of them, *Procoptodon goliah,* must have been about 3 metres in height.

Wabula means "long time ago" in the language of the Aborigines of Queensland's gulf country and *Wabularoo* is a particularly appropriate name for one of Australia's oldest fossil kangaroos. Fossils of this species have been found preserved in limestone at "Riversleigh", northwestern Queensland, and are probably about 14 million years old. At this time, most of Australia received a higher rainfall and the area around "Riversleigh" may well have supported much wetter forests than it does today. Along with the remains of *Wabularoo naughtoni,* the fossil bones of many other extinct kinds of animals, including five other species of kangaroos, have been found in the Riversleigh deposit. All of the kangaroos from this remote period of Australia's history were small primitive types. By the Pliocene epoch, 5 million years ago, the climate had become much drier with a consequent increase in grasslands in place of the forests. During the Pliocene there was a marked radiation of forms adapted for grazing. The biology of modern species is related to their distribution in and adaptation for hot, arid areas. Kangaroos are efficient heat regulators (they lose heat in high temperatures by panting, sweating, and saliva-spreading, and by a low level of oxygen metabolism); the large kangaroos have the marsupial characteristic of low body-water turnover and they are also well adapted to the utilization of poor quality foods. The kangaroos reached a peak in variety, numbers and size during the Pleistocene epoch, about a million years ago.

The customary view has been that climatic deterioration since the end of the Pleistocene was the primary cause of the extinction of the Pleistocene large fauna, although the Aborigines may have been a contributing factor. Aborigines could have had a profound effect on the vegetation, chiefly by their use of fire for hunting. The extensive burning of the countryside by Aborigines is attested to by numerous observations in history. Continued burning could have caused habitat modification on a vast scale.

Although modern taxonomic studies have thrown much light on

the relationship to each other of various South American and Australian marsupial groups, there has not been any great change in the composition of the family Macropodidae. This family includes those diprotodont, syndactylous marsupials in which the fourth digit of the hind foot is greatly elongated and larger than the other digits, and in which locomotion is generally by bipedal hopping, with the long tapering tail used as a balancer; the second and third digits of the hind foot are very small and are joined together (syndactylous), appearing to form a single toe with a split nail; dentition is highly specialized for a herbivorous diet with a single pair of forward-projecting lower incisors.

The early history of the Macropodidae (some prefer to call it a superfamily, Macropodoidea) is uncertain and considerably more needs to be known of kangaroo diversity and palaeogeography and on the temporal relationships of the sediments before radiations can be determined with confidence. The later history is much better known although it is evident that every new site discovered adds new dimensions and complexity to kangaroo radiation.

At the time from which the earliest fossil records of the family Macropodidae are known (the late Oligocene or early Miocene), there were already two distinct subfamilies – the Potoroinae and the Macropodinae. A third subfamily – the Sthenurinae – arose from the Macropodinae in the late Miocene/early Pliocene, but disappeared during the Pleistocene. The two extant subfamilies are most easily distinguished by characteristics of the teeth. The relationship between faunal evolution and the vegetational changes, especially the evolution of grasses, is still poorly documented. The relatively few genera of marsupials found in Australia and North and South America represent a pattern of mammalian organization at least as old as that of placental mammals.

It is perhaps appropriate to remember that although the marsupials were known since around the year 1500, and a wide variety was available from 1788, the Europeans did not recognize the unity of the family until 1816. In their classifications until then, marsupials known to them were distributed among various orders of mammals depending on external resemblances. Some conservative mammalogists continued this practice until as late as the 1830s.

Members of the kangaroo family Macropodidae occur only in Australia, New Guinea, Indonesia and some neighbouring islands. The family comprises some fifty-eight species, grouped into two subfamilies, the larger of which (Macropodinae) includes the well-known kangaroos and the wallaroos, wallabies, and tree-kangaroos;

the smaller subfamily (Potoroinae) consists of the rat-kangaroos (including potoroos). The subfamilies differ fundamentally in numerous dental characteristics. The species are listed by their common and scientific names in table 1, with the twenty-nine species occurring in Queensland appearing in bold type.

Table 1   List of Macropodidae by common name and species

Common name	Species
Potoroinae	
Rat-kangaroo	
Musk rat-kangaroo	***Hypsiprymnodon moschatas*** Ramsay 1876
Potoroos	
Broad-faced potoroo	*Potorous platyops* (Gould 1844)
Long-footed potoroo	*Potorous longipes* Seebeck & Johnston 1980
Long-nosed potoroo	***Potorous tridactylus*** (Kerr 1792)
Bettongs	
Brush-tailed bettong	***Bettongia penicillata*** Gray 1837
Burrowing bettong	*Bettongia lesueur* (Quoy & Gaimard 1824)
Tasmanian bettong	***Bettongia gaimardi*** (Desmarest 1822)
Rufous rat-kangaroo	***Aepyprymnus rufescens*** (Gray 1837)
Desert rat-kangaroo	***Caloprymnus campestris*** (Gould 1843)
Macropodinae	
Hare-wallabies	
Central hare-wallaby	*Lagorchestes asomatus* Finlayson 1943
Eastern hare-wallaby	*Lagorchestes leporides* (Gould 1841)
Rufous hare-wallaby	*Lagorchestes hirsutus* Gould 1844
Spectacled hare-wallaby	***Lagorchestes conspicillatus*** Gould 1842
Banded hare-wallaby	*Lagostrophus fasciatus* (Peron & Lesueur 1807)
Nailtail-wallabies	
Bridled nailtail-wallaby	***Onychogalea fraenata*** (Gould 1841)
Crescent nailtail-wallaby	*Onychogalea lunata* (Gould 1840)
Northern nailtail-wallaby	***Onychogalea unguifera*** (Gould 1844)
Rock-wallabies	
Black-flanked rock-wallaby	*Petrogale lateralis* Gould 1841
Brush-tailed rock-wallaby	*Petrogale penicillata* (Griffith, Smith & Pidgeon 1827)
Godman's rock-wallaby	*Petrogale godmani* Thomas 1923
Little rock-wallaby	*Petrogale concinna* (Gould 1842)
Proserpine rock-wallaby	*Petrogale persephone* Maynes 1982
Rothschild's rock-wallaby	*Petrogale rothschildi* Thomas 1904
Short-eared rock-wallaby	*Petrogale brachyotis* Gould 1841
Unadorned rock-wallaby	*Petrogale inornata* Gould 1842
Yellow-footed rock-wallaby	*Petrogale xanthopus* Gray 1855
Tree-kangaroos	
Bennett's tree-kangaroo	***Dendrolagus bennettianus*** De Vis 1887
Grizzled tree-kangaroo	*Dendrolagus inustus* Muller 1840
Lumholtz's tree-kangaroo	***Dendrolagus lumholtzi*** Collett 1844
Matschie's tree-kangaroo	*Dendrolagus matschiei* Forster & Rothschild 1907
Ornate tree-kangaroo	*Dendrolagus goodfellowi* Thomas 1908
Unicoloured tree-kangaroo	*Dendrolagus dorianus* Ramsay 1883
Vogelkop tree-kangaroo	*Dendrolagus ursinus* Muller 1840

Table 1 (cont'd)

Common name	Species
Pademelons	
Dusky pademelon	*Thylogale brunii* (Shreber 1778)
Red-bellied pademelon	*Thylogale billardierii* (Desmarest 1822)
Red-legged pademelon	***Thylogale stigmatica*** Gould 1860
Red-necked pademelon	***Thylogale thetis*** (Lesson 1827)
Quokka	
Quokka	*Setonix brachyurus* (Quoy & Gaimard 1830)
Wallabies	
Swamp wallaby	***Wallabia bicolor*** (Desmarest 1804)
Agile wallaby	***Macropus agilis*** (Gould 1842)
Black-striped wallaby	***Macropus dorsalis*** (Gray 1837)
Parma wallaby	*Macropus parma* Waterhouse 1846
Red-necked wallaby	***Macropus rufogriseus*** (Desmarest 1817)
Tammar wallaby	*Macropus eugenii* (Desmarest 1817)
Toolache wallaby	*Macropus greyi* (Waterhouse 1846)
Western brush wallaby	*Macropus irma* (Jourdan 1837)
Whiptail wallaby	***Macropus parryi*** (Bennett 1835)
Forest-wallabies	
Lesser forest-wallaby	*Dorcopsulus vanheurni* (Thomas 1922)
Papuan forest-wallaby	*Dorcopsulus macleayi* (Miklouho-Maclay 1885)
Black forest-wallaby	*Dorcopsis atrata* Van Deusen 1957
Common forest-wallaby	*Dorcopsis veterum* (Lesson 1827)
Great forest-wallaby	*Dorcopsis hageni* Heller 1897
Wallaroos	
Antilopine kangaroo	***Macropus antilopinus*** (Gould 1842)
Black wallaroo	*Macropus bernardus* (Rothschild 1904)
Wallaroo	***Macropus robustus*** Gould 1841
Kangaroos	
Eastern grey kangaroo	***Macropus giganteus*** Shaw 1790
Western grey kangaroo	***Macropus fuliginosus*** (Desmarest 1817)
Red kangaroo	***Macropus rufus*** (Desmarest 1822)

Source: Based on the *Mammal Index List of Species and Distinguishable Forms of Australian Mammals* for Australian species. After *A World List of Mammalian Species* for New Guinea species.
Note: The most recent fashion in listing the family elevates it to a superfamily, Macropodoidea, with two families – Potoroidae and Macropodidae – corresponding to the subfamilies Potoroinae and Macropodinae recognized in this book.

Conservation vs preservation

The matter of conservation of kangaroos by any statutory agency must be considered at the species level. The law recognizes only the biological validity of the species; to recognize the other real entity – the individual – is to impose practical problems of enormous magnitude. In any event, this would be the endeavour of preservation rather than conservation.

Some elements in the field of preservation must not be overlooked, of course. In the main, in Queensland for example, these are the concern and responsibility of the Royal Society for the Prevention of Cruelty to Animals under *The Animals Protection Acts, 1925 to 1981.* Where that concern for individuals extends to the "damage" (such as disease transmission) which they may cause indirectly, authorities in Queensland such as the Department of Primary Industries (on behalf of the Commonwealth Animal Quarantine Service) have powers and means to act appropriately.

This does not mean that the conservation agency can afford to ignore the individuals that in the end make the whole (that is, the species population). Without delving into the infinite number of individual variations that go to make up these populations, some more obvious components are mentioned in the next two sections.

Incipient species – subspecies, varieties, forms

Twenty-three forms of rock-wallaby, included as species or sub-species of the genus *Petrogale,* have been described by the criteria of size, coat colour, and skull dimensions, characteristics that may vary markedly among some of the species (see figure 1). There are serious doubts, therefore, whether all of the named forms are "true" species, or merely "species in the making", and many are virtually indistinguishable in the wild to zoologists and wildlife managers alike. Plans for basic research and for conservation have been severely hampered by the uncertainty in identification and in the basic nomenclature.

The status of the twenty-three named forms is currently the subject of an exhaustive study undertaken by the School of Biological Sciences at Macquarie University (New South Wales) in collaboration wherever possible with the Queensland National Parks and Wildlife Service. The modern taxonomic techniques of chromosome cytology, immunology, protein and DNA electrophoresis, coupled with studies of host-parasite specificity (particularly lice) and fertility of hybrid offspring in captive colonies and from the wild, are all used to determine the degree of relatedness, and the extent of cross-breeding (if any) among forms.

The confusion has been somewhat lessened by the inclusion of some forms as geographical varieties or subspecies of other species. The genus *Peradorcas* can now be included within the genus *Petrogale.* On the other hand, several "new" chromosomally distinct

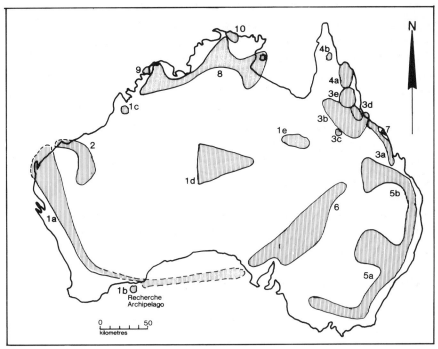

Figure 1   Distribution pattern of the twenty-three forms of rock-wallabies (*Petrogale* species). Chromosome races are: 1a *lateralis*, 1b *hacketti*, 1c Western Kimberley, 1d MacDonnell Ranges, 1e *purpureicollis*, 2 *rothschildi*, 3a *inornata*, 3b *assimilis*, 3c *puella*, 3d Mt Claro, 3e Mareeba, 4a *godmani*, 4b Cape York, 5a *penicillata*, 5b *herberti*, 6 *xanthopus*, 7 *persephone*, 8 *brachyotis*, 9 *burbidgei*, 10 *concinna*, *canescens* and two *indet*. (after Briscoe et al. 1982 and Close 1983).

groups of uncertain taxonomic status have been found, and the data indicate that the evolution of some existing species has involved occasional interbreeding between some forms leading to introgression of specific chromosomal rearrangements and protein variants across species' borders.

The significance of this introgression is still not clear but it may help to maintain genetic variation and thereby increase the animals' chances of withstanding vagaries of the environment. Certainly, the robust groups of northeastern Australia carry far more genetic variation than do the isolated, struggling populations of Western Australia.

Several rock-wallaby taxa are distributed allopatrically (that is, in a geographically distinct way) and allopatric methods of speciation obviously apply in some instances. However speciation in the brush-tailed rock-wallaby groups may also include clinal, area-effect or stasipatric patterns.* (The technically precise terminology involved reflects the complex processes on the one hand and the confusing and obscure results that appear publicly on the other.)

The genetic variation found in most colonies of rock-wallabies is low relative to that of many vertebrate species, but is none the less higher than theory would predict for populations of strictly limited size and great geographical isolation. There is considerable variation among populations in the form of alleles (protein variants) unique to particular populations. The distribution of these alleles can provide clear evidence of reproductive barriers between colonies. For example, the Proserpine rock-wallaby carries variants of several classes of protein which are not found in nearby colonies of the unadorned rock-wallaby. Had there been cross-breeding between the two groups then the alternative alleles of each protein would have been found in both groups of animals with the relative frequencies of the alleles indicating the degree of cross-breeding.

This work by Professor G. B. Sharman and his colleagues goes far towards relieving the basic decisions of biological status that the wildlife manager currently faces. It is impossible to formulate a valid and workable conservation policy without knowledge of such status and species' distribution. The confusion that can be caused by lists such as that of the authoritative Heber Longman (then Director of the Queensland Museum) in 1930 are obvious. Even by present incomplete standards, his catalogue of thirty-two species of Macropodidae contains seven species not valid as such and therefore of less than first concern to the wildlife manager. Still, no one can be adamant about either the previous whereabouts or the fate of *Thylogale bedfordi*. This was exhibited by Mr Oldfield Thomas at the Zoological Society of London on 20 February 1900; it had been presented to the British Museum by the society's president, the Duke of Bedford, after the adult female animal had lived some little time at Woburn. It was *said* to have been brought from Queensland *or* North Australia, and differed from its near ally *M. eugenii* (the tammar wallaby) in its long fur and peculiar, pale body colour. No species would be defined on such characteristics nowadays.

The earlier debates about the real identity of "Captain Cook's kangaroo" (*Mus canguru*) — now settled in favour of the wallaroo *Macropus robustus* — offer another example of the problems of nomenclature. Because of the long-standing use of the specific name

---

* Cline: character-gradient; stasipatric: resulting from the origin within the range of the species of chromosomal rearrangements that are superior as homozygotes to the inferior heterozygotes.

robustus for the wallaroo, confusion would be caused by reverting to the first given (and therefore priority) name *canguru*. This latter name has now been placed on the list of invalid names in zoology by the International Commission of Zoological Nomenclature and may not now be used for any species of *Macropus*.

In more recent times, the late N. A. Wakefield described *Bettongia tropica* as a new rat-kangaroo species akin to the brush-tailed bettong (*Bettongia penicillata*) occurring (from a specimen collected in July 1924) at Mount Spurgeon on southern Cape York Peninsula. An investigation of the chromosomes, allozymes, and the speciation process in rat-kangaroos (in collaboration with Professor Sharman's team) concluded that *B. tropica* did not appear to be a "true" species. It has been argued subsequently that while the chance of *B. tropica* and *B. penicillata* being found to be sympatric in northern Queensland is remote, this possibility has not been eliminated because no comparison was possible on the living animal to determine if the morphological characters of its skull and dentition were of the form described by Wakefield. To add further confusion (if that is needed), the premolar morphology of the type specimen of *B. penicillata* from "New South Wales" agrees with that from present-day Western Australian populations of that species and not with that from bettongs now found in southeastern Australia.

The point here is that the status of *B. tropica/B. penicillata* is arguable on relatively obscure technical grounds. For a state fauna conservation authority, the discovery of a population in Queensland that may be legally recognizable as a species confined to only a few localities should attract appropriately urgent measures of investigation and protection. In practice, the manager must err if he can towards the conservative view until such debates are resolved. A factor that alleviates urgency in this matter, however, is that one locality is within Davies Creek National Park (near Mareeba on the Atherton Tableland) (see plate 1[a]).

A nature conservation authority must maintain continuation of the process of speciation as much as maintaining the species themselves. In the rock-wallabies of far northern Queensland, for example, Godman's rock-wallaby may be endangered by the natural chromosomal spread of the Mareeba race of the unadorned rock-wallaby and there is no basis on which this should be artificially impeded.

Hybrids and major colour variants

It should not be overlooked that in the population of any kangaroo species unusual individuals may occur, the future of which need not attract undue concern.

Hybrids are widespread. In enclosures at Hermitage Research Station (Warwick), a male agile wallaby was observed on separate occasions mating with two female red kangaroos; these females later carried furred pouch-young* of phenotypic appearance intermediate between the species. The mitotic chromosomes of the parent species are $2n = 16$ for the agile wallaby and $2n = 20$ for the red kangaroos; both progeny (male and female) in this cross had a count of $2n = 18$. After eviction from the pouches, both hybrids were extremely active in comparison with normal red kangaroo young and spent most of the time for some months suckling, attempting to suckle, and generally clawing at the pouch opening. Under such continual harassment the mothers lost condition.

Palpation of the scrotum of the male hybrid indicated that the testes were either absent or vestigial. There is no reason to suppose that the natural fate of other hybrid individuals is any more substantial than this, even under enclosure conditions where observations also have been made of grey kangaroo × agile wallaby, eastern and western grey kangaroos × red kangaroo, red kangaroo × wallaroo, eastern grey kangaroo × whiptail wallaby, eastern grey kangaroo × western grey kangaroo, black-striped wallaby × red-necked wallaby, agile wallaby × swamp wallaby, agile wallaby × red-necked wallaby, red-necked wallaby × swamp wallaby, and red-necked pademelon × red-legged pademelon. The capacity to form hybrids is evidence of close genetic relationship; such a relationship is not unexpected within the species listed in table 1.

Luteistic individuals are those of paler than usual colour. Again, the appearance is not unknown in individuals of many species. From 640 agile wallabies studied from around Townsville during 1965–72, one was examined; other individuals have been noted in the eastern grey kangaroo and the swamp wallaby.

In 1922, Heber Longman described *Macropus welsbyi*, as the red Stradbroke wallaby, from an undated specimen collected near Amity Point on North Stradbroke Island. While Longman considered the possibility of affinity with the swamp wallaby, he noted anatomical differences (in particular in the nasal bone and nasal opening [nare]). The *Checklist of the Mammals Recorded from Australia* (Iredale and Troughton, 1934) accepted the status, although the authors later

---

* Joey is a popular term for a juvenile kangaroo that is in one of the following growth stages: in pouch, *pouch-young;* out of pouch but suckling, *young-at-foot;* independent of mother, *sub-adult.*

suggested the possibility of its derivation as a hybrid from the swamp and the agile wallabies. These cadmium-yellow individuals continue to attract comment and interest on Stradbroke Island where extensive urban development is expected. A young animal most likely to be this wallaby was collected near Mudgeeraba on the mainland nearby (and therefore it may be more widespread than previously believed); conservation action is clearly of priority only if this is established as a "true" species.

The skulls of eight specimens of the red Stradbroke wallaby held in the Queensland Museum were compared with the skulls of typically coloured swamp wallabies obtained from North Stradbroke Island (see plate 1[b]). The skulls of a male of each form, with a similar molar index (as defined by T.H. Kirkpatrick in 1964) suggesting these were of similar age, revealed no morphological difference that would allow distinction of the skulls at a species' level. The reproductive system of a young female collected near the type locality was normal in appearance and the sectioned ovaries contained numbers of Graafian follicles, suggesting that the potential for development of a reproductive capacity existed — meaning that it was unlikely to be a hybrid. The chromosomal complement did not differ from that recorded for a male swamp wallaby. The parent of a male pouch-young red Stradbroke wallaby displayed the markings and coloration of a typical swamp wallaby. Finally, that pouch-young eventually mated with two swamp wallaby females and two male young were produced. One of these survived to become a typical swamp wallaby in appearance, again suggesting that hybridization is not involved. In technical jargon, then, *Macropus welsbyi* is merely a junior synonym of *Wallabia bicolor,* and the conservation of the red Stradbroke wallaby — however picturesque and unusual this isolated form might be — must therefore be of lesser priority.

Likewise, albinism occurs, with a recorded incidence of 1 in 120 rufous rat-kangaroos studied in northeastern Australia. Albino grey kangaroos, red kangaroos and red-necked wallabies have been observed also, the last two bred in captivity.

Field identification

The identification of kangaroos in the field has long posed practical problems. Their cryptic nature makes for little impact on the casual observer. Use of colour alone, so long a characteristic means of separating such animals as the birds, is of little use. Thus in 1968 it could be said (by T.H. Kirkpatrick) of the wallaroo:

The general body colour of males is a mixture of black and rusty red; either colour may predominate in a particular specimen. Females are generally pale blue-grey with an infusion of rusty red that may vary from slight to extensive.

Occasional specimens of either sex are found with a wide reddish band across the neck and shoulders. In both sexes the fur is paler on the belly than on the back, and pale orange fur is usually present at the ear entrance and on the forearms and tail.

The variability in coat colour tends to follow a pattern throughout Queensland. Males and females from the southeastern corner are mostly black and blue-grey respectively, with the amount of rusty-red increasing in those taken from farther west and farther north. However, this is only a tendency, and in some districts the full range of colours may be found in specimens from a small area.

A certain amount of controversy exists in the naming of wallaroos. The range of colour variation throughout Australia is greater than that found in Queensland, and as many as six species, based on colour and locality, have been recognized over the continent by some authorities. Others prefer to distinguish the various types only as subspecies or even as colour varieties.

Today only one species is recognized throughout most of Australia.

For the red kangaroo, simple popular descriptions along the lines of "*Red* kangaroo or *plains* kangaroo: Australia, mid-latitudes, wherever there are extensive grassy plains" can confuse or mislead the inexperienced onlooker. In fact, female red kangaroos are usually blue-grey in colour as some males also may be; the sexes differ markedly in size, adult males sometimes exceeding 95 kg, females rarely reaching even half that weight. In Queensland, the species occurs discontinuously in the eastern part of its range where it is found in suitable "pockets". Habitat types include forests and open plains; the extent to which each type is utilized depends on the area available, the weather and the availability of suitable food. Grazing is confined to pasture; open plains are grazed more extensively when pasture in forested areas is relatively unavailable. The species is nomadic, particularly during dry times when many kilometres may be traversed in search of fresh growth. However, the sudden appearance of large numbers of red kangaroos in an area is more likely to be the result of movement out of the cover of the adjacent forest in search of food rather than a movement from a distant area.

In more accurate terms, the red kangaroo must be described as most readily distinguished from other large kangaroos by a partly hairy muzzle and a faintly grooved, third upper incisor tooth (in the unworn condition) – hardly convenient field guides!

The distinction among the common names of kangaroo, wallaroo and wallaby is one of size rather than anatomical difference, and the size varies with the age and sex of the individual. Colours vary greatly and are an unreliable guide. To add to the confusion, animals rarely are watched at close quarters standing immobile in open habitat. It may be argued that an observer who can presently distinguish most kangaroo species has no use for a field guide; yet sound management demands that all who come into contact with kangaroos for one reason or another should have the means then to recognize whether the identified species is common or endangered, protected or unprotected, and so on.

Ready field recognition of the various species of Macropodidae has been attempted previously using still photography and line drawings. Early lithographs (for example, in John Gould's *The Mammals of Australia* Vol. 2 [1863] or popular versions of this such as Joan M. Dixon's *Kangaroos/John Gould* [1973]) remain impractical sources for most field users because of their cost, size, and style. The key diagnostic features of species of the family are not found simply in anatomical appearance. Behaviour and distribution can provide clues for the instant that an individual may be available to be recognized. Bearing in mind, then, the idiosyncracies provided by colour variations, incipient species, hybrids and so on, a special style of field guide was obviously needed.

In the course of her work an artist (Ruth Berry), trained in interpreting visual character, accompanied skilled scientific observers in the field; she later viewed for prolonged periods the same species in captivity. Where no live animal could be examined, either museum study skins and drawings were used where satisfactory (desert rat-kangaroo) or the species was not depicted because it was indefinable (Godman's rock-wallaby) or for fear of being misleading (Tasmanian bettong). Her outline drawings were subjected to critical examination by the zoologists and then organized to portray social relationships, and to demonstrate simple silhouettes — a more usual form to which the observer is exposed. Finally, the plates were allied with pertinent brief diagnostic descriptions of features that are not readily illustrated — habits and overall habitat. The fourteen plates illustrating the twenty-nine species are presented, with captions, following page 70.

Habits

Many mammals are saltatorial, that is, they progress by a series of leaps with the hind limbs providing the main propulsive force. Some of these, such as rabbits and hares, are quadripedal; their leap is termed a spring and all four feet are involved. Several only distantly related saltatorial mammals (kangaroos, jumping mice, jerboas) are bipedal. Their leap is termed a "ricochet" and the forefeet are not utilized.

The two most commonly used gaits are the "fast hop" (the leap referred to above) and the "slow walk". For the slow walk in the larger species such as the eastern and the western grey kangaroos, the red kangaroo, the wallaroo and the antilopine kangaroo, the forefeet are placed on the ground in the front of the animal, and the basal half of the large muscular tail is positioned so that it is vertical to the ground and able to support the weight of the hindquarters. The basal half of the tail is then tautened, which allows the hindfeet to be lifted and brought forward in unison between the forefeet. For all species other than the tree-kangaroos and the musk rat-kangaroo, the slow walk is similar in action except for the part played by the tail. In this group, the tail is held at an angle to the body and appears to leave most support of the body to the forearms. This permits the hindfeet to be swung forward in unison, with the tail dragging behind. The slow walk for the musk rat-kangaroo is similar to that of the larger kangaroos; the tail, however, does not act as a support and is held stretched out above the ground.

The fast hop for all species except the musk rat-kangaroo (with its five digits) is digitigrade (toes only, the metatarsals and metacarpals never contacting the surface during locomotion) with the tail extended stiffly behind for balance. Fast locomotion for the musk rat-kangaroo is a quadripedal, accelerated version of its slow walk, again with the tail extended and not used as a ground support.

Habitat appearance

The use of habitat as a means of identifying the species of macropodids is impossible at any broad scale of either habitat or kangaroo species. Thus across Australia, some sixteen categories of vegetation types on an appropriate scale are usually illustrated (see, for example, *The Australian Environment*); forty-eight species of kangaroos inhabit these types with a noticeable reliance on the transitional zones among the categories for their obvious beneficial edge effects. Even on a smaller scale, such a vegetation classification for Queensland comprises thirty-three categories (see *Queensland Resources Atlas*) with one category (coastal and subcoastal hills and mountains)

Plate 1 (a) Reserved habitat of *Bettongia penicillata tropica*, Davies Creek National Park, via Mareeba, northern Queensland; (b) limited insular habitat of *Wallabia bicolor welsbyi*, North Stradbroke Island, southern Queensland

(a)

(b)

containing as many as seventeen macropodid species, and two species (the eastern grey and the red), occurring in at least twenty-three (not coincidental types) of these.

Of course, characteristics of the habitat other than vegetation also play a part. Both biotic (living) and abiotic elements may be important in the structure of an animal's habitat. There are few detailed studies of the habitat of a particular species of macropodid, and fewer still of habitat use. Comparisons among species are fewer still, and the extent of ecological differentiation is little known. Shelter including ground cover and nest sites may be described but the dependence placed on this by an individual is rarely demonstrated. Most studies of food concentrate on what is eaten but the nutritional aspects of this are usually neglected. Clearly, while precise habitat descriptions are of importance for management purposes, their value for comparative identification is extremely limited.

It remains to be said that apart from the problems of identifying some rock-wallabies (described earlier), there are still some differences between species that defy field illustration. The distinction between the brush-tailed bettong and Tasmanian bettong is a fine one. Identification of the Tasmanian bettong (which once, at least, occurred in Queensland) rests on the few grooves (4) and small size (4.5 millimetres) of the deciduous third premolar tooth, the grooved enamel of which was 2.4 millimetres in vertical depth at both anterior and posterior ends (as compared with about 4 millimetres and 2 millimetres, repectively, for these measurements in brush-tailed bettongs). Besides the differences of shape and insertion of the fourth premolar tooth, the cranial proportions said to distinguish Tasmanian bettongs from brush-tailed bettongs are: (1) greater interorbital width, (2) wider nasal opening, (3) shorter and shallower bullae, (4) larger molars, (5) tooth rows closer to parallel.

Where is proof that 'roos face extinction?

Would like to reply to Jacki Kent about letter (Daily Sun, April 5) telling Mr ... don to get his ... right.

DAVID FLEAY'S NATURE NOTES

To the rescue of a special wallaby

Kangaroos not endangered

SYDNEY (AAP) — Kangaroos "breed like rabbits" and are in no danger of extinction, according to a kangaroo researcher.

Wallaby's future secure

Back from the brink

Save the 'roo demo in Rome

ROME: Staff at the the killing of kangaroos, Australian embassy in Australia. confronted yester— Similar demonstra- by 20 people and a tions are planned in tall inflatable kanga- Zurich, Bonn, London protesting against and Paris United Press International

Export ban urged to save roos

CANBERRA.— The Australian Conser- comed the American decision. It ... vation Foundation has called for a total ban representative to the US to co... on kangaroo exports. the screening of the controversi...

THERE are more than 40 species of kangaroos in Australia — or there were when Europeans arrived. One species is now certainly extinct and a number of others are on the brink of extinction.

Roo commen... was ludicrous

I have lived in south-east, south-west and central ...nsland for the past 10 ... and have been ...nsed shooter for part ...

...ing my travels ...d the State as an ...nce inspector a... ...net and known do- ...responsible,...

Roos pushed t... 'breaking point...

SIR — Comments (Country L... April 14) were made that cons... vationists have found the argu- ment that the three species ... kangaroo commercially harves... in Australia are facing extin... is hard to sustain. We have found,... non-stop resear... ...ought and the...

A BULLDOZER, disease, a serious drought or one bushfire could eliminate a species of wallaby in Queensland.

Such a fragile balance might come as a surprise to many people, par- ...icularly those who still hold the ...that kangar-

WILDLIFE

Save, don't shoot, the 'roo

Following our Februa John Shaw on kanga the right of reply to

Tracing our vanishing animals

Commonwealth and State wildlife authorities believe that controlled harvesting of kangaroos by profes- sional shooters working to annual quotas is far preferable to allowing in- discriminate shooting and poisoning to occur and they generally support the re-introduction of imports of

WALLABY AID

The Federal Government has offered $200,000 to help save an endangered wallaby species.

The money will help the State Government buy the Red Hill property, near the town of Dingo, which comprises most of the habitat of the the...

Rare wallaby survives in Queensland

GRANT FOR PROTECTED MARSUPIAL

In view of the renewed ...n Govern... public interest in the ...he fut... harvesting industry, espe... relation to the controvers... "Goodbye Joey", it is pe... 'perhaps to reiterate some ...0 contribution 'comments made in a feature ...nsland Newslett... on kangaroos in Q...

(ADVERTISEMENT)

Which politician will save the 'angaroo?

Rare wallaby sheds light on disease

By PETER TERRY

QUOKKAS, those rare, rat- shaped wallabies now found

have the inbuilt ability to re- build muscle tissue naturally. He said the discovery means diseases such as muscular

Medical colleagues had been having trouble with sick quok- kas and a paralysed animal had been brought...

Chapter 2
Scarcity and extinction

Change and conservation priorities

Former US President Carter's book *Global 2000* has warned us to expect by the year 2000 that some six hundred thousand species of animals and plants will have become extinct, the greatest part of the earth will be "settled land", and few significant terrestrial ecosystems will be surviving in their present form. Furthermore, some scientists and others argue that there is simply no point in sustaining species that have outlived the ecosystems in which they have evolved (including those of man).

Such cynicism denies that living creatures can offer us anything to learn from, to wonder at, or even to profit by. It is perhaps equally extreme to suppose that the best hope for wildlife lies in the proven consistency of man's inability to predict the future.

In a way, zoos that deal with species one at a time have an easier set of problems than those facing the guardians of wild populations, where action on one species inevitably affects others. One approach is to try to preserve the greatest breadth of diversity; this results in the giving of preference to protecting orders before families, families before genera, and so on. Thus, groups that are monotypic (one species per genus/family), or nearly so, receive preference. The action taken, of course, must be influenced by the status of the animal in the wild. Certainly, the overall process of choice is both complex and uncomfortable.

There have developed in nature conservation two technical pathways by which a satisfactory conclusion is regarded as attainable. One uses the "tool" of the national park (or equivalent reserve), by which means broad ecosystem management is achieved. This cares for landscapes in particular, often on the economically justifiable basis of recreation. Its use in relation to macropodids is seen elsewhere in this book, particularly where the range of an unusual species is restricted by habitat type. The second pathway employs the devices of wildlife management, concentrating on the fauna rather than the habitat and often justifying this economically in the rural industries (either in relation to controlling abundant pests or to sustaining commercialized species).

Into this latter applied ecology pathway in more recent times has come a community concern for the "endangered species" — a species that in the light of current knowledge is uncommon and occurs in a limited, fragile, and/or threatened habitat. The notion is born of compassion, aesthetics, economics, and the indirect benefits to man; it is the current *cause célèbre* in the field of nature conservation. Many such situations prove, on closer examination, not to be zoological challenges but problems of economics and sociology. Quite often, no great insight is required to determine why a population is declining and to prescribe countermeasures that are at least theoretically correct. The main problem undoubtedly lies in persuading people to take appropriate action.

Extinction is neither remarkable nor rare. G. G. Simpson, formerly of the American Museum of Natural History, estimated that there might be two million species of animals and plants surviving from an all-time total of five hundred million. To put it another way, more than ninety-nine per cent of the species that have ever existed are now more than endangered — they are extinct. By way of further illustration, the historian Arnold Toynbee summarized that of twenty-one civilizations of man, fourteen are now wholly extinct. In fact, we can witness the extinction of local populations of even the most abundant species going on around us all the time. With the best will in the world, we may never have the scientific resources to investigate, or the management resources to develop and implement, programmes that will save more than a small percentage of those species that may be recognized as endangered.

The following is an account of the practical approach taken to one such species, although any conservation authority must allow for some broader considerations. The subject area as a whole is an emotive one, far removed from science. For all that has been written about the parlous state of the Australian environment, the quantitative evidence is less convincing. By way of example, scientists consider that there is no conclusive evidence for the extinction of any mainland insect since European settlement of Australia, and no single species of eucalypt yet appears to have been lost through the agency of Europeans. Others, applying their attention to wildlife over the vast area of northeastern Australia, have concluded that the most obvious advantage of scientific surveys has been improvement in the inventory of species and the extent of their distributions. For example, some half dozen new or rediscovered (thought extinct) species of Australian mammals have been described in the last decade.

Any scientific outlook about endangered species must therefore embrace some of the following broader questions, still mostly unanswered by those who would direct the research. What allowance is to be made for the fact that most species sooner or later become extinct? The term used for selected species is "endangered", but is this correct for all species so termed when so little is known about status at the time of selection and when they are considered in such isolation? How many species should or can be included on any "endangered" list when this recognition immediately imposes long-term commitments on the one hand and a situation of "diminishing returns" on the other? Is such a list fixed in any way, bearing in mind the commitments entailed and the largely unknown circumstances, as well as an unpredictable public interest? How are the widely different situations that apply to a species to be reconciled in any list? Is there, in fact, common ground by which (in Queensland, for example) bizarre but common species such as the platypus, vagrants such as the leatherback turtle, endemics such as the Herbert River ringtail-possum, "lost causes" such as the paradise parrot, widely spaced small populations such as the rock rat, little-known species such as the Darling Downs hopping-mouse, and highly prized uncommon species such as the golden-shouldered parrot, can be related? What is the relationship of a sovereign state's tasks to those of other states where the same species may be common, or "endangered", or not present (now, or in the past)? Who pays, and how? What proportion of any funds should be spent in the national park "pathway" compared with the wildlife management "pathway"? In the latter regard, what role is apportioned to relocation, and what to zoos? Can, in practice, the national park system survive without the initial educational input of zoos, where the most appealing element of nature is highlighted in convenient surrounds? When a species is selected, what proportion is spent on habitat acquisition, on research, on day to day management? Without these decisions, how can we effectively conserve such species as the bridled nailtail-wallaby?

Saving the bridled nailtail-wallaby

The bridled nailtail-wallaby is one of those previously abundant and widespread species of kangaroos that has all but disappeared following European settlement of Australia (see figure 2). It provides an excellent opportunity to examine and build a case history for conservation management purposes, one that contains all the characteristic elements of such a problem: an early abundance, a carelessly allowed decline with the misguided attention of settlers, a barely lamented slide into apparent oblivion, an awakening of public conscience, the excitement of rediscovery, and finally the testing reality of an attempt at rehabilitation.

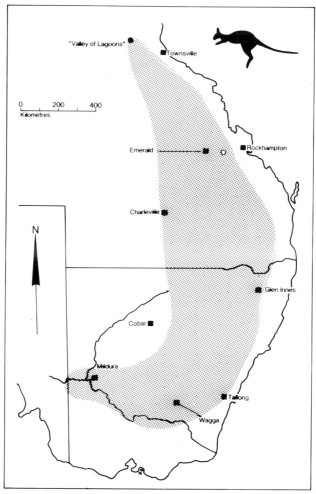

Figure 2 Eastern Australia showing former range of the bridled nailtail-wallaby. Stipple: area covered by records; circle: present range.

History of the species

That the species was previously commonplace, or at least locally abundant in a number of places, is well documented. The zoologist Gerard Krefft, during a fauna survey in the Mildura–Gunbower area of Victoria between 1852 and 1862 found the bridled nailtail-wallaby "common in the northern part of Victoria and the most common of all the smaller species of the Kangaroo tribe". In New South Wales it was known to be common, ranging along the western slopes and plains of the Great Dividing Range from Wagga Wagga to Glen Innes, and as far west as the Namoi River at Cobar. So common was it that, under the name of "pademelon", government bounties were paid on its scalps throughout its distribution range until the early 1900s. In Queensland, too, the collectors John Gilbert and Carl Lumholtz during the second half of the nineteenth century were able to describe it as "common" on the Darling Downs, "numerous in the scrubs" of central Queensland, and occurring as far north as the Burdekin River catchment of northern Queensland. Even as recently as 1930, Heber Longman of the Queensland Museum noted that the bridled nailtail-wallaby was "not uncommon in some parts of southern Queensland, and its pelts were frequently seen in sales two or three years ago under the name of pademelon".

By the early 1900s, however, a decline had set in through the southern Australian areas of its range, a decline that was clearly welcomed by the pastoralists who firmly believed that their livelihoods were at risk in competition with virtually the entire mammalian fauna of Australia. They were encouraged by governments of the day that made "marsupial destruction" a condition of land leases.

There were those who perceived and deplored the decline – John Gould, A. S. Le Souef, Professor Frederic Wood Jones, H. H. Finlayson and E. LeG. Troughton were among those who wrote pleading for a wiser and kinder approach not only to the bridled nailtail-wallaby but to the total native fauna. They were rare voices, however, and their sounds were barely heard. There was one well-meaning attempt to save the species from impending oblivion when a group of animals were released on Bulwer Island off the coast near Newcastle (NSW) but colonization was unsuccessful.

By the time the advancing spread of pastoral conquest began to slow down in eastern Australia and governments began to heed pleas for a more protective approach to Australian fauna, it appeared to be too late to save the bridled nailtail-wallaby. Basil Marlow, then Curator of Mammals at the Australian Museum, wrote in 1958 that the species was at least scarce in New South Wales where the last

official record of its occurrence was at Manilla (north of Tamworth)
in 1924. It had seemingly vanished from Victoria long before this.
The last Queensland sighting in this period was by H. H. Finlayson
of South Australia who, in a survey of the Dawson Valley in 1930,
described the species as scarce or absent over most of the surveyed
area (he observed it only twice).

Following the gradual awakening of public interest in native fauna
that began soon after World War II, committed searches for this (and
other) apparently extinct species in the eastern Australian mainland
states failed to locate a single individual and hopes for its survival
had all but vanished. This was despite occasional obscure references
to it in books, for example in Jean Devanny's *Travels in North Queensland* about the late 1940s, and uncorroborated letters, for instance
from J. K. Wilson to David Fleay of West Burleigh (in 1963) noting
observations of a few of these animals approximately fifty kilometres
outside Tambo in central Queensland in February 1950.

In 1973 a fencing contractor, Mr D. Challacombe of Duaringa,
reported a sighting near the town of Dingo in central Queensland.
He had identified the animal from a colour plate of Gould's *Mammals
of Australia* reproduced in the magazine *Woman's Day* in a series on
scarce fauna. Zoologists of the (then) Fauna Conservation Branch of
the Queensland Department of Primary Industries arrived in the
area soon afterwards and confirmed the identification; they then
proceeded to define the extent of the colony, thus beginning the
latest chapter in the story of this picturesque species. It is a story
that is still incomplete but today, more than ten years and hundreds
of thousands of dollars later, the rehabilitation of the bridled nailtail-
wallaby is under way.

The major part of the range of the colony located so fortuitously by
Mr Challacombe was found to be almost entirely within the boundaries of two cattle grazing properties, "Taunton" (see figure 3) and
"Red Hill", with a combined area of 11,240 hectares. Much lower
densities occurred in a peripheral region as far as twelve kilometres
away, indicating that the two properties were indeed the core area
for the species (figure 4). Clearly, if survival was to be ensured, it
was on these two properties that work had to begin as soon as possible; fortunately, the owners were prepared to cooperate.

There were two immediate problems. The first and most obvious
was, with the cooperation of the landholders, to "freeze" the habitat
in a state that had kept the colonies alive at the time of rediscovery.
The second was to determine what the factors were that had allowed
the bridled nailtail-wallaby to persist there; this included the need to

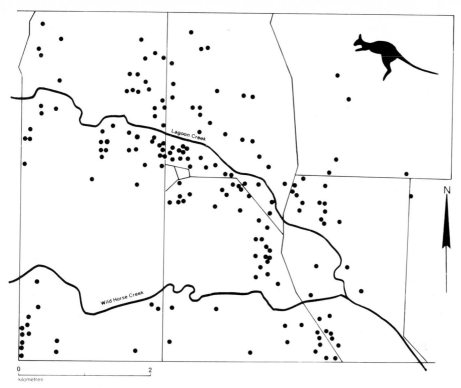

Figure 3 Distribution of sightings of the bridled nailtail-wallaby on "Taunton", central Queensland: 1980 to 1984. (Fences indicated.)

Figure 4 District of Dingo in central Queensland showing recent survey sites and locations of observations of bridled nailtail-wallabies on properties other than "Taunton" and "Red Hill". Stipple: property spotlighted and residents interviewed; hachure: residents interviewed only; dot: animals sighted.

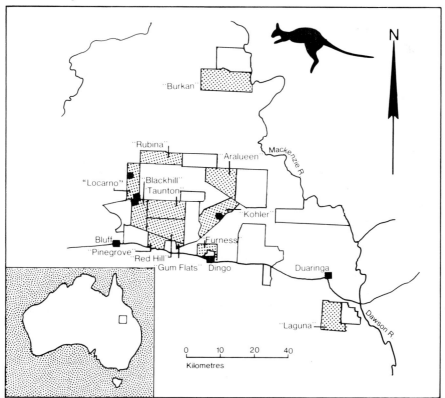

establish whether any of the factors that had caused decline elsewhere were operating. These constituted mammoth tasks indeed!
The final question, of course, would be to determine those measures
that would be needed to ensure survival into the foreseeable future
(including perhaps to allow it to extend its range). All of these
matters would incur costs that would require community decisions
as to its preparedness to bear such expenses.

The first hurdle proved to be the easiest. Landholders Mr V.C.
Turvey of "Taunton" and Mr F. Draper of "Red Hill", were much
concerned at the newly found notoriety of their properties and justly
concerned about the future of their lands. Were these to be sacrific-
ed for an admittedly attractive but otherwise rather inconsequential
animal that everybody else had been permitted to eliminate with
impunity? Nevertheless, the owners were willing to cooperate. That
they were later prepared to return their properties to the government
for a fair price must be acknowledged as a most generous contribution to the conservation of Australia's endangered fauna. The authority to do something real about the second problem was secure.

The second problem, however, is still in the process of being
answered, as is the question about benefit–cost deriving from its
solutions. There has been no single answer, as the following account
demonstrates. The only way with such a delicate programme is to
proceed steadily, feeling for each step forward but prepared to
retreat or change direction at any time that the colony even *seems* to
be reacting adversely. In reality, the rediscovery of the bridled nailtail-wallaby has demanded that the academic question of why an
animal population declines and disappears must be supplied with
non-academic answers – circumstantial evidence, if you like!

A clue to the decline of the species probably lies in that it survives
in the northern sector of its once substantial range (figure 2). Conventional reasoning would surely conclude that a population under
normal stresses would retreat from its marginal distribution to core
or "reservoir" areas of the most suitable habitat, which logically
would be near the centre of its range. Thus, for a species to survive
only in the northern portion must signify extraordinary pressures
elsewhere and diminishing from south to north; this so obviously
coincides with, and indicts, the effects of European colonization that
one hardly needs to search for any other cause. But of the many
features of European occupation of the land, were any more important than others in contributing to the decline? Are some of these
tolerable?

The most evident instruments of change have been the axe and the gun, and the introduced predators, particularly the fox. Less obvious, but probably more insidious, are the competing herbivores, both domestic and feral. Less apparent still are the pasture and other plants introduced to replace the native vegetation with something more acceptable to the introduced livestock.

Reviewing the circumstances of the bridled nailtail-wallaby's survival, several features stand out. The first, and perhaps the most important, is that large scale habitat destruction – land development – did not begin in the Dingo area of central Queensland until 1962, when the Fitzroy Basin Brigalow Land Scheme was introduced. The vast stands of brigalow and associated softwood vegetation communities of inland Queensland (incorporating Dawson gum, yapunya, yellowwood, bastard sandalwood and leopardwood) had long frustrated the efforts at large scale clearing; methods finally were devised, however, and the entire area had been thrown open to government-financed subdivision. The rate of destruction of the natural habitat, aided by enormous post-war increases in the capabilities of land clearing machinery and associated technology, was probably unparalleled in the history of Australian land development up to that time; thus, despite a late start, settlers were well able to make up for any delays.

Fortunately for the bridled nailtail-wallaby, the so-called brigalow belt is really a complex of soil and vegetation types (see, for example, figure 5). Parts of the region were unsuitable for pastoral development, particularly those not associated with brigalow vegetation. Further, the poor monetary returns during the 1970s from beef cattle grazing (the purpose of the brigalow lands development scheme) ensured that both the finance and the incentive to clear land was reduced, granting a (temporary) respite to much of the present area of distribution of the wallaby.

Another point in the circumstances of the species' survival is that, of all the grazing competitors, only cattle were in substantial numbers in its central Queensland range. The notable absentees included the rabbit, surely the most destructive of all introduced mammals to Australia; this has only just reached central Queensland and even now is not established in any significant way.

A third point to be recalled relates to predation by the dingo which certainly includes the bridled nailtail-wallaby in its diet. Since the opening up of the region for grazing, invading dingoes have been subjected to a systematic and sustained trapping campaign that has undoubtedly reduced numbers of the dogs. The survivors have a readily available food source in the black-striped wallaby of the

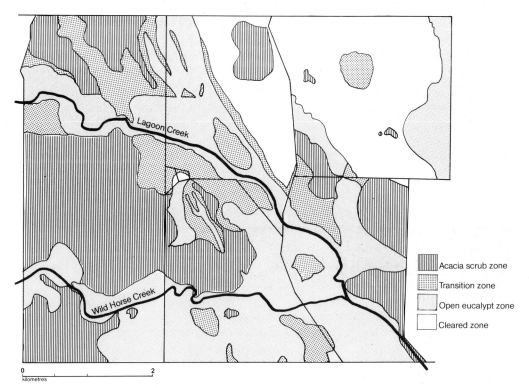

Lagoon Creek

Wild Horse Creek

Acacia scrub zone

Transition zone

Open eucalypt zone

Cleared zone

0   2
kilometres

Figure 5 Main vegetation zones in the bridled nailtail-wallaby study area at "Taunton", near Dingo, in the central Queensland brigalow belt. (See also figure 3.)

undisturbed scrubs; this is a prey that they readily utilize, as attested to by the frequent discoveries of its remains left by dingoes. It seems highly likely that the abundance of the black-striped wallaby in the same areas as the bridled nailtail-wallaby has, in conjunction with the dingo control programme, considerably reduced predation pressure on the scarce species.

The overriding importance of the first factor — retention of the natural vegetation — is given added weight by the fact that, during the past seven years, the bridled nailtail-wallaby seems to have disappeared from much of the peripheral area where it was located in 1974. This has occurred concurrently with a marked increase in land clearing for grazing and agricultural cropping in that area. Indeed, the rediscovery of the bridled nailtail-wallaby at all was an accidental result of the push to develop more land which had involved the observant fencing contractor.

There can be little doubt that the major factor in the decline of this animal was the extention of European methods of agriculture into its habitat (see plate 2[a]). This conclusion, reached early in the review of

(a)

(b)

Plate 2 (a) Cleared brigalow habitat of the bridled nailtail-wallaby at "Taunton" near Dingo, central Queensland, 1978; (b) rocky range shelter of the yellow-footed rock-wallaby at "Wakes Lagoon" near Adavale, western Queensland, 1974 (G. Gordon); (c) restricted hillside habitat of Godman's rock-wallaby at Black Mountain near Cooktown, far north Queensland, 1973 (C.M. Weaver).

(c)

its rediscovery, contained a most important implication for the future of both the wallaby and the landholders on whose properties it was found. And that, simply, was that the survival of one had to be at the expense of the other. Given the sizes of the properties and their accepted land use, there was no obvious, certainly no easy, way to maintain the presence of the wallaby and an economically viable farming enterprise at the same time. Thus was raised the critical question of the value the community was prepared to place on the survival of a small relict population of unusual animals that had been allowed to become almost extinct without much concern at all. The way the problem has been solved, however, has raised new and as yet unanswered questions in the rural community; for example, if a scarce species is found on my land, will this land be taken from me? If the land is taken, will I get a fair price, given that the value of the land varies greatly with annual weather conditions?

Developing a management programme

The solution to the dilemma came in 1979 as a clear reflection of the changing times. With the assistance of the federal government, the Queensland government purchased "Taunton". The entire Australian community, through its national and state governments, had committed itself to the survival of one of the most attractive and most endangered kangaroo species and its rehabilitation became the responsibility of the Queensland National Parks and Wildlife Service. At the time of writing, a similar land purchase was being approved for "Red Hill".

The first action required under an interim management plan prepared in anticipation of the acquisition of "Taunton" was to remove all domestic stock as quickly as practicable, and by the end of 1981 only twenty "scrubbers" remained. These proved impossible to muster from the dense vegetation on the western side of the property and were allowed to remain there for at least the time being. Inhabiting as they do only a one thousand hectare paddock, these exert minimal grazing pressure and are not at present regarded as any sort of threat to the environment of the wallaby.

At the same time as the cattle were being removed, a qualified management officer (P.J.Tierney) was employed to commence a study to determine how many bridled nailtail-wallabies were present, their habitat requirements, and their behaviour, particularly where this was related to the way the animals used their habitat. The study was regarded as necessary to provide a basis for the implementation of strategies to ensure the survival of the species and, if necessary, to promote its population increase.

Because only one population of the species is known, the research programme had to be undertaken without the advantage of a concurrent comparative study, a resource normally considered invaluable (if not essential) in work of this type. This meant that progress could only be measured against the data collected from a population which was in the process of manipulation – a hazardous scientific procedure to say the least.

Matters listed as research priorities included the need to know the size of the population and whether it was increasing, static, or declining, and the species' daily and seasonal use of its habitat – including the animals' movements, diet, water usage, and predators and competitors. The area comprising the western half of "Taunton", roughly rectangular in shape, was subjected to the study (figure 3). Some three-quarters of this area was in a seemingly natural state; the remaining one-quarter was primarily of brigalow that had been "pushed" (by bulldozers) between 1974 and 1977 but had not been burnt, an action that produces a regrowth far thicker than the original condition (and a bane of the early developers of brigalow lands).

Within this study area a set of forty-one transects – predetermined survey lines through the bush from which observations were to be made – was established at approximately 140-metre intervals from its eastern boundary to the western boundary. Suitably marked with painted posts, these transects were to be traversed on foot three times each year for several years. The times for traversing the transects were planned for February, just after the finish of the summer wet season, for May, when the vegetation was due to be at its peak of growth after the wet for the year, and for October, when the vegetation usually is in its worst condition, just prior to the first summer storms. During the walking of the transects, a distance totalling 180 kilometres and taking at least three weeks to complete, data collected included the location and behaviour of every bridled nailtail-wallaby seen, and the description of a set of floristic and structural characteristics of the vegetation present at each position. In addition, these same vegetation measurements were to be made at another thirty-two randomly selected sites during each sampling period.

During the two years and six sampling periods since the study began in 1981, the data that have been collected have provided much information on wallaby numbers and habits as well as on the vegetation characters of both the study area as a whole and on the particular locations occupied by the animals. More work is required, of course, before satisfactory answers are available for the questions posed at the outset. But much of use for practical management purposes has been learned already, which is certainly more likely to give correct results than if no such study had been conducted.

The questioner must be warned to have reservations about the answer to the question of universal interest – how many individuals remain? Because counts of wild animals are invariably and at best estimates, their reliability and use to which they may be put depends on an understanding both of how these were gathered and how they were analysed. Not only is the accuracy of the data taken along the transects critical – including correct identification of animals seen and the careful measurement of "flight distance" (explained below) – but the theory underlying the calculations using the observational data is at least as significant in the results obtained. The problems and dangers associated with population estimation are described in the last chapter of this book. The bridled nailtail-wallaby, however, is a species of such scarcity and restricted distribution that an attempt to obtain a population estimate is justified.

The data on which the estimations of total numbers are made are actual numbers seen and the distance from the observer that a wallaby makes itself visible (the "flight distance" or "flushing distance"). This normally occurs when it emerges, always in great haste, from its daytime shelter. During daylight hours (when the transects are undertaken) these animals spend most of their time (at least ninety per cent) resting in a "form", a depression worn in the ground by repeated use, usually in the shelter of a tree or shrub. When approached by a person on foot, the quickly alert animal first "freezes" in its form and, if approached closer than a prescribed distance (the flight or flushing distance), it bursts out of its form and rapidly hops some hundred metres or so to take shelter behind available vegetation. Secure in the invisibility provided by the shelter and its protective coloration, it reviews the situation. This flight distance is critical to the calculation of abundance; it must be carefully assessed, and measured separately for each vegetation type because the more open the vegetation is, the greater is this distance. For the four broad vegetation types present in the study area, the flight distance has varied from twenty metres in dense acacia scrub and brigalow regrowth, to sixty metres in open eucalypt forest (such as of poplar box, narrow-leafed ironbark and silver-leafed ironbark) and riverine vegetation, to ten metres in "cleared" regrowth areas (the densest of all).

Using a calculation based on such flight distances, the frequency of sightings in each vegetation type present, the percentage of each transect covered by each vegetation type, and the proportion of the total area actually seen from the transects, the 144 sightings made during the six survey periods to date have been translated to a calculated population of some eight hundred individuals. It is anticipated that future counts will allow changes (if any) in population abundance to be measured. It is this change, rather than the absolute numbers, that is of major interest and importance.

The subject of preferred habitat is addressed by reference to the data shown in figure 3 and in figure 5, where the sightings can be linked with the vegetation type occurring at the location. It is immediately apparent that the wallaby prefers to spend the daylight hours in the area identified as transitional vegetation, which occurs where the open eucalypt forest and the acacia scrub meet. The transition zone includes species from both forest and scrub, but usually comprises smaller plants than in the "pure" areas, and usually includes currant bushes and turkey bushes. Within it, the trees and bushes tend to be in clumps some ten to fifteen metres across, separated by interclump spaces of about the same distance.

An additional observation is that most of the sightings are also related to the watercourses flowing through the area, and a first impression is that proximity to water is important to the bridled nail-tail-wallaby. The only observed occasion of drinking, however, was when an individual encountered a pool of water after rain during grazing movements. Because it has rarely been seen to drink, the association with water may only be because the transition zone is also largely associated with the creeks in the study area. There may be, of course, some preference by the wallaby for other vegetation associated with the waterways.

The as yet uncompleted analysis of foods eaten, based on "droppings" (faeces), appear to confirm the general observation that a wide range of plants, including grasses, herbs and shrubs are consumed; this work may permit preferences to be determined. Such a study will require comparison of measurements made of the vegetation at the locations where each of the animals was sighted with what is found in the droppings. Such comparisons will of course need to include consideration of seasonal changes in the vegetation, and promise to be highly complex.

While much is still to be learned from the investigations, these early and more evident conclusions have provided the basis for a number of practical management decisions that are being introduced at "Taunton" to promote at least stability, and perhaps to increase the bridled nailtail-wallaby population.

An obvious need has been to encourage as far as possible establishment of the transitional vegetation type so clearly preferred. Where this can be done to best advantage is in the area cleared by former owners and which is now being allowed to regenerate. This involves permitting regrowth in some areas and controlling it in others to create "patchiness". It has necessitated the trial use of a range of control methods including slashing, clearing and burning, as well as grazing by cattle. The seeding, and even irrigating, of selected native grass and bush species in suitable areas is also under consideration as is the possible control of some exotic plants. These await conclusions from the food preferences study. The careful use of cattle as a management tool is also under review, largely to prevent excessive growth of exotic grasses at sites where these have been introduced. This is both to reduce the chance of serious damage to the habitat in a wildfire outbreak and to minimize grass competition with young shrubs and trees; of course, high numbers of cattle also can destroy these young plants.

Equally important as the vegetation to the survival of the bridled nailtail-wallaby are the other native mammal inhabitants of its environment. These must be carefully considered in any management plan. The perceived importance of the dingo has already been mentioned and, at this juncture, it seems necessary to continue to keep its numbers low. This may well result, however, in an upsurge of black-striped wallabies because of their importance in the dingo's diet; the possibility of having to cull this macropodid must be considered, particularly during the dry period before the summer rains, to reduce competition. It appears desirable to ensure the continued presence of the black-striped wallaby in the managed area, however, if for no other reason than that it has always occurred wherever bridled nailtail-wallabies have been found in the region; the possibility must be allowed that these are in some way important for the bridled nailtail-wallaby's survival. Because the black-striped wallaby occupies the thick acacia scrubs of the region, and the maintenance of these is included in the strategy for the bridled nailtail-wallaby, ensuring the survival of the former seems to be a straightforward matter. To control its numbers without the help of the dingo, however, may be a problem.

If, as it appears at the moment, the bridled nailtail-wallaby has been retained in its central Queensland redoubt, the question must arise as to how secure it really is. The area involved in both

"Taunton" and "Red Hill" is only some eleven thousand hectares, by world standards small for a reserve containing the last remnant of a comparatively large animal species. Further, such a tiny, isolated population may well lose some of its genetic viability over the years, perhaps resulting in an increasing susceptibility to an infrequently experienced adverse environmental pressure, such as disease. It is clearly desirable, therefore, to save more than one population. It may be, of course, that a carefully managed reservoir of animals will eventually provide surplus stocks that will emigrate and manage to colonize surrounding areas successfully. The likelihood of this is small, however, particularly if the deduced cause of decline of the species is correct. If additional populations are to be preserved, these must be free of the presence of European agriculture, on reserves to which they will probably have to be reintroduced. This raises questions of how large such reserves must be, and how reintroduction is to proceed.

Theoretical considerations have provided some answers. For a viable population, it has been calculated that a minimum of fifty individuals will permit the maintenance of short term (five hundred years) genetic fitness; five hundred individuals are needed for long term fitness. This means that once the desirable density of bridled nailtail-wallabies has been determined (from current studies), minimum areas can be specified to contain other populations. To prepare for reintroduction, it is necessary that an intended area first be located within the previous range of the species; it must be established that the species is in fact absent there; and the causes of its disappearance must be positively identified and effectively eliminated.

If the survival of the bridled nailtail-wallaby at the most desirable population level is to be ensured, planning for reintroduction must start now, when the opportunities for identifying and securing suitable potential reserves still exist.

It should be noted, finally, that reintroduction necessarily incorporates the establishment of captive breeding colonies. The techniques for gathering these, for their effective husbandry (including use of foster parents such as the unadorned rock-wallaby), and for obtaining additional information on the basic biology of the species, are now being obtained. The major contributions that can be made by zoos in this field also are being closely observed.

The final management programme – if indeed finality can ever be achieved in the unstable environment of central Queensland – will surely involve a balanced, and probably opportunistic, combination of many management techniques. Most of these will have been designed to destroy the natural environment but, we believe, can be converted for maintenance of the ecology in a condition conducive to securing one of the most endangered kangaroo species.

The solutions to such problems of conservation go far beyond the conventional prescriptions for helping wildlife – legal protection and habitat preservation. Instead, it becomes necessary for biologists to devise highly manipulative procedures that intervene into the precise stage of the life cycle of the endangered species where it has proved to be vulnerable to adverse environmental pressures.

Other threatened species

Without placing undue emphasis on the species per se, it must be recognized that management of species has outdistanced the management of ecosystems, just as the knowledge about individuals has outstripped that of species. Based on the experience of the bridled nailtail-wallaby, other species of kangaroos may eventually demand singular attention. These may occur in widely different circumstances and with different reasons for the interest in them, as the following examples show.

"Bizarre" species

The musk rat-kangaroo is sometimes stated to be the most primitive living member of the family Macropodidae. The distribution of vibrissae (whiskers), limb proportions, structure of the hands and feet including the presence of a mobile hallux (first toe), the galloping (rather than saltatory) gait, presence of a vestigial lower second incisor tooth, and an unsacculated stomach, provide a significant array of characters that appear to be retained from a premacropodid ancestor. The species is endemic to northern Queensland, with distribution restricted to the belt of evergreen closed forests (figure 6 and plate 3[a]), where conservation of habitat is a most contentious public issue.

"Marginally distributed" species

The long-nosed potoroo occurs uncommonly throughout south-eastern Queensland (figure 7) as an extension of its fundamental southern Australian coastal (Bassian) distribution range. Some of the

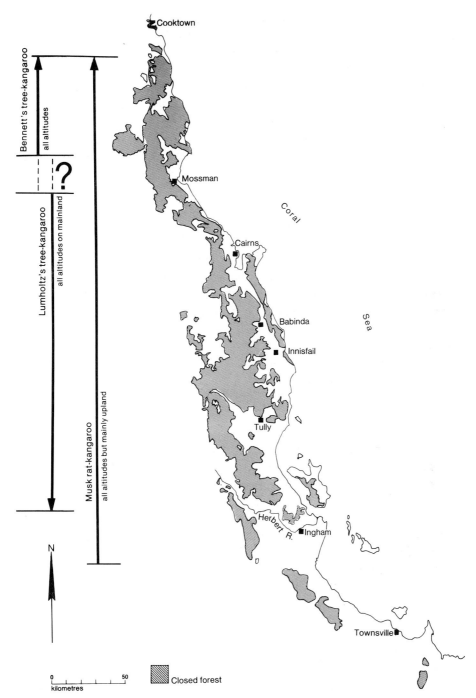

Figure 6 Evergreen closed forest distribution (shaded areas) in northeastern Australia showing occurrence of the musk rat-kangaroo, Lumholtz's tree-kangaroo and Bennett's tree-kangaroo.

(a)

Plate 3 (a) Closed forest habitat of the musk rat-kangaroo and the red-legged pademelon, Wallaman, northern Queensland; (b) Cape York Peninsula habitat of the antilopine kangaroo, Mt Surprise district, northern Queensland (see colour plate N for details).

(b)

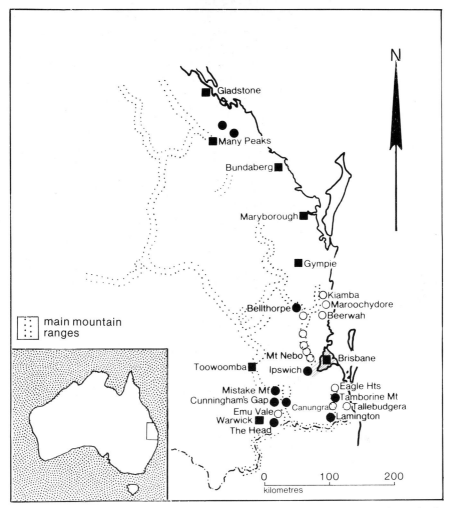

Figure 7 Distribution of records of the long-nosed potoroo in southeastern Queensland. Circle: specimen in Queensland Museum; dot: captive individuals and those recently observed or captured.

last recorded specimens held in the Queensland Museum are forty to fifty years old and it is doubtful if the animals still occur in the localities from which these were taken.

Even more isolated in the north of the continent is the brush-tailed bettong, previously widespread across southern Australia and now known only from a relict population (*B. penicillata tropica* described earlier) in Davies Creek National Park and from Windsor Tableland in northern Queensland (see plate 1[a]). Previous records by Professor R. Collett note it or a related species as "extremely numerous" in the Dawson River Valley (130 kilometres southwest of Rockhampton) and "other places" in central Queensland (1882) and G. H. H. Tate described it from Ravenshoe (1922) and from Mount Spurgeon (1932). The most extreme distribution of this type is illustrated by the Tasmanian bettong, known in Queensland from the skull of a sub-adult male collected at Pine Mountain near Ipswich in 1869. The retreat of the species south to Victoria more than sixty years ago and its subsequent isolation in part of Tasmania poses a conservation problem that now would appear to be approachable only in that island state. The capture of an adult male individual, presumably a relocated escapee, on a main highway in Brisbane in June 1983 only further emphasizes the extraordinary management questions that can be posed within one sovereign part of a species' distribution range.

"Apparently extinct" species

The desert rat-kangaroo was last recorded in central Australia in 1935. It appears to have occurred usually in small numbers within an estimated 155,000 square kilometres stony plains range, though an irruption in numbers on the lower Diamantina River in 1931 is suspected (figure 8). The record is confused by a specimen reputedly taken (by Professor Ralph Tate in 1878, then President of the Philosophical Society of Adelaide) from the Bunda Plateau at the head of the Great Australian Bight where there were allegedly many individuals. Of all the potoroines, the dental character of its incisors, "canines", premolars, and molars makes it the only one similar to the macropodine subfamily; while it is closest in body appearance to the rufous rat-kangaroo, and most closely related to the long-nosed potoroo, identification of the desert rat-kangaroo depends ultimately on its teeth (figure 9). Recent rediscoveries of other kangaroos give hope that this species may survive in remote areas or as relict populations.

Isolated populations

The complex distribution pattern of rock-wallaby species has been described earlier in this book. The yellow-footed rock-wallaby, much the most attractive of all the rock-wallabies, occurs in the Grey Range habitat (figure 10 and plate 2[b]) and reports suggest that the distribution may be more extensive than was previously known. The species may have undergone a great decline there. Such a decline would correlate with the less rugged nature, lower altitude,

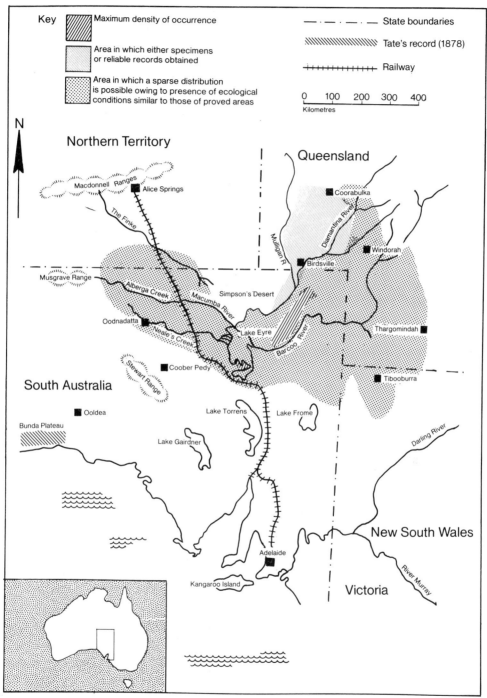

Figure 8 Former range of the desert rat-kangaroo in central and southern Australia (after Finlayson 1932).

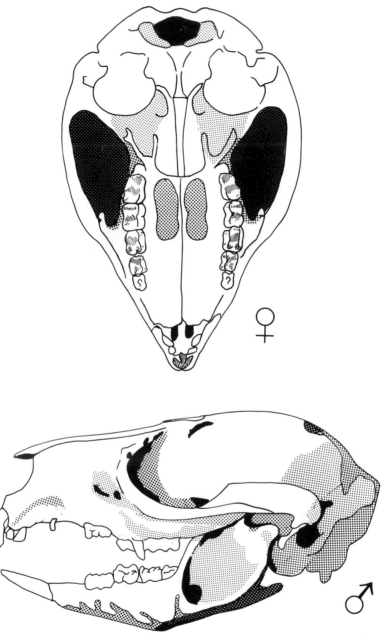

Figure 9 Outline of the skull (side and palatal views) of the desert rat-kangaroo. Top: sub-adult male. Bottom: adult female (after Finlayson 1932).

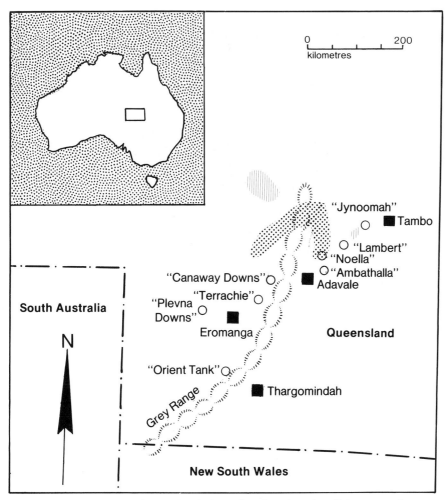

Figure 10 Distribution of records of the yellow-footed rock-wallaby in southwestern Queensland. Stipple: common sightings by zoologists; hachure: uncommon sightings by zoologists; circle: other reports.

and less extensive area of mountainous country compared with the southern Australian part of the rock-wallaby's range; these factors could increase the effects of introduced herbivores on the species and its food supply. Reports also suggest a recent and rapid decline after European settlement, rather than a long-term one due to climatic change. Ridge country in southwestern Queensland shows extensive erosion of the slopes and flats nearby, a consequence of earlier overgrazing. One of this species sighted on such a flat had been feeding on vegetation growing there.

Such erosion could cause a permanent decrease in the food supply and lower the carrying capacity of the habitat. The decreased food supply, when accentuated by severe drought, could be the immediate cause of local extinctions, rather than factors such as fox predation or indirect competition with introduced herbivores for food. Conservation should be based initially on the exclusion of introduced herbivores from the remaining habitat to prevent its further deterioration.

Godman's rock-wallaby, on the other hand, is the most northerly representative of the rock-wallabies in Queensland. It occurs north from Mt Molloy to beyond Coen, where it lives on sandstone ridges and granite boulder outcrops such as Black Mountain, near Cooktown (plate 2[c]). Two chromosomal races or subspecies are recognized. These are a northern, as yet unnamed, form that occurs around Coen and "true" *P. godmani* which occurs in the Cooktown area. Tropical grasslands with varying densities of dry schlerophyll trees, such as ironbark gum, surround most Godman's rock-wallaby colonies; it has not been found in apparently suitable rocky areas surrounded by wetter vegetation such as evergreen closed forest. It apparently feeds primarily on kangaroo grass and spear grass which occur widely throughout its range; these are almost certainly supplemented by other plant foods including herbs, fruits, and shrub leaves.

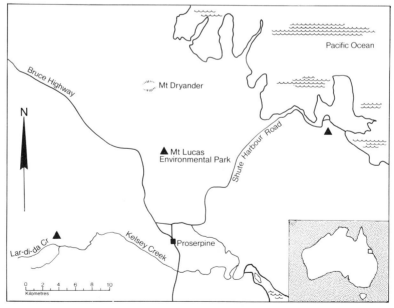

Figure 11 Distribution of records of the Proserpine rock-wallaby in northeastern Queensland. Triangle: specimen collected.

As noted earlier, the continued existence of Godman's rock-wallaby is seemingly threatened (for example, at Black Mountain) by the natural chromosomal spread from the adjacent unadorned rock-wallaby population, a conservation problem thus of a vastly different complexion from that confronting the yellow-footed rock-wallaby.

Again, confined populations can be extremely threatened. The distinctively large Proserpine rock-wallaby is recorded from only three sites (see figure 11) where it may also overlap with the unadorned rock-wallaby. Although part of its habitat is now gazetted parkland and although it is possible that this recently discovered species (1976) may be encountered outside its presently known range, the absence of information by which to manage the situation in the midst of extensive agriculture is a severe impediment to its conservation.

Little known species and zoo animals

Several zoos have listed Bennett's tree-kangaroo among their stocks in recent years, yet little is written of its husbandry, let alone its biology and ecology. Both Australian tree-kangaroos are endemic to northeastern Queensland in the mountainous region of evergreen closed forest (figure 6). Their management and conservation is clearly that of the management of their limited and exploited habitat, and much attention is likely to be given to this in the future for a variety of reasons. Estimates suggest that Lumholtz's tree-kangaroo may be marginally more secure, with twelve per cent of its 574,409 hectare habitat reserved in national parks compared with one-quarter of the 126,400 hectares of the habitat of Bennett's tree-kangaroo.

Selection for particular notice, even from among this short list, will be difficult. Whether we are optimists or pessimists, there is no reason to suppose that long-term ecological decisions will soon replace short-term economic ones in human affairs. There is only one systematic method of selecting species for "saving" that has received general attention. This is *triage,* based on the method of selecting the most time-effective cases on which French surgeons operated during the overwhelming casualties of World War I. It is a considered attempt to maximize return for effort expended. Regrettably, this still fails to confront the "enemy", and it fails to recognize that different resources may be available to respond to the plight of different species at different places and times (and not in accordance with a preconceived ranking of importance). In more recent years, decision analysis had provided techniques that make *a priori* judgments explicit so that they can be subjected to scrutiny, and it makes logical inconsistencies apparent so that these can be corrected.

At the very least the preservation of a small number of species, even if only for a generation or two, is the preservation of options.

Conservationists seek ban on 'roo products export

By JANE CADZOW

E Fund for Animals and Australian conservation ask the Federal

exports in an attempt to bring about the cessation of kanga roo "harvesting".

Roos and sheep both eat grass

I READ, with absolute amazement, the letter from Elizabeth Ashcroft (C-M. September 19) regarding kangaroos.

Surely she can't be serious! Has she never had a pet kangaroo and watched what it ate? Has she never watched what a sheep eats? Let me assure her they certainly do compete for the same feed. Also, does she know that a new born joey certainly does not eat grass

It seems to me that people like Eli

The roo versus rui

TV linku highligh roo killin

More roos in West now'

EWS from the United es this week that bans on garoo products look like g lifted could not have come better time for Charleville ed kangaroo abattoir opera Phil Capewell.

hil, who has been in the kangaroo oting business for 34 ye ised a deputation to Prima

KANGARO IS COWA

I AM opposed to th of a kangaroo in change of the Au tional flag

WANTED
A PILOT WHO CARES ABOUT WILD

We are concerned starving and flood wildlife in S.W. QUEENS We seek a pilot who wou willing to give his/her tim fly our representatives to area for an aerial surve YOU'LL HELP, PLEASE PH Jacki Kent (after 6 pm). (07) 378 7

Inserted by ANIMAL LIBERATION (QLD) LTD.

Roos a few hops in front

CANBERRA. — There are more kangaroos in Australia than people, according to figures sup plied by the Com monwealth Scientific and Industrial Research Or ganisation.

garoo skin products be tentative rder usiness is r ii said.

"The final nail i movie 'Goodbye scenes of cruelty ly meant to typif

extent dlife Asso each

The federal government quota for the commer cial killing of kangaroos announced on Monday has reawakened contro versy on one nation'

"Anybody wi

'Roo plight' | f GENTLE JEDDA

Kangaroos are protected fauna. rotected by what? Governments ch allow millions to be massacred.

RECENT aerial sur a population ex ed and grey kan as occurred in weste properties carry oos for every

NSW with

WANTED
000 'ROO RANGERS

ne, the market oducts is con it less attrac ial shooter

hich have cial harv uth Aus ensland nts well ndustry

An Aussie 'stew' at roo talks

WASHINGTON: The Au Government and United Sta Australian conservationist clashed in Washington at a mental hearing on the future kangaroo industry in the US.

They presented conflicting testimo a sub-committee of the US Interior partment which later will make rec mendations to Congress on whether red, western grey and eastern grey k garoo should be taken off the US thre

Society wants wal
in Shire emblem

Reward on joey killers

A man was recovering yesterday after being attacked by a kangaroo

Ten kangaroo os were let loose n the street ch early yesterday morning after va ls cut the chain on their Queens Pa closure w young cou

Roo disease

THOUSANDS of kangaroos are though have died from a myster swept through the tricts reco were coax

THE KANGAROO LAUGHTER

by the ROME.— Demonstrators yeste ant kangaroo-shaped balloon to the-kangaroo campaign. The 3 m plastic balloo named Joanna, will be used in protests in five oth European countries that import kangaroo meat a skins, organisers of the demonstration said.

Kangaroo prot

Fight for 'roo too

Roo's death

A COLLISION between a big red kangaroo and a Fokker Friendship plane has caused a

kangaroo hopped from the pi lot's left on to the runway. The kangaroo died instantly.

rks airport safety probe

tence and Walgett with stock-proof tence to keep kangaroos away. Townsville

mptoms of partial

pictures which follow o are horrific. Th al sy

hey're gunning for 'roos

at of arms al heri

ll for action kangaroos

Goondiwindi

ENSLAND'S major conserva organisations do not oppose olled kangaroo harvesting

SYDNEY. — Kangaroos "breed like rabbits" and are in no

They say it is wrong to kill kanga roos because they are endangered,

Chapter 3

The red kangaroo
and the arid environment

The desert ecosystem

Because most Australians live along the continent's seaboard, it is difficult for them to comprehend that their country is more than two-thirds desert. In eastern Australia, once across the Great Dividing Range and into the great open plains of the west, the vision of an arid land becomes real.

Arid lands are often described as lands that can not support farming without the use of irrigation. Semi-arid country will support dryland farming, though not reliably, and is usually classed with the dry regions of Australia. A description depending on the absence of agriculture as a criterion for aridity may be satisfactory for farmers and other land users, but not for those undertaking any serious study of desert animals. Such studies require a much more profound knowledge of desert ecosystems.

There is one feature characteristic of all deserts of the world: the lack of water. Within a desert, rainfall is so low that water becomes a dominant controlling factor of biological processes. Rainfall in deserts is highly variable throughout the year, often infrequent and usually unpredictable. Consequently, inland Australia may suffer drought conditions for many years and suddenly, within a few days, become isolated by floods.

This unpredictability of the supply of water leads to similar irregularity of growth of vegetation. Plants respond to rain and soon after reasonable falls the apparently barren countryside may be covered with green grasses and flowering shrubs. The animal inhabitants respond in the same way, although there is necessarily a greater time lag in the reactions of the fauna. Overall, as the plant life increases, so does the number of those animals dependent upon vegetation as food, the herbivores. Later, the predators follow.

The great majority of herbivores of desert ecosystems are not the usually seen and illustrated grazing sheep and cattle but much smaller animals such as termites and other invertebrates. In one situation (in the Northern Territory) for example, it has been estimated that one species of subterranean termite has a biomass (living matter expressed as weight of organisms per unit area, or volume of organisms per unit volume of habitat) of 20–25 kilograms per hectare of land, while in the same area cattle are stocked at the rate of 10–15 kilograms per hectare and kangaroos have a density of about 0.16 kilograms per hectare. The termites eat 50–100 kilograms of plant life from each hectare, about the same as that consumed by cattle.

Dependent on the herbivores are the many carnivores and scavengers that, predictably, increase in numbers following any increase in their prey. So life in the deserts mainly comes in pulses that are governed by the frequency and extent of the rainfall.

Following a long dry period, in contrast, the desert ecosystem reverts to an inactive state. An effective rainfall activates many biological processes and the growth of plants and animals builds up as described. These processes gradually exhaust the ration of available water supplied by the rain and after an initial growth period – often staggering in its proportions – the biomass of both the plants and the animals again diminishes to a steady small level in readiness for the next burst of rain; it has been described as a "pulse and reserve model" of an ecosystem. The trigger that sets off a pulse of production in plants and animals is rain; the energy of the pulse is mostly lost by mortality or consumption. Fortunately – perhaps better, sensibly – some is diverted back into a reserve of seeds, eggs, and other drought-resistant forms of "resting" life. This reserve compartment holds its energy during the non-rain period and from it comes the next growth pulse.

The red kangaroo and the wallaroo: desert species

Probably the most recognized animal living in the Australian desert is the red kangaroo. It occurs nowhere else in the world and to many people it symbolizes the national character of this country.

The major part of the species' distribution includes the arid parts of the continent; it appears to be an animal that prefers a dry existence. When observing red kangaroos in a zoo during a rainstorm, one quickly appreciates that these animals are not at all partial to wet conditions; they quickly lose their shiny-coated appearance and they are always the first to seek shelter, long before their more temperate relatives such as the eastern grey kangaroo and swamp wallaby.

Although the physiology and reproductive strategies of the red kangaroo are indicative of animals adapted to desert living, it is the way in which the behaviour of the species fits into the general arid ecosystem of the desert that is addressed in this chapter.

Behaviour and its modification in different environments is vital for the survival of mammals. Thus the behaviour of an animal within a predictive climate, whether hot or cold, wet or dry, will be different from that displayed by those from an unpredictable arid area such as exists over much of Australia. As described earlier, the general characteristics of the inland regions of Australia include, as a most important aspect, the lack of certainty of the extent and even occurrence of water.

Many animals avoid crises induced by adverse climate by hibernating or aestivating, that is, reducing metabolic rates to permit a state of "sleep". This strategy is utilized in Australia by frogs, reptiles, and several small mammals; many invertebrates remain in cocoons during these times, and indeed many species survive only as eggs hidden away in the ground, under bark of trees, or in the dry mud of evaporated waterholes in riverbeds. Large animals such as the red kangaroo cannot use these tactics, of course, and so employ other ways of tolerating drought.

The physiological adaptations of the two main "desert" species, the red kangaroo and the wallaroo, are well developed. The regulation of water loss from the kidneys of these animals is an excellent example of their ability to survive dry conditions. Both the red kangaroo and the wallaroo have glomerular filtration rates (GFR), renal plasma flows, and urine flow rates, when hydrated and dehydrated, which are lower than those of similarly sized eutherian mammals.

The low GFR and urine production and the responses of the two species to dehydration categorize these marsupials as superior to most larger eutherian mammals in renal function. The red kangaroo has a flexible kidney in regard to water and electrolytes, being able to filter and handle relatively large amounts of these substances. This would be important for the nomadic red kangaroo in its varied environment, with its large water requirements for temperature regulation and so on. While the red kangaroo may prefer green grass for food, it may at times depend on the halophytic succulent shrubs such as saltbushes (*Atriplex* species) common in much of arid Australia. These shrubs contain high levels of salts that require extra water for their excretion.

On the other hand, the wallaroo tends to avoid the heat of the desert by sheltering in caves and thus has a lower water requirement. If suitable shelter is available, the principal ecological problems of the wallaroo are nutritional. In its restricted home range, the wallaroo may be affected more readily by overgrazing during drought and thus have to rely on poor-quality herbage. The wallaroo has the ability to conserve more urea in its kidneys than the red kangaroo and this ability is used to advantage during drought.

One part of the strategy of the red kangaroo — probably the most obvious part — is to utilize mobility, moving long distances to locate areas that will supply their needs of food and water. Red kangaroos move to and from areas best suited to their particular needs at the time. This pattern of habitat use is found in many other animal groups including mammals; the movement of the large mammal herds of the Serengeti Plains of eastern Africa is a spectacular example.

Habitat preferences

Traditionally, red kangaroos have been regarded as "plains kangaroos"; they are pictured usually as inhabitants of the vast grasslands of the semi-arid zone of the Australian continent. Yet, the red kangaroo's choice of habitat ranges from heavily timbered areas, particularly beside creeks and low-lying swamps, to stony rugged hills that are more readily associated with the wallaroo. To add further to this apparent inconsistency, these habitat types are not all utilized at the same time, their occupancy being usually temporary and dependent mostly upon seasonal conditions.

Several studies of the habitat preferences of red kangaroos have been undertaken in central Australia and, in 1974, a six-year study began in southwestern Queensland, northwestern New South Wales and northeastern South Australia (figure 12). This work was designed to find out how the red kangaroo fitted into the relatively complex mosaic of habitat types found in western New South Wales and Queensland. Because of the importance of the work to management of the kangaroos, particular emphasis was placed upon the need to identify the extent of both movements and habitat use by these animals in the context of human development.

A first priority was to define a small study area, which was done in the vicinity of Tibooburra, New South Wales, and to mark individually as many kangaroos as possible within it. The trapping of kan-

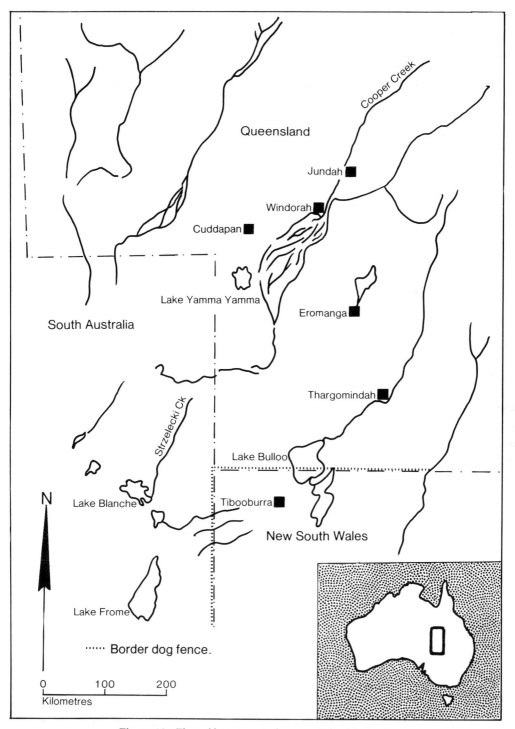

Figure 12 The red kangaroo study area in inland Australia.

garoos is not difficult: the scarcity of water in inland areas forces
kangaroos during the summer months to watering points such as
earth tanks built by landholders to water their stock. Incidentally,
these have probably allowed more kangaroos to survive during
droughts than any other manmade feature. Tanks enclosed by a
netting fence, with funnels in the corners, prevented animals that
entered the area to drink from leaving. However, handling kangaroos trapped this way is difficult; they do not stand stand still to be
caught! After many exhausting trapping sessions, nearly seven
hundred red kangaroos were trapped and released into the study
area wearing white collars with individually coded colour markings
(plate 4[a]).

Following this marking session, the precise locality of any animals
seen when travelling through the study area was recorded. Collars
from marked animals shot by hunters were returned also with
comments on localities and the condition of the animals. Because
the population of red kangaroos in the study area was estimated to be
150,000 at the time, the chances of seeing many of the marked individuals was small and results from this approach were inadequate as
the sole basis for firm conclusions about habitat choices.

Alternative approaches were then adopted. The first was observation of the number of red kangaroos found in different habitat types
during the same period; these were undertaken from vehicles in
regions of New South Wales, Queensland, and South Australia
(figure 13). Set courses (transects) within this study area were
followed during summer and winter. Many land types, including
those within the large Sturt National Park, were included, as were
lands grazed by sheep and cattle.

The transects were driven by vehicles with roof, windscreen, win-
dows and doors removed to give 360 degrees visibility; all transects
were driven in the early mornings before kangaroos settled down to
rest beneath trees and shrubs. In summer, cool morning conditions
were pleasant, but in winter, with temperatures below zero, the
open vehicle was definitely chilly!

As well as the ground-driven vehicles, a second set of observations
was made from an aircraft. The technique used for this involved
counting red kangaroos from a plane flying at a set speed and
altitude. The number of kangaroos within a fixed width of some one
hundred metres on each side of the plane gave usable estimates of
density within the many habitat types.

All of these methods of approach were employed for more than
four years and, from the results, a pattern of habitat use by red
kangaroos in the dry interior was obtained.

(a)

(b)

Plate 4 (a) Handling and collar-marking the red kangaroo for movement studies (M.J.S. Denny); (b) the border dog fence; (c) drought-killed red kangaroo

(c)

Home range

Of the 692 caught and marked with collars, only 117 were resighted. The majority of relocations (eighty per cent) were within ten kilometres of where the individual was originally caught; the remainder were found as far as three hundred kilometres away. This value of ten kilometres may be regarded as the radius of the "home range" of the majority of red kangaroos, at least during favourable seasons. Much the same value has been suggested by other zoologists working on the species. (The term home range is used to describe the total area occupied by an animal during its life.) For most red kangaroos the results indicate that the home range is roughly a circle with a radius of ten kilometres (or 314 square kilometres).

The attractions of a home range area of this size are easily visualized. Within such an area are usually found several watering points (either natural or artificial) as well as a variety of habitat types. It is not difficult to understand why many marked kangaroos were sighted repeatedly within this range of their original capture point year after year.

To see if the home range area was as attractive as it seemed, a group of red kangaroos was transported sixty kilometres from their point of capture. Many of these left their point of release and some were found later in their home ranges, suggesting inherent values at these locations.

What of the twenty per cent of marked kangaroos that were resighted more than ten kilometres from their capture point? Some moved from New South Wales to South Australia. Some moved relatively slowly at a calculated rate of only a hundred metres a month. Some moved quickly at a rate averaging thirteen kilometres a month. Interestingly, most of these far-ranging individuals were males. The females were nearly all sedentary and the males from the sedentary group were significantly heavier and larger, and thus probably older, than the mobile males.

These observations permit the simple interpretation that when dispersion takes place in a red kangaroo population, it mainly involves young males that are unable to mate with females because they are dominated by older males. They leave the home range of their birth for another location where they might be able to locate a female and breed.

Long-distance movement, however, is more than mere dispersion, an interpretation that was helped by results of the counts made while looking for marked animals, and from the air. The majority of individuals resighted a long way from their point of release were found in areas where freshly grown grass — green pick, as it is called in the west — had become abundant. Such areas were usually either a consequence of localized rainstorms or an aftermath of fire. In areas recently burnt, the density of red kangaroos was as much as four times that found in unburnt parts of the same habitat; in areas where rain had recently fallen, the kangaroos were found in densities up to 270 times those occurring in dry areas.

Preferred vegetation

The characteristics of the vegetation in wet localities were those most attractive to red kangaroos — low, dry biomass and high proportions of water and nitrogen. To attain high densities in wet areas, red kangaroos do not have to move long distances. In an area of about thirty square kilometres where rain had recently fallen, red kangaroo densities were calculated to be as high as 94 per square kilometre, an estimate that when applied to the whole area meant that some 2,800 kangaroos had crowded on to the site. Because over-all density before the rain was only 12 per square kilometre, 360 animals were probably there before the rain — which means that 2,460 red kangaroos moved into the area from surrounding country. That this had indeed happened was demonstrated by the fact that the countryside surrounding the 30 square kilometres of land had a density of only 0.2 kangaroos per square kilometre. At the same time, it must be realized that for 2,400 kangaroos to move into the wet area an area of only 205 square kilometres would have had to lose its animals — an area in fact smaller than one home range (314 square kilometres from the data above).

Sightings of marked kangaroos in wet areas, however, showed that some of these must have moved as far as thirty kilometres to take advantage of a localized rainstorm. Because it is possible in this relatively flat country to see and to smell rainstorms thirty kilometres away, it is obvious that such distances were not too great to prevent the movement of individuals to a preferred area. It is easy to understand from this experience how the high densities of red kangaroos within isolated areas can give the impression of a "kangaroo plague" that people so often talk about. Here, more than two thousand red kangaroos were in sight at one time!

Another reliable observation was that red kangaroos are capable of great sensitivity when choosing those areas where rain provides the greatest benefit. In one district where rain fell upon a mix of two distinctly different habitat types, stony downs and alluvial flats, the animals selected the stony downs to move to, where vegetation contained a higher proportion of water and nitrogen compared with that of the alluvial flats.

The other principal aspect studied was habitat utilization, because habitat preferences manifestly have to be a major reason for kangaroo movement. Within the study area, there are numerous habitat types all used to some extent by red kangaroos. These include open grassy plains (stony downs), swamps, stony hills, sand dunes, and creek beds; each habitat can in fact be described in terms of vegetation cover, soil type, and geomorphology, although greater detail is required to explain the reasons for the particular attraction to red kangaroos of each habitat type.

On the reasonable assumption that food preferences must have something to do with habitat preference, several features of plant growth were measured within each habitat type studied. Variations in these were then related to any changes in habitat use by red kangaroos. Measurements made included tree height and shrub height, dry biomass, and percentage of water and nitrogen contents of grasses and forbs. Tree and shrub height and density showed little change from season to season but the measures of grasses and forbs altered significantly. These variations coincided with the amount of rainfall (figure 13).

Within each habitat type, changes in exploitation by red kangaroos also vary from season to season. If the results from the above study are separated into summer and winter seasons, it is apparent that some habitat types have higher kangaroo densities in one than in the other; for example, a habitat associated with creeks has a relatively higher kangaroo density in summer than in winter. Alternatively, kangaroo density is higher in winter than in summer on stony downs. It was not possible to associate these differences with the amount of food available, but they evidently were associated with the amount of cover from the sun. Creek habitat has a much denser cover of tall shrubs and trees than the stony downs, and in summer red kangaroos are attracted by the shelter. In winter, however, the more exposed stony downs allow red kangaroos greater access to the warmth of the sun.

Another fairly obvious reason for the red kangaroo distribution pattern lies in the need to seek shelter from the cold winter winds. The most suitable shelter for this purpose is in the form of small bushes that serve as wind breaks yet permit sufficient sunlight for basking. Such a situation occurs within swampy habitat, where the shrubs (usually lignum about one metre in height) provide a suitable

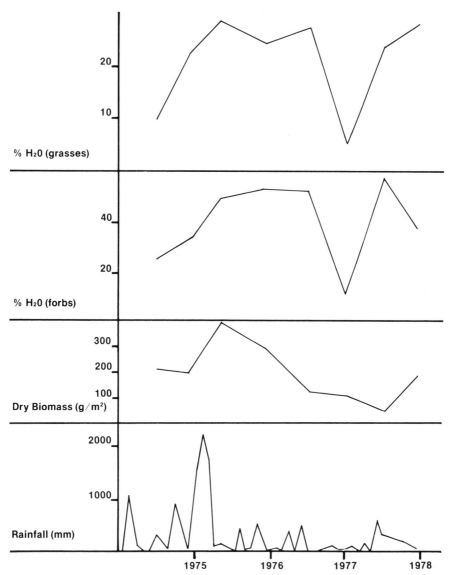

Figure 13 Changes in water content of grasses, of forbs, and in dry biomass of grasses and forbs compared with rainfall in the inland Australia study area: 1975 to 1978.

cover in winter even though food is limited. Changes in red kangaroo densities in sheltered areas during summer and winter can be illustrated. In an area of approximately three square kilometres, the red kangaroos counted in June 1975 (winter) numbered 182, in November 1975 (summer) 48, in May 1976 (winter) 123, and in November 1976 (summer) 34. The high densities in winter are readily attributable to the incidence of the shrub *Bassia quinquecuspus,* of ideal height (24–40 centimetres) to be used as shelter against the wind. During the colder months, the area provided much less food than other areas nearby, yet attracted many more red kangaroos.

Perhaps the strongest decider for the changing habitat preferences of red kangaroos, however, is food availability. Other studies have pointed out the relationship between red kangaroo density and the amount of short green pick. More recently, it has been shown that red kangaroos consistently seek green, growing pastures; yet grey kangaroos were much more evenly distributed than red kangaroos, suggesting that that species is less concerned about the presence of fresh green grass so sought after by red kangaroos.

The study reported here also has demonstrated a strong connection between green grass and red kangaroo numbers, but it went a step further by relating red kangaroo density to the amounts of water and nitrogen in the grasses. In habitat types where the dry biomass of grasses was low but water and nitrogen content high, it could be predicted that many red kangaroos would be found. The dry biomass of grasses in wet areas was low compared with that of dry grasses (30 grams per square metre and 77 grams per square metre, respectively), but the percentage of water and nitrogen of grasses and forbs was high in wet areas. Thus, grasses were forty-one per cent water in wet areas and seven per cent water in areas where no rain had fallen.

Man's effects on dispersion

An interesting aspect of the movement patterns of red kangaroos in the desert ecosystem has arisen from observations made on the numbers of animals near the border dog fence (plate 4[b]).

The border dog fence extends along the borders between New South Wales, Queensland and South Australia. This two-metre high netting fence was established early this century as a barrier for dingoes entering New South Wales from other states. Because of its height and length (more than six hundred kilometres), it also stops the movement of kangaroos.

Driving along the track that runs beside the fence, it is quickly apparent that large numbers of red kangaroos congregate there, particularly on the New South Wales side. Both ground and aerial counting in the vicinity reveal that within one kilometre of the fence kangaroo density is more than twice the average value for the region, prompting the obvious questions of why so many kangaroos are associated with the fence and is the fence interfering with one of the patterns of red kangaroo movements. A study was undertaken to examine these concerns.

Because most of the border dog fence passes through sandy country, estimates of fence effects could be obtained by the simple expedient of smoothing a one-metre wide strip of sand at selected intervals along it. The strips were smoothed out by broom and to any passing motorist the sight of somebody "sweeping the dog fence" must have seemed strange indeed! The strips were left overnight and the numbers and directions of any kangaroo prints on each strip were counted the following morning.

Results varied widely. Sometimes as many as a hundred red kangaroos travel along the fence, at other times none. One reason for the observed differences was that wind direction apparently influences both the position and direction of travel by red kangaroos. For instance, when the wind was blowing from the west, most kangaroos were found along the South Australian rather than the Queensland border and the animals were moving in a westerly direction. When a northerly wind was blowing, red kangaroos were found in greater numbers along the Queensland border and heading northwards. This pattern is similar to that found in sheep, which tend to graze into the wind.

Thus, from the results of these studies, it has been possible to explain many of the basic patterns of movement of red kangaroos in inland Australia as dispersal of young males and as grazing into the wind, with concentrations caused by movement in response to localized areas of grazing. Other types of movement do occur, such as movement away from disturbance caused by shooters; there is some evidence of long distance migration at least by some animals. Overall, there can be no doubt that the ability and preparedness to move is a vital aspect of the success of the red kangaroo in a desert ecosystem.

Implications for management of movement patterns

The overall implications of these studies of movement and habitat preferences for red kangaroo management are extensive. The main pattern of movements is within relatively short distances and takes place in response to changing habitat characteristics and red kangaroo needs. Within the typical home range are many habitat types for which red kangaroos show changing preferences through the year and a most important consequence of this is that any area of land set aside for conservation of them must allow for this variety.

The absolute minimum size of a conservation area must be no smaller than a home range area, that is about thirty thousand hectares; this was the extent of area utilized by the sedentary kangaroos in the present study area with its diverse habitat types. In other areas, it has been found that red kangaroos require smaller home ranges.

Other scientists have suggested that in Australia the minimum population size for macropodids should be between 250 and 3,000 individuals; others have tripled these numbers. Some 1,000 red kangaroos present in a home range area would give a density of about three animals per square kilometre. This relatively low figure could be used as a guide when red kangaroos are being harvested; that is, no cropping should be permitted once this level of density has been reached (at least in the landforms where the present study was made).

Reserved land, such as a national park, containing one or even several home ranges will not contain all of the red kangaroos in a population, of course. At least one-fifth of the population is sufficiently mobile to move outside such a reserve and, during prolonged drought, an even higher proportion could be expected to do so. Thus, if successful conservation of red kangaroos is to be achieved, an area is required that is large enough to contain the more mobile individuals. If a distance of 210 kilometres is accepted as the radius of such a conservation area (because several red kangaroos have been recorded as travelling this far), then the area would have to be about fourteen thousand square kilometres (or about one-half of all of the land held currently as conservation reserves throughout Australia). It is unnecessary to be concerned for every individual in a population, of course, but when drought occurs and a higher proportion of red kangaroos becomes more mobile, such large areas must be contemplated. Thus, on commonsense grounds, conservation of longer-ranging kangaroos must involve acceptance of the principle of multiple-purpose use of land: a simple approach to this is merely to give protected status to red kangaroos on land surrounding, say, a national park, particularly during periods of stress.

As pointed out above, large concentrations of red kangaroos in localized areas can easily mislead an observer about overall population density. This leads to an incorrect assessment of the status of the species and results in an overestimate of the numbers that may be harvested. Movements of red kangaroos into a preferred area can occur in less than a week after rain and the large numbers found there can diminish soon afterwards. If wildlife managers are too slow to respond to complaints of kangaroo damage, then inspection may not reveal the high densities that may have occurred. Where verification of damage is also required (as in New South Wales) authorities must react quickly to complaints to avoid unnecessary antagonism with landholders.

Movement by red kangaroos occurs for many reasons but some level of predictability may, in fact, be applied to distribution in an area. Once some knowledge of an area's immediate history is gathered it is possible to predict precisely where the highest density of animals may be expected. Suitable practical guidelines would include such observations as: areas of ten-kilometre radius surrounding watering points will maintain a stable population; areas experiencing rain will temporarily support a high density of animals; a prevalent wind will influence the direction of movement of individuals; habitat with trees will attract animals in summer and open bushy areas will attract red kangaroos in winter.

Population sizes of red kangaroos, like so many animals of the desert, fluctuate according to prevailing climatic conditions. During a series of good wet seasons, numbers can build up to high levels, while in drought these can decline dramatically. In the study area discussed above during the period 1973 to 1977, the density of red kangaroos increased from 2.2 per square kilometre to 17.9 per square kilometre, a rate of increse of 0.54 each year. Studies at Kinchega National Park (south of Broken Hill, NSW) have shown a maximum rate of increase of 0.74 per year. Thus the natural increase in a population of red kangaroos during a series of wet years approaches the maximum likely rate.

In the current investigations, the increase in red kangaroo population size was paralleled by a gradual increase in plant productivity (see figure 14). There was also an improvement in the body condition of red kangaroos between 1973 and 1977. When, however, in late 1977 and into 1978 a minor drought occurred in the study area, plant productivity fell and density rates steadied. Had the population kept increasing at the earlier rate, red kangaroo density would have been about 38 per square kilometre; instead, it was 15 per square kilometre.

This "stabilization" of population size did not appear to be due to a cessation of reproduction; eighty-five per cent of the females caught still had pouch-young. More likely, the steadying of population growth was due to greater mortality, particularly among the less fit individuals. Many old kangaroos were found dead or dying in or near evaporated waterholes and the general body condition of all red kangaroos declined during this drought period (plate 4[c]).

This is, of course, a classic animal–resource relationship. In better seasons, plant productivity increases and is followed by increased red kangaroo numbers. Then, as a consequence of drought, influenced by overgrazing and other effects, plant productivity falls and population sizes fall soon after. Thus in this study, red kangaroos were in peak numbers in 1978 (when in fact plant productivity was dropping as was kangaroo body condition).

At such time, management decisions must be made which recognize that alternative events are possible:

1. Should it rain, the resulting increase in plant productivity will cause an upswing in the red kangaroo population.
2. Should it not rain, the downward trend already established will continue, with a resultant fall in numbers.

The correct management decision then undoubtedly is that this is the best time to crop (harvest) the population, particularly of males. If it does rain, there will remain a viable breeding population that can increase to its past level. If not, the lower number of kangaroos have more chance of survival on the limited food resources. Such a suggested management tactic is little different from that used on every grazing property in inland Australia, where stock is sold at the beginning of an impending drought. The real question is whether the kangaroo population should be allowed to reach environmental saturation before harvesting is permitted.

Attitudes to the red kangaroo

A proper study of red kangaroos cannot depend solely on information derived from present situations; it must also rely on information from the past. When Europeans first settled in Australia, this country bore little resemblance to Europe, either culturally or environmentally. In Europe between 1770 and 1800 works by Beethoven, Mozart, and Haydn were performed publicly; Balzac, Hugo, Pushkin, Sheridan, Scott, and Austen were popular novelists; and the poetry of Byron, Blake, and Keats was widely read. The culture of Australia belonged to the Aborigines.

The history of European development of Australia is closely allied with our attitudes to and exploitation of the larger kangaroo species,

COLOUR PLATES

PLATE A

An Aboriginal engraving of a kangaroo track, located in the floor debris of Cathedral Cave, Carnarvon National Park, central Queensland in 1979 (G. Walsh). The engraving – made by abrading the sandstone with a harder rock – portrays the toes-only imprint left by a kangaroo moving at a "fast hop" (see p. 20 for details). The representation of one foot slightly ahead of the other is true to life of the moving animal.

PLATE B

Musk rat-kangaroo (*Hypsiprymnodon moschatas* Ramsay)

[*Top to bottom:* male, female, subadult]

Features: scaly tail; ("thumb", giving five toes on hind foot)

Size: average length (incl. tail), 37 cm; average weight, 0.5 kg

Habits: "Galloping run"; diurnal; searches litter of forest floor with its forepaws for food; builds "nest" as resting site, using (like other rat-kangaroos) the tail to carry the necessary plant material

Habitat: found only in mature closed forest on rugged, elevated regions of north-eastern Australia and the adjacent coastal plain (see figure 6); more commonly sighted in wetter areas near rivers, creeks and springs. Occasionally it can be observed in regenerating forest when the canopy has been partly disturbed as a result of logging. Fruits and animal life from the leaf litter provide the basis of its diet; some of the fruits are from such trees as the Kuranda satin ash and Alexandra palm. Large plank buttress roots, lawyer vine clumps and occasionally, small rock piles provide "nest" sites. (See also plate 3)

PLATE C

Brush-tailed bettong (*Bettongia penicillata* Gray)
[*Top:* male, male]

Features: triangular-shaped ears; distal one-third of tail black and bushy
Size: average length (incl. tail), 64 cm; average weight, 1.3 kg
Habits: "nest builder"; low, hunched, fast, hopping gait with tail held straight out.
Habitat: occupies rugged, elevated areas of open forest and adjacent woodlands with a grass and shrub understorey; outcrops of granite on parent basalt rock may be present. Vegetation of the open forest includes black she-oak, acacias and grevilleas. The understorey comprises blady grass, giant speargrass and kangaroo grass.

Rufous rat-kangaroo (*Aepyprymnus rufescens* (Gray))
[*Centre:* female]

Features: white underparts to "grizzled" grey body; (also furry nose)
Size: average length (incl. tail), 74 cm; average weight, 3 kg
Habits: typical stance of head withdrawn in shoulders, though upright when alarmed; arms stiffly down beside body; long, low hissing call when alarmed when (like many other kangaroos) it also stamps its hind feet; digs for food; builds a "nest" that is often re-used at the base of a grass tussock, against a log, or in a depression in the ground; usually solitary
Habitat: occurs on flat to undulating country of the eastern uplands that consists mainly of sedimentary and volcanic soils. The habitat is open forest (black gidgee, brigalow, tea-trees and a wide range of eucalypts) with a well-grassed understorey of wire grasses, desert bluegrass, kangaroo grasses, giant speargrass, black speargrass and pitted bluegrass. Found occasionally on the margins of closed forests and agricultural lands. (See also figure 17.)

Long-nosed potoroo (*Potorous tridactylus* (Kerr))
[*Bottom:* male]

Features: rounded ears; scaly tapered tail covered at base with fur; (also pointed, bare nozzle)
Size: average length (incl. tail), 60 cm; average weight, 1.1 kg
Habits: usual macropodid locomotion (with forepart of body held close to ground), though when stationary or excited the tail may display serpentine-like movements; digs conical holes in the ground when searching for food; rests in "nests" at the base of grass tussocks or grasstrees during the day; (species often confused with bandicoots)
Habitat: in southern Queensland, the northern extent of its Australian distribution, inhabits eucalypt open forest with a thick understorey of grasses and shrubs in moist situations; within the Moreton region, the animals are restricted to the ranges where such open forests are usually in close association with rainforest in which individuals occasionally have been observed. The species also inhabits coastal wallum country where it occurs in woodlands composed of scribbly gum and banksias, and in low heath of banksias and grasstrees (much of these lands have been cleared for agriculture). Potoroos excavate depressions under grasses and grasstrees, suggesting that ground cover created by fires and other disturbance especially in marginal areas is important. Such cover includes kangaroo grass, blady grass and bracken fern; where a shrub layer is present this comprises mostly acacias, though the dominant trees (and the ground cover for that matter) can vary greatly. (See also figure 7.)
Note: The Tasmanian bettong (*Bettongia gaimardi* (Desmarest)) is not illustrated. The only northern record is of a skull; the species apparently is extinct on the Australian mainland.

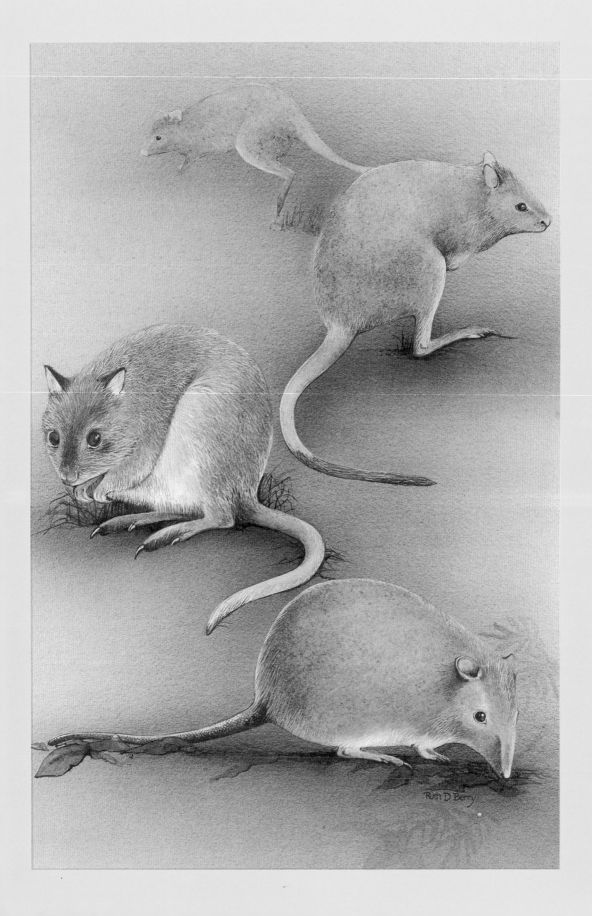

Ruth D Berry

PLATE D

Desert rat-kangaroo (*Caloprymnus campestris* (Gould))
[All females]

Features: short, blunt head in profile with long, narrow ears, short forearms and long tail

Size: average length (incl. tail), 58 cm; average weight, 0.9 kg

Habits: uses a shallow "nest" under bushes or in the open where it is loosely thatched over with leaves, grasses and sticks; solitary; fast, easy, uniform stride, with one foot placed down before the other rather than in parallel as with other rat-kangaroos; leans well forward when hopping, with tail straight out

Habitat: in transition areas between gibber plains and loamy flats with sparse shrub cover mainly of bluebushes, saltbushes, burrs and corkwood. (See also figure 8.)

Ruth Berry.

PLATE E

Spectacled hare-wallaby (*Lagorchestes conspicillatus* Gould)

[*Top to bottom:* female, female, male, male]

Features: rufous-brown eye-rings; thickset body

Size: average length (incl. tail), 80 cm; average weight, 4 kg

Habits: accentuated slow walk; nocturnal; solitary; shelter is a shallow depression at the base of a large grass tussock.

Habitat: occurs in open forest with a grass understorey on the eastern coast, through grassland and low woodland (of eucalypts, tea-trees and acacias) in the central part of Queensland to woodland with a grass understorey in the far west; topography generally flat or undulating. The plant communities of the open forest consist of narrowleaf ironbark, silverleaf ironbark, box communities, and coolibah, poplar gum and ironwood; the plant communities of the woodland of the far western areas consist of eucalypts, acacias and spinifex grasses. (See also figure 17, top right.)

PLATE F

Bridled nailtail-wallaby *(Onychogalea fraenata* (Gould))
[All males]

Features: white "bridle" behind relatively short arms; (also black-tipped tail)

Size: average length (incl. tail), 110 cm; average weight 5 kg

Habits: fast, smooth movement with body held low to ground; like the northern nailtail-wallaby and the spectacled hare-wallaby, species may lie prone in long grass to avoid detection

Habitat: presently in country of dense plant communities of shrub species mainly, though not exclusively, dominated by brigalow communities, other scrubs (of bastard sandalwood, wattles and yellowwood), eucalypt communities and cleared areas; these include regenerated open forest and shrubland, and areas with partly disturbed canopies. Relevant land systems consist of the more fertile soils such as cracking clays and alluvial soils. (See also figures 3, 4 and 5.)

Ruth Berry.

PLATE G

Northern nailtail-wallaby (*Onychogalea unguifera* (Gould))
[All males]

Features: long ears; brown stripe along back; distal one-third of long, thin tail black

Size: average length (incl. tail), 120 cm; average weight, 6 kg

Habits: low, crouched hop with long thin tail held upcurved; the peculiar rotary action of forearms when animal is moving rapidly has led to its names of the "organ grinder", "lefthander", and "righthander".

Habitat: found most commonly on the flat floodplains of river systems (such as around the Gulf of Carpentaria) on parent soils of granite, sandstone and basalt. Most of the floodplains are treeless with grasses such as bluegrass and browntop forming a pasture. Structural forms of the vegetation range from woodland with a grass understorey to Mitchell grass plains. The woodlands contain such trees as ironbark, Georgetown box and ironwood. (See also figure 17, bottom left.)

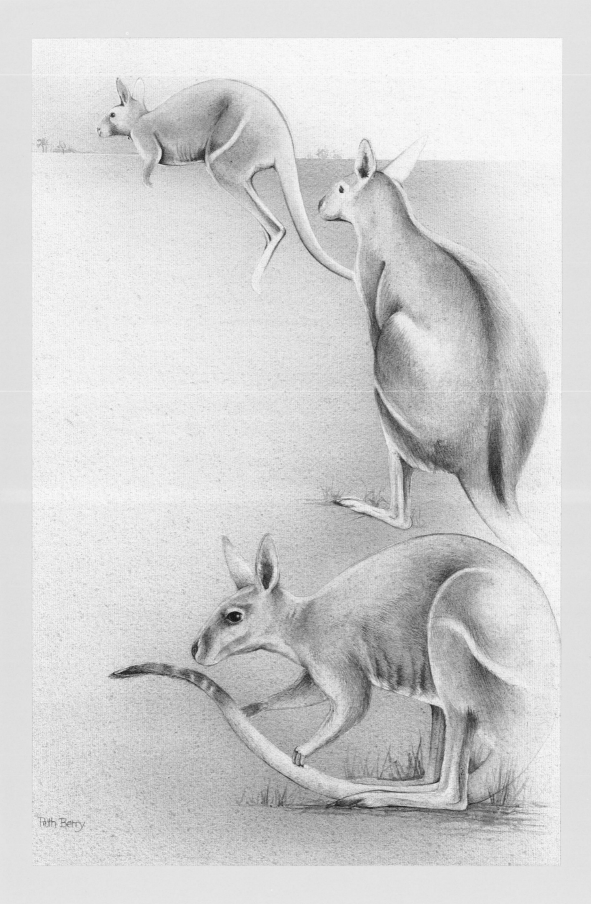

Ruth Berry

PLATE H

Brush-tailed rock-wallaby (*Petrogale penicillata* (Griffith, Smith & Pidgeon))
[*From top down crest:* female, male, female]

Features: black furry feet; long, heavily furred, black-tufted tail
Size: average length (incl. tail), 104 cm (northern form); average weight 6 kg
Habits: typically hops with great agility on ledges of well-lit rockfaces; also climbs sloping trees; lives in colonies
Habitat: on boulder-strewn hillsides of granite and sandstone where protection from predators and extreme temperatures can be found (in fissures, crevices and caves). Vegetation ranges from tropical open woodland in the north through brigalow scrub to temperate open forest and woodland in southern Australia. Grasses such as those of the genus *Poa* and kangaroo grass (*Themeda*) are common in addition to a variety of herbs and the fruits and leaves of shrubs and small trees. (See also figure 1.)

Black-flanked rock-wallaby (*Petrogale lateralis* Gould)
[*Centre right:* male]

Features: purple coloration around head and neck (in northwestern Queensland form)
Size: average length (incl. tail), 108 cm; average weight, 5.5 kg
Habits: as for all rock-wallabies
Habitat: in rocky granite hillsides associated with a variety of vegetation types from xerophytic (dry) hummock and tussock grasslands to mulga shrublands. Spinifex grasses, Mitchell grasses, Flinders grasses and lovegrasses prevail. (See also figure 1.)

Unadorned rock-wallaby (*Petrogale inornata* Gould)
[*Second from bottom:* subadult]

Size: average length (incl. tail), 104 cm; average weight, 4.5 kg
Habits: as for all rock-wallabies
Habitat: vegetation on the escarpments and rock-strewn hillsides varies from brigalow scrub to dry mid grass and tussock grassland. Grasses such as wiregrasses, bluegrasses and Flinders grasses are abundant but a wide range of herbs and the fruits and leaves of shrubs must also be present to provide supplementary foods. (See also figure 1.)

Proserpine rock-wallaby (*Petrogale persephone* Maynes)
[*Bottom:* female]

Features: relatively large size; few body markings
Size: average length (incl. tail), 120 cm; weight 5–8 kg (males noticeably larger than females)
Habits: as for all rock-wallabies.
Habitat: on rocky hillsides. The vegetation is of low vine forest. (See also figures 1 and 11.)
Note: Godman's rock-wallaby (*Petrogale godmani* Thomas) is not illustrated. Found only in far north Queensland, it is indistinguishable in appearance from the unadorned rock-wallaby.

PLATE I

Yellow-footed rock-wallaby (*Petrogale xanthopus* Gray)

[*Top to bottom:* female, male, female, male]

Features: long pointed ears; dark rings around tail

Size: average length (incl. tail), 110 cm (northern form); average weight, 6 kg

Habits: as for all rock-wallabies

Habitat: along cliff-lines formed at the edges of low stony tablelands and ridges, with sloping sides and precipitous walls towards the top, usually one–two metres in height and reaching ten metres; occasionally on low hills with vegetation cover only. Flats with temporary watercourses occur below the tablelands. The principal vegetation on the stony tablelands and slopes is mulga, with other tree and large shrub species such as lancewood, bendee and bastard mulga on almost bare ground and tree cover on grassy floodplains on the flats. Communities of coolibah and gidgee are common near the watercourses. (See also figures 1 and 10 and plate 2(b).)

Ruth Barry

PLATE J

Lumholtz's tree-kangaroo (*Dendrolagus lumholtzi* Collett)

[*Top:* male]

Features: pale-coloured band across forehead; rounded ears.

Size: average length (incl. tail), 120 cm; weight 6–7.5 kg

Habits: vertical tree climber; tail hangs loosely; leaf and fruit eater; hindlegs can move independently of one another

Habitat: in closed forest of volcanic and sedimentary soils over mountainous areas and on to the coastal plain. (See also figure 6.)

Bennett's tree-kangaroo (*Dendrolagus bennettianus* De Vis)

[*Bottom:* male]

Features: dark brown colour overall; rounded ears

Size: lengths (incl. tail), 130–160 cm; male weight 13 kg (males noticeably larger than females)

Habits: as for Lumholtz's tree-kangaroo

Habitat: as for Lumholtz's tree-kangaroo and sometimes into open forest, but with different geographic range. (See also figure 6.)

PLATE K

Red-legged pademelon (*Thylogale stigmatica* Gould)

[*From top right:* female, female, young-at-foot]

Features: red coloration on thighs

Size: average length (incl. tail), 85 cm; average weight, 4.5 kg

Habits: extremely timid; leaf and fruit eater

Habitat: occurs in mountainous closed forests and associated smaller, low, dry vine forest areas (generally to the west of the ranges); the dense understoreys are on volcanic and sedimentary soils. (See also figure 17, bottom right, and plate 3.)

Red-necked pademelon (*Thylogale thetis* (Lesson))

[*Bottom:* female]

Features: rufous brown coloration on shoulders

Size: length, (incl. tail), 77–95 cm; weight, 4–7 kg (males much larger than females)

Habits: moves out at night into open areas, returning to cover at daybreak

Habitat: uses both closed forest and open grassy pastures, but does not penetrate far into either. (See also figure 17, bottom right.)

R.Berry

PLATE L

Agile wallaby (*Macropus agilis* (Gould))
[*From top:* male, female]

Features: pointed face; black border to ears
Size: length (incl. tail), 130–155 cm; weight, 11–19 kg (males noticeably larger than females)
Habits: hops with forearms extended; often props when alarmed; usually in small groups
Habitat: open forest with grass understorey along coastal areas of flat or gently undulating terrain. Trees are mostly eucalypts (such as grey ironbark, poplar gum and ghost gum) and the grasses include speargrasses, bluegrasses and kangaroo grass. Occurs in pastures and agricultural crops adjacent to natural. (See also figure 18, top right.)

Whiptail wallaby (*Macropus parryi* (Bennett))
[*Centre right:* male]

Features: white underparts to grey body; distinct white facial stripe; long slim tail
Size: length (incl. tail), 155–185 cm; weight, 11–16 kg (males noticeably larger than females)
Habits: hops erect (like the eastern grey kangaroo) often in groups.
Habitat: in and adjacent to mountainous and hilly country with open forest, woodland and open woodland (usually of eucalypts) and grass understorey. (See also figure 19, left.)

Swamp wallaby (*Wallabia bicolor* (Desmarest))
[*Bottom:* male]

Features: dark colour with black stripe above eyes and behind shoulders
Size: length (incl. tail) 140–150 cm; weight 13–17 kg (males noticeably larger than females)
Habits: apparently uncoordinated gait, with tail held high; leaps high in long grass; solitary
Habitat: requires vegetation with moderate to dense ground cover either as shrubs or tall grass. Habitat is shrubland and timbered country including open forest, woodland and open woodland; uses both eucalypt and non-eucalypt communities including acacia scrubs such as brigalow; it also occurs in grassy open forest, timbered watercourses, semi-evergreen and deciduous vine thickets, heathlands and high dunes. The species is by no means limited to swampy areas, more frequently being found on slopes of hilly country. It also commonly invades young grain crops. (See also figure 18, top left.)

PLATE M.

Red-necked wallaby (*Macropus rufogriseus* (Desmarest))

[*From top:* female, female]

Features: stocky appearance to head and forequarters; no black stripe down middle of back; tail with brushy tip

Size: length (incl. tail), 100–160 cm; weight, 14–18 kg (males noticeably larger than females)

Habits: usually in large groups, though basically solitary animals as adults

Habitat: includes forested areas with a moderate to dense undergrowth of brush. The species invades open grasslands, cultivated pastures and crops adjacent to forested areas, especially during winter and months of low rainfall. (See also figure 18, bottom right.)

Black-striped wallaby (*Macropus dorsalis* (Gray))

[*Bottom two:* male, male]

Features: black stripe down middle of back from neck

Size: length (incl. tail), 110–160 cm; weight 6–16 kg (males much larger than females)

Habits: moves with head low and arms stretched out; timid, tending to flee when disturbed; communal.

Habitat: in and near vegetation with a moderately dense to dense shrub or tree layer. The communities include the denser forms of eucalypt open forest, acacia open forests such as lancewood and brigalow grassy open forest, and shrub-dominated communities such as eucalypt shrub woodland, vine thicket (softwood scrub or bottle tree scrub) or brigalow shrubby open forest. Invades adjacent pastures and croplands. (See also figure 18, bottom left.)

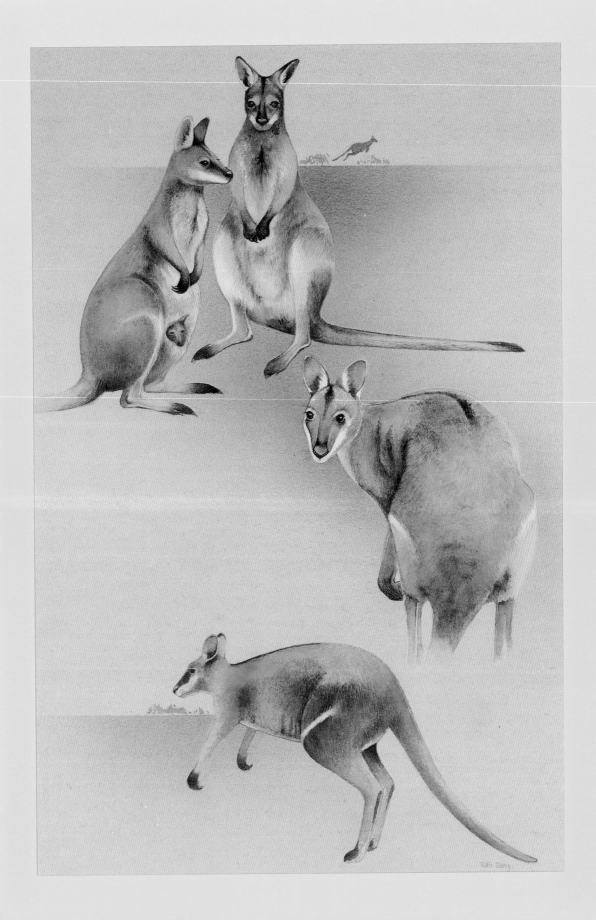

PLATE N

Wallaroo (*Macropus robustus* Gould)

[*From top:* female, male, subadult]

Features: large, heavy, shaggy appearance (including furry nose); tail thick and relatively short; (there is enormous colour variation)

Size: length (incl. tail), 130–190 cm; weight 25–55 kg (males much larger than females)

Habits: usually solitary

Habitat: mostly in the vicinity of rugged country (including rocky creekbeds); usually on or near hills and mountain ranges where cover in the form of forest or, in lightly timbered country, caves, is available. Though rarely in non-rugged country, the species sometimes uses dense vegetation such as eucalypt shrub woodland with dense shrub understorey. Grazing is largely confined to pastures, and wallaroos will readily graze sown pastures and forage crops, particularly during dry times.

Antilopine kangaroo (*Macropus antilopinus* (Gould))

[*Bottom three:* male, male, female]

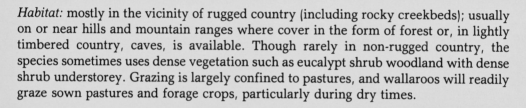

Features: no *distinctive* black and white face markings

Size: length (incl. tail), 150–190 cm; weight 17–37 kg (males much larger than females)

Habits: highly gregarious (in small mobs)

Habitat: occurs in flat and undulating woodland areas where there are grass understoreys, and on open plains. Dominant eucalypt trees include Georgetown box, narrowleaf ironbark, gum-topped bloodwood and ghost gum, while common grasses include bunch speargrass, kangaroo grass and wiregrasses. (See also figure 19, right, and plate 3(b).)

PLATE O

Western grey kangaroo (*Macropus fuliginosus* (Desmarest))
[*Top left:* female]

Features: black face; furry nose
Size: length (incl. tail), 155–220 cm; weight, 27–54 kg (males much larger than females)
Habits: hops erect; gregarious (in small mobs)
Habitat: inhabits open forests and adjacent open areas

Eastern grey kangaroo (*Macropus giganteus* Shaw)
[*Top right:* female, young-at-foot]

Features: uniform colour overall with dark terminal one-third of tail; furry nose
Size: length (incl. tail), 170–250 cm; weight, 32–66 kg (males much larger than females, with occasional individuals to 95 kg)
Habits: hops erect; gregarious (in large mobs)
Habitat: inhabits timbered country and adjacent grassland, with both eucalypt and non-eucalypt communities of open forest, woodland and open woodland structure and grass or shrub understorey. Adjacent areas including pastures, crops and timber plantations are grazed particularly during dry times. The wide range of native pasture grasses occurring in the habitat are all eaten.

Red kangaroo (*Macropus rufus* (Desmarest))
[*Bottom:* male, male, male, female]

Features: distinct black and white face markings; nose partly furred
Size: length (incl. tail), 180–205 cm; weight, 26–66 kg (males much larger than females, with occasional individuals to 95 kg)
Habits: hops with body held horizontally; often in small mobs
Habitat: in low rainfall areas of the forests and open plains of the inland; mulga-annual grass communities, mulga–perennial grass and open woodland communities including flood plains, gilgaied plains, foothill fans and treeless plains

(a)

Plate 5 European development influencing red kangaroo populations includes (a) spread of domestic stock; (b) use of trees (mulga) for fence posts; (c) building of artificial water impoundments; (d) tolerance of feral pests

(b)

(c)

(d)

especially the red kangaroo. The subject has been described in detail elsewhere; the more important conclusions are outlined here.

Many attitudes towards red kangaroos by European settlers have developed since these animals were first sighted; all are still current. These include the kangaroo as a curiosity, as a pest, as an object for sport, food, and commercial exploitation, and as an animal in need of special protection. Such a diverse set of attitudes within a society makes it extremely difficult to institute a management plan that will satisfy most people – hence the continual controversies surrounding the subject.

There is increasing evidence that the numbers of red kangaroos in pre-European settlement times were as large in some areas as they now are. Many authorities presume that populations were low prior to the development of water impoundments and the increase in pasture grasses (both encouraged for domestic stock) (plate 5). Nevertheless, the numbers of animals noted by early explorers, particularly along the western slopes of the Great Dividing Range, were often in the hundreds; this reflects densities as high as nowadays.

Massive numbers of red kangaroos have been killed in the past, yet the populations are as extensive as any other time for which records exist. For instance, between 1880 and 1890 the estimated population of red kangaroos in New South Wales fell from 5,484,000 to 921,500; this estimation of a dramatic fall of over 4.5 million kangaroos was seen to be due to the combined influences of hunting and drought. In this period of time, kangaroos were regarded as vermin attracting a bounty (on heads); many people earned their living by destroying these animals. Even though numbers evidently were low at the turn of the century, by the 1950s red kangaroos were so abundant as to be described by the rural community as in "plague proportions", and again destroyed in large numbers. It has been estimated that three-quarters of the population in southwestern New South Wales disappeared again in the 1960s. Now, twenty years later, the numbers of red kangaroos in inland Australia have appeared in extremely large numbers. It is evident that, despite the efforts in the past of a large proportion of landholders to eradicate kangaroos, such a campaign even in conjunction with prolonged droughts has had no long term effect on present-day distribution.

The red kangaroo is, in fact, an ideal occupant of Australia's vast inland. It is physiologically and behaviourally adapted and suited to the desert ecosystem. It has a flexible approach to an erratic and unpredictable environment that has allowed it to cope also with modifications brought about by European settlement.

Approval for roo culling

Eight species of kangaroo and wallaby may be taken during the open season in Queensland next year.

No 'roo in pet foo
— canne

PET food manufacturers do not use kangaroo meat and it is not

KANGAROOS—OUR NEW MEAT EXPORT TO EUROP

Roo meat has royal approval

SIR — I would like to ask questions of the head ranger Fund for Animals who adv in the press recently for 10 rangers.

Has he seen kangaroos in c thousands in grazing and farm

Roo quota

CANBERRA. — The Federal ment yesterday announced quota

THE documentary Goodbye Joey showed "one or two set-up ex amples" of cruelty to kangaroos, the Federal Environment Minister, Mr Cohen, said

It's on the Australian coat-of-arms . . . some West Germ'n menus. Here it is put on th urker

but kangaroo and sauerkraut will soon be o allowed to be sold only as a delicacy like venison and wild pig. The opening of a n as a pet food but there it s inflame the current controversy over the survival of ZVARD reports on this new in the

Kangaroos 'too few for quota'

The Cattlemen's Union yesterday asked the State Government to endorse a national management plan for the control of harvesting of kangaroos.

members have claimed that on a three found too few kan-

Pet meat trade the loser

Shooters rule 'roos

in the turmoil backlash

THE pet meat tr

'The kangaroo is a national emblem adorning the coat of arms . . . conversely it is an abundant, renewable resource.'

Within a millisecond he was dead, shot through the eye. In death, he reared back, nerve endings recording nothing.

ONY

controls permits, tags, licenses o on, but export meat is the Com-

harvest and mark lines which are u "If something i

Shoot permit for 1.5m. roos

US. Lifts Roo Ban

US pleas for new roo import ban

Mr. Don Neal, Member for Balonne LICENSED will again be able to tal s an

American conservation and animal welfare groups have appealed to the Prime Minister, Mr Hawke, to ask the US Government to ban imports of kangaroo products.

The 'roo shooters

Permits needed for kangaroo shooting in '8

Major conservatio organisation no opposition to 'roo culling

EXPORTING

Farmers and graziers wishing to shoot kangaroos pply to the National Parks and Wildlife Service in Toow A Crop Damage Permit is available to farmers and graziers f ervice is satisfied that significant damage is being caused to crops ar nd wallabies.

US authorities retain ban on kangaroo goods

THE Wildlife Preservation Society Queensland has pointed out that Queen land's major conservation organisations not oppose kangaroo culling. At its recent meeting in Brisbane the Societ

Chapter 4
The kangaroo industry

Aboriginal exploitation of kangaroos

It may be confidently assumed that kangaroos have been hunted by man since the first appearance of Aboriginal man in Australia, a view supported by the faunal remains aged between 6,000 and 3,000B.P. in the "Early Man shelter" at Laura (on Cape York Peninsula). These deposits included approximately 2,600 bone fragments – one-half of a single species (Godman's rock-wallaby) and two thirds of the remainder wallaroo and agile wallaby. The hunting methods used were presumably those employed by other primitive peoples – spears, snares and pit-traps, and running gregarious species over cliffs. Modern Aborigines were still using pits for trapping wallabies at the time of European settlement, and Moore in his extracts from the 1848–50 *Rattlesnake* journals of O. W. Brierly noted: "On the way back observing that the grass had been burnt on portions of the flats, the Blacks said that the rain that was coming would make the young grass spring up and that would bring down the kangaroos and the Blacks would spear them from the scrub".

By the time Europeans arrived on the Australian scene, macropodids were well established as a vital part of the Aboriginal economy, providing meat and skins for food and covering, and sinews, bones and teeth for a variety of functional and ornamental uses. The advent of Europeans caused no immediate change, at least from the point of view of the kangaroos; the newcomers continued to hunt them and for much the same reasons. As the modern-day colonization of Australia developed, however, the taking of kangaroos increased from serving a basic subsistence need to a commercial activity; this chapter reviews this development into the regulated industry it is today.

The Aborigines, it is generally believed, had developed a conservative approach to kangaroo hunting, born of the necessity to ensure continuation of the resources of the natural environment on which they depended totally. It is certain that their conservative ways were discovered by trial and error, and that they made mistakes along the way from which they learned. These may even have been on as grand and spectacular a scale as the mistakes from which European man is currently learning. There is an increasing body of evidence that a drastic change occurred in the vegetation of Australia, associated with a massive increase in soil erosion and coinciding with the earliest signs of human habitation. This is not unreasonable considering that the entire Australian continent may well have been populated by the descendants of the first handful of immigrant Aborigines in no more than two thousand years, involving virtually instantaneous exposure of the environment, and its fauna, to a new exploiter. These massive changes are readily attributed to them through the extensive and uncontrolled use of fire characteristic of the Aboriginal lifestyle; there can be little doubt that the pristine fauna was similarly affected. Whether Aborigines were involved in the extinction of the giant marsupials of the Pleistocene epoch is uncertain, because the chronology of this extinction is not established. It is likely. There certainly is proof that marsupial inhabitants of many of the islands off the coast of northern Australia were eliminated by Aborigines. The introduction of that efficient predator, the dingo, also had a major and deleterious effect on the fauna, including the extinction of the thylacine which survived only in Tasmania where the dingo was not released.

The large kangaroos of today's commerce, however, have been conspicuous survivors of all the actions, including the mistakes, of both Aboriginal and European man; they remain in abundance, and are the basis nowadays of one of the world's largest industries using a wild terrestrial animal.

European exploitation of kangaroos

The way to the current status of the industry – which entails the application of procedures that are as conservative as available knowledge allows – has involved many changes. The first colonizing Europeans regarded the kangaroo family with curiosity, but were grateful for it as a source of fresh meat even though they preferred the flesh of their domesticated ruminants and hastened to introduce these to their new homeland. Later colonists, introducing the tastes and habits of the English gentry, were happy to substitute the kangaroo and the dingo for the deer, hare and fox of England in the sport of coursing, and considered that the "sport" so provided was equivalent to that provided by the animals of their homeland; so seriously did they pursue it that a special breed of "kangaroo dog" was developed (figure 14).

As settlement expanded, and with it the area of land occupied by introduced crops and herds of domestic stock, the kangaroos began to be seen in a new light – as pests, and serious ones at that. The pest status of the macropodids is examined elsewhere in this book; here it is introduced because of the part this status has played in the development of a kangaroo industry.

The still existing conflict between the kangaroo family and the farming community began in earnest in the mid-nineteenth century, when the perception of kangaroos as a threat to the livelihoods of the rural community had developed to the extent that the state governments of eastern Australia enacted draconian legislation requiring the destruction of "marsupials" (meaning kangaroos) by all landholders. Monetary rewards – bounties – were offered by both farmers and governments for the scalps of all macropodids to stimulate greater destruction, and uncounted millions of these animals

Figure 14 Style of small-scale kangaroo-hunting in the 1870s. (Photograph courtesy John Oxley Library, Brisbane.)

Plate 6 Styles of large-scale kangaroo shooting in western Queensland in the 1890s
(Photographs courtesy John Oxley Library, Brisbane)

were destroyed throughout Australia during the nineteenth and early twentieth centuries. That much of the problem attributed to kangaroos, particularly in the rangelands, was equally attributable to the gross overstocking of domestic animals by graziers who were unable to comprehend and react to an environment radically different from that of their homeland took many decades to be appreciated, at least by the majority of the rural community. The kangaroos were large, obvious animals that had clearly taken advantage of the improvements wrought by the colonists for their domestic livestock and had increased greatly in numbers; they were obviously the cause of their problems. Ecological principles, too, were hardly understood in those days. The conservative use of land, developed in Europe over the centuries, had been established by trial and error; the attempt to understand the principles involved is a twentieth century phenomenon still in progress.

Development of the kangaroo industry began during this period of attempted extermination, when the superior quality of kangaroo skins began to be appreciated by overseas manufacturers of leather goods. The enormous supply made available by the pest destruction operation was exploited by shooters and dealers (plate 6) who extended this into an industry even in Western Australia before the agriculturalists and pastoralists developed there. Records of this period are difficult (if not impossible) to obtain, but every capital city had its skin market and associated port from which hides were shipped to Europe and North America. Annual sales in each of these centres were in the hundreds of thousands. Only since the enactment of the conservation legislation of the 1950s about the taking of native fauna and control of the kangaroo industry have records been kept. The Queensland experience in the collection and publication of such records is representative of the experiences of other states. Thus, while it was possible for the director of the Queensland Museum to be advised in 1923 by a dealer that annual "marsupial" skin sales in Brisbane were "between 300,000 and 400,000", since 1954 the annual commercial harvest has been known, according to species, with some accuracy. These figures are summarized in table 1 (the significance of these data will be discussed later).

Conservation legislation

It is somewhat ironic that an industry that developed during a time of dramatic and frequently disastrous change to the Australian environment had a significant part in the development of today's conservative attitude and legislation about the kangaroos; it gave a positive commercial value to animals that otherwise were regarded as useless vermin to be exterminated if at all possible. Because of its importance to the economy of rural Australia both in terms of invest-ment and cash flow, pressures were created on industry and govern-ment, to act and legislate respectively, for the conservation of the resource on which the industry depended. The pressures from other sources, including the increasing softening of community attitudes towards wild animals and the development and community accept-ance of ecological concepts that require a planned approach to environmental changes, have in fact only become significant enough to influence governments in recent years, and certainly *since* Queens-land's conservation legislation of 1954 was enacted. Application of at least some conservation principles by the kangaroo industry long preceded community espousal of the conservation ethic. Today's legislation relating to kangaroo harvesting, industry practices, and community attitudes all have a common objective that seeks the preservation, or more accurately conservation, of the harvested species of kangaroos.

The acceptance by the farming/grazing community of this conser-vative legislation depends in no small way on its belief that kangaroo harvesting is an acceptable way to have its pest problem managed. The legislation is seen as maintaining a precarious balance between the anxiety of the rural community to have its perception of kangaroos as pests suitably provided for and its preparedness to tolerate the protective attitude of the unaffected (and often unaware) urban dwellers provided the pest problem is recognized.

While the legislation controlling the kangaroo industry differs in detail among the several Australian states that allow kangaroo shoot-ing, all are derived from the basic perception of the large, harvested kangaroo species as highly successful and abundant animals that represent a pest problem to rural enterprise. All acts have as common objectives the maintenance of viable populations of kangaroos throughout their natural range and control of the industry with no heavier a hand that is necessary to ensure cooperation between industry and government in their mutual interest (if for different reasons) in the welfare of harvested species.

In Queensland, the industry is based mainly on the eastern grey kangaroo, which normally accounts for more than one-half of the take (table 2). Next in importance is the red kangaroo, followed by the wallaroo and the whiptail wallaby. The other species listed in table 2 are taken mainly as pests; they are of little value for skins and even less for meat, and the numbers that now enter the trade have decreased over the last decade as the cost of taking these continues to increase relative to returns.

Relevant Queensland legislation dates back to 1877, but in its current conservation form only to 1954; the earlier legislation virtually demanded that extermination be undertaken. The *Fauna Conservation Act 1954–1979* (the current legislation) requires that all shooters and dealers be registered annually and involves the payment of licence fees; it requires that all shooters name the properties on which they intend to operate, with signed approval for entry from the owner/occupier, and that all dealers and shooters declare each month the numbers of each species taken or handled. Royalties are payable on the four main commercial species; since 1975 these royalties have been collected in advance through the purchase of non-reusable, numbered, self-locking tags that must be attached to each harvested animal. Also controlled by registration and fee payment are the sites and premises from which dealers operate; since 1970 the number permitted in any year has been set, and the locations of premises must be approved. A general rule is that a new site must be a minimum of eighty kilometres from any other (most distances are much greater) and the volume of refrigerated storage for carcasses at any non-abattoir site must not exceed a prescribed maximum. Permits for both intrastate and interstate movements of kangaroos, whether as skin or carcasses, are required from dealers and shooters. Fees are charged for all permits issued under the act, and appropriate penalties including revoking of permits and fines are provided for non-observance of the regulations.

The effectiveness of the regulations, from the point of view of both ease of enforcement and survival of populations of harvested species, is under constant review. As the need, or demand, for new regulations is established, the necessary steps are taken to have them introduced. Permit fees were increased considerably and further controls including quotas and tags introduced during 1974. Despite the introduction of quotas (see below) which in theory at least should serve by themselves to prevent overharvesting, it is still desirable to ensure an even distribution of the kangaroo harvest in both space and time if for no other reason than to ensure control of the pest problem. Shooters' licences help to ensure a reasonable distribution in space, and a suitable distribution of dealers is necessary to prevent the likelihood of excessively high harvests in some areas (particularly around large towns) with consequent filling of the quota early in the year.

Table 2 Numbers of Macropodidae, by species, harvested annually in Queensland: 1954 to 1983

Year	Eastern grey kangaroo*	Red kangaroo	Wallaroo	Whiptail wallaby	Red-necked wallaby	Black-striped wallaby	Swamp wallaby	Agile wallaby
1954	127,753	68,683	3,295	6,429		7,907***	1,678	2,714
1955	155,956	93,616	11,155	11,580		15,581	12,848	4,900
1956	183,663	111,034	21,642	13,800		13,923	12,167	5,233
1957	283,137	276,125	29,987	13,781		14,756	6,959	6,379
1958	172,437	78,248	12,212	11,164		7,063	3,168	528
1959	319,829	588,807	55,031	91,773		25,141	6,784	2,154
1960	488,118	250,059	10,319	5,478		8,059	6,642	1,273
1961	293,365	161,063	3,374	11,038		2,208	592	nil
1962	369,631	163,712	8,377	4,945		1,227	879	nil
1963	444,607	175,284	6,727	11,026		3,462	846	111
1964	596,775	496,439	13,328	7,800		3,299	1,172	nil
1965	787,955	353,223	13,365	8,662		4,139	1,455	88
1966	640,985	269,377	4,703	8,082		1,210	272	nil
1967	662,319	198,294	3,601	3,323		1,350	2,413	nil
1968	612,323	235,123	5,524	6,214		1,467	2,330	nil
1969	774,881	322,727	5,817	9,732		1,678	1,230	nil
1970	604,932	232,017	42,372	13,850		5,856	1,088	nil
1971	402,322	139,010	27,931	7,604		4,423	381	8
1972	741,493	240,684	26,367	31,746		23,072	10,135	135
1973	340,751	83,067	14,263	14,293		3,950	1,336	55
1974	222,568	58,959	11,672	22,847		1,107	300	26
1975	363,520	95,225	6,026	31,642		711	14	nil
1976	421,808	106,971	31,949	45,259		12,719	1,203	646
1977	402,808	110,254	27,201	34,497		7,711	1,165	4,768
1978	378,432	152,455	23,372	41,793	1,774	nil	687	1,869
1979	866,395	342,622	34,054	53,908	9,714	262	370	6,935
1980	649,534	237,282	22,005	29,431	2,337	253	545	1,712
1981	398,860	220,216	27,937	31,981	241	nil	49	100
1982	682,583	352,117	67,191	33,823	197	238	nil	649
1983**	502,161	263,346	62,100	20,559	91	19	109	nil

* Some western grey kangaroos were included in these totals.

** Provisional.

*** Both species included as "brush" wallabies prior to 1978.

Since 1954, the Queensland government has had the responsibility of declaring open seasons annually for each harvested species, a responsibility that demands some assessment of the capacity of populations to withstand harvesting – the basis of the research programme described elsewhere in this book. Open seasons are declared for each species for such periods as are considered suitable; to date the period has been a full year throughout the state. Persons in possession of the necessary permit and landholder permission may take the number of kangaroos equal to the number of tags with which they have been issued by the fauna conservation authority.

Harvest quotas

The total number of the four commercially harvested species that may be taken, termed a quota, has been determined since 1975 at the

Table 3 Relationship between annual harvests of Macropodidae in Queensland and number of shooters, market value of skins and weather: 1954 to 1983

Year	Total no. kangaroos harvested	No. of registered shooters	Estimated average price per kg for first-grade skins	Seasonal weather conditions
1954	218,459	1,100	$1.63	wet
1955	305,616	1,513	$1.72	wet
1956	361,462	1,802	$1.74	wet
1957	631,034	2,466	$1.37	dry
1958	295,820	1,210	$1.10	average
1959	1,006,919	1,773	$1.74	dry
1960	769,948	1,775	$1.37	average
1961	471,640	1,470	$1.26	average
1962	548,771	1,514	$1.43	average
1963	642,063	1,711	$1.70	average
1964	1,118,813	2,198	$1.48	dry
1965	1,168,887	2,155	$1.46	drought
1966	924,629	1,281	$1.90	drought
1967	871,390	1,433	$2.20	drought
1968	862,981	1,445	$2.54	drought
1969	1,116,065	2,042	$2.54	drought
1970	900,115	1,907	$2.76	drought
1971	581,679	1,678	$1.15	average
1972	1,073,632	2,018	$1.12	drought
1973	457,720	1,550	$0.60	drought
1974	317,479	752	$0.60	flood
1975	497,138	935	$0.60	wet
1976	620,555	1,104	$0.60	wet
1977	588,404	1,309	$1.00	average
1978	600,382	1,437	$1.30	wet
1979	1,314,260	2,141	$2.10	dry
1980	943,099	2,578	$1.80	drought
1981	681,292	1,558	$0.90	average
1982	1,136,798	1,484	$0.95	drought
1983	848,385	1,404	$0,90	wet

beginning of each year and controlled by the issue of tags. Before the introduction of this system, numbers taken were governed by kangaroo availability, related to the season and market forces (see table 3). In fact numbers are still governed by this: the quota merely represents an arbitrary upper limit which the harvest is not allowed to exceed.

The way the quota is determined varies among the states. In New South Wales and South Australia it is based on an aerial survey of kangaroo numbers using techniques discussed elsewhere in this book (chapter 7); some fraction, usually of the order of ten per cent of this "count" is set as the maximum harvest permitted. In Queensland, the recorded harvests since 1954 are used as a primary basis for quota determination. These records, covering thirty years, demonstrate the capacity of populations to withstand the harvests taken under a wide range of weather conditions. Data on species' distribution (obtained from observations by field staff and from shooters' returns) and the sex and age distribution of the take (obtained from samples provided by shooters in selected harvesting areas), which allow the detection of any level of overharvest, combined with harvest records, provide a sound basis for setting the maximum permitted take for the next year. The use of these data is further discussed in chapter 7.

Commercial harvesting procedures

The primary product of the kangaroo industry is, of course, a dead kangaroo. The necessary equipment to secure it includes a utility, light truck, or four-wheel-drive vehicle with a trailer, a centre-fire rifle of a calibre somewhere between 0.22 and 0.310 fitted with a telescopic sight, and a vehicle-mounted spotlight for night shooting. Commercial shooters normally work from a town or from a base camp in the hunting territory; today most are "casuals" in the sense that they operate part-time, with employment in other rural work – fencing, shearing, ringbarking, and so on – the time spent at each occupation varying with the circumstances. A full-time shooter may operate for as many as four or five nights a week when conditions are suitable, meaning no heavy rain or high winds. A night's shooting normally begins a few hours before dusk and continues through the night with the return to camp shortly after daylight, the "skin shooter" with the skins for salting or pegging out, the carcass shooter after delivery of the prepared carcasses to a "chiller box" (mobile refrigerated room). Kangaroos are shot in the head, preferably; neck and high chest shots are also acceptable and normally cause instant death. An older technique, acceptable to an earlier generation, of shooting kangaroos low in the body with a high velocity soft-nosed bullet, which "anchored" but did not necessarily kill the animal (normally effected later by a blow to the head) has been abandoned by the industry for many years. Individuals so shot are unsuitable for the meat trade and there has been an increasing sensitivity to animal suffering in the community that has extended to kangaroo shooters. The charge that such wounded animals were left longer than the time to walk from the shooter's vehicle to the grounded kangaroo − for example, for as long as several days for the shooters to collect on a return circuit when they would still be alive − is not only unrealistic but has never been confirmed by the authors of this book.

Preparation of a carcass for pet food, its normal use, involves removal of head, tail, feet, forearms, and viscera; carcasses taken for the (small) export game-meat trade are prepared by removal of the alimentary tract only. For these, the retained viscera must undergo veterinary inspection in view of export approval.

The rise of the kangaroo meat trade began in the late 1950s (see table 4) and coincided with the dramatic reduction of rabbit numbers following the successful introduction of myxomatosis, a mosquito-borne virus introduced for the purpose of rabbit control. This loss of the rabbit industry, which had supplied the meat trade for more than a century (providing in a peak year 100 million carcasses and furs) resulted in there being a large number of unused chiller boxes in southern inland Australia. A few operators took the opportunity to adapt them for the previously unused meat of kangaroos and this proved highly successful in commercial terms. Between 150 and 500 kangaroo carcasses, according to the size of the chiller, can be frozen and stored (for several weeks if necessary) awaiting transport to an abbatoir by truck; this may involve distances of up to 1,300 kilometres. The idea spread and a trade in kangaroo meat for pet food developed rapidly, reaching a peak in the 1960s, when nearly two-thirds of the harvest served the dual purpose. As the meat trade rose in importance, the skin became a part of a carcass to be removed by the dealer at an abbatoir rather than the primary product of the shooter, and the old method of preparing "flint" skins by pegging out and air-drying gave way to the preparation of skins by salting, as is done in the abbatoirs. When the industry changed again in the mid 1970s so that the majority of kangaroos were being taken only for

Table 4 Weight of kangaroo meat sold, and estimated numbers of carcasses in Queensland: 1959 to 1980, showing change in harvest use over time

Year	Weight (tonnes)	Estimated no. of carcasses	Percentage of total kangaroo harvest
1959	39.6	2,500	0.27*
1960	838.2	67,100	9.08
1961	863.6	85,000	18.70
1962	986.9	97,130	18.21
1963	840.5	82,720	13.34
1964	2,341.1	230,413	21.07
1965	4,134.0	406,871	35.65
1966	5,890.2	579,720	62.70
1967	6,763.8	567.274	65.10
1968	5,884.3	579,135	67.11
1969	7,196.3	708,266	63.46
1970	5,456.5	537,030	59.66
1971	7,116.0	350,195	60.20
1972	8,574.2	421,950	39.30
1973	5,106.2	251,290	54.90
1974	4,374.9	215,300	67.80
1975	2,188.0	107,696	22.00
1976	2,940.0	144,697	23.30
1977	2,362.0	116,338	19.75
1978	2,998.0	147,538	24.60
1979	3,899.5	191,903	14.60
1980	12,263.3	603,513	63.90

* The year 1959 was the first year when the use of harvested kangaroos for carcass meat was recorded (it began in a very small way in 1958).

skins, salting remained the preferred trade practice. It is important to note that the industry, ultimately, depends on the skin trade. The market for meat is generally limited and fiercely competitive.

Carcasses may be delivered direct to an abbatoir by the shooter but they are usually transferred there by open truck from the field chiller box. In the abbatoir, kangaroo carcasses are skinned using hydraulic or air-operated skinning machines, and the meat removed from the bones, packed, and frozen. Average carcass weight is about fifteen kilograms, and a carcass entering a pet food abbatoir consists by weight of about sixty per cent meat, thirty per cent bones and ten per cent skin. Typically, the amount of fat is negligible. Bones and unusable meat may be reduced to blood-and-bone fertilizer, sometimes also meat meal. Meat is sold in bulk, chilled or frozen, to pet food shops and to canneries where good quality canned pet foods are prepared. The export market for game meat requires a more refined system which is expensive to operate: the carcass must be frozen within a few hours of slaughter and must pass veterinary inspection before processing, which then proceeds in much the same way as the pet food operation although under more hygienic conditions.

The kangaroo, in theory at least, is highly desirable as a source of edible animal protein because its body consists of a large proportion of carcass muscle and negligible fat; moreover this muscle is concentrated in the high-value regions of the loin, rump, and thigh. This has led frequently to suggestions that kangaroos ought to be farmed in some way to profit from its advantages; why this has not been attempted successfully is discussed later.

Kangaroo hides are mostly tanned to produce leather which has outstanding strength for weight. This leather is used extensively in high quality footwear. A good quality fur suitable for some fashion garments may be obtained from the red kangaroo. Although it is not much used for this purpose today, the potential certainly exists. Other uses for furred hides are as floor mats and rugs and the manufacture of souvenirs, particularly of koalas for which the skins of the whiptail wallaby were once preferred.

Some of the by-products of the industry are illustrated (figure 15,

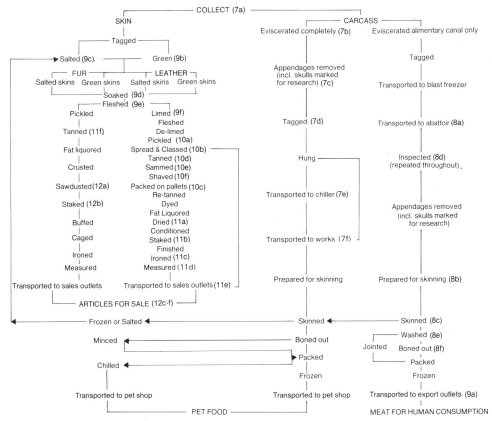

Figure 15   Schematic diagram of kangaroo industry processes and procedures in Queensland (1984). (Numbers refer to plates illustrating the particular procedures.)

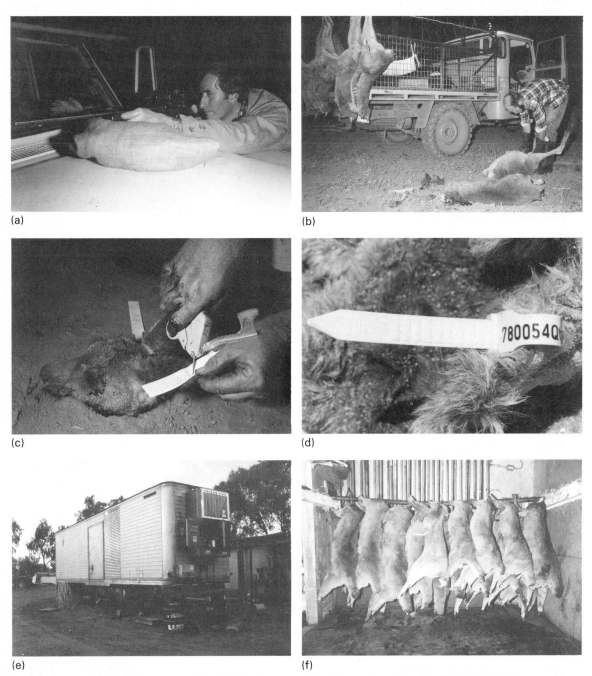

(a)

(b)

(c)

(d)

780054Q

(e)

(f)

Plate 7   Some stages in collecting kangaroos (a) and preparing pet food (b–f) (See figure 15 for place of each stage in the industry.)

(a)

(b)

Plate 8 Some stages in preparing meat for human consumption (a–f) (See figure 15 for place of each stage in the industry.)

(c)

(d)

(e)

(f)

(a)

Plate 9 Some stages in preparing meat for human consumption (a) and in the initial preparation of skins for fur and leather (b–f) (See figure 15 for place of each stage in the industry.)

(b)

(c)

(e)

(d)

(f)

(a)

(b)

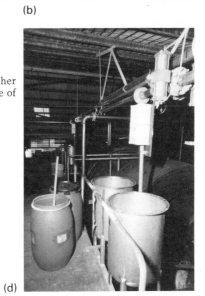

Plate 10 Some stages of leather preparation (See figure 15 for place of each stage in the industry.)

(c)

(d)

(e)

(f)

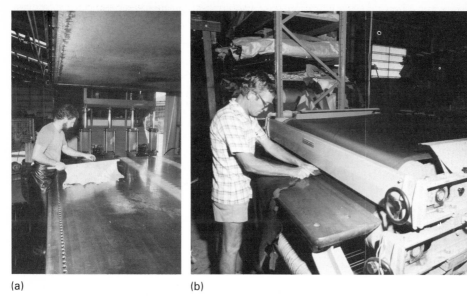

(a)

(b)

(c)

(d)

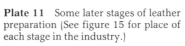
(e)   (f)

(c)

Plate 11 Some later stages of leather
preparation (See figure 15 for place of
each stage in the industry.)

(a)

(b)

(c)

(d)

(e)

(f)

Plate 12 Some stages of leather preparation (a) and of fur preparation (b); and subsequent articles for sale (c–f) (See figure 15 for place of each stage in the industry.)

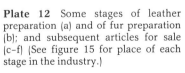

plates 7–12). To describe in detail the processes and uses of kangaroo products would require its own book. Similarly, an account of
the history of monetary values of the industry to shooters, dealers
and manufacturers would require a full chapter but would do no
more than indicate that returns fluctuate considerably, with those to
the shooter, particularly for meat, ranging around a fairly low figure.
None the less, the annual Australian harvest of some 2 to 3 million
kangaroos, the preparation of the meat and skins, and the extensive
uses to which the skins in particular are put represent a small but
significant investment and cash flow to the Australian economy,
particularly in rural areas.

   If one defines the kangaroo industry to include not only shooters
but meat wholesalers and retailers, canners (mostly in the pet food
industry), tanners and fur processors, exporters, manufacturers, and
wholesalers and retailers of skin products, the industry appears even
more significant. In terms of their meat and skins alone, kangaroos
are a valuable national resource.

Kangaroos vs. domestic livestock: the economic analysis

Although the overall values above are of interest, they are of little
significance from the point of view of economic analysis. To examine the economic use of resources, it is necessary to consider the
value of alternatives that are forgone. Is the ratio of production of
kangaroos and domestic livestock on the land economically optimal?
Does the additional social value obtained from a larger kangaroo
population exceed the value of livestock production that is forgone?
It has been pointed out elsewhere that, because kangaroos are so
mobile, landholders find it difficult to appropriate them and to
ensure for themselves any reward for husbanding them. On all
except the largest properties, landholders find that the number of
kangaroos is virtually independent of their own activities and that
they can gain little by husbanding them. On the other hand, landowners can appropriate all gains from husbanding domestic livestock and can expand the number of these wherever this is profit-
able, even if the increase in profit from the additional numbers of
livestock is less than the loss in collective profit from kangaroos.
Moreover, landholders have little incentive to prevent kangaroos
being taken on their properties for commercial purposes; they may
in fact gain from this, believing that it will lead to a reduction in the
animals they regard as pests.

   Thus, kangaroos are really a common-property resource, with

some undesirable economic attributes; too many factors of production from an economic efficiency viewpoint are attracted to exploiting the resource. Further, some of the smaller species of kangaroos have little commercial value and some are extremely vulnerable to land use by domestic stock because of habitat changes. It follows that if all species are to be conserved and, indeed, if the industry also is to be conserved, then intervention by government is inevitable.

Professor Clem Tisdell of Newcastle University (NSW) has described how the basis on which "ideal" land use can be defined and the means by which this can be brought about are complex issues, especially where governments exert no control over livestock numbers or over wildlife habitat on private property. Interdependence of production of kangaroos and livestock demands a far more extensive knowledge of kangaroos than presently exists if an economically optimal mix is to be prescribed. The problems of managing such a mix have not been examined; they are sure to be complex.

The effect of harvests on populations

The annual Queensland harvests recorded in table 2, which serve to indicate the scale of the kangaroo industry's operations (see also figure 16), need careful interpretation if these are to be used as a basis for inferences or predictions about populations. In a general sense, a large annual take of a wild animal that continues without dramatic change in either the harvest or the population over many years indicates that the harvest is sustainable and that overharvesting, at least in the long term, is not occurring. Substantial differences from year to year require explanation, particularly when a low harvest follows a high one, because this may well indicate that populations were so adversely affected by the high harvest that they were unable to recover. The Queensland kangaroo harvest data fit the general picture of stability well, but the virtual trebling of the harvest during the 1960s, had it been allowed to happen on the basis of harvest records alone, would have been a major step in the dark. Some of the fluctuations about the pre and post 1960 harvest have been large; to explain this requires identification of the reasons and the way these operate. They are seen to include industry forces, the weather and, theoretically at least, the kangaroo populations themselves.

From table 3, it is apparent that there have been large changes from year to year in the numbers harvested of all species, but there is

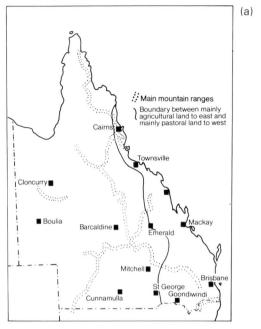

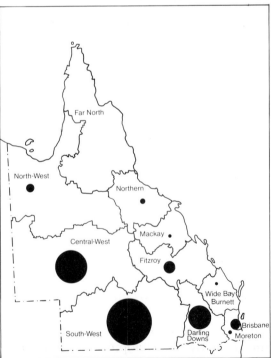

Figure 16 Queensland statistical divisions showing (a) some main cities and towns and the major land use differentiation; and (b) the proportional distribution of A class fauna dealers' site locations in relation to these.

no real evidence that the size of the take in any one year has had any direct effect on the harvest of the next. Thus the 1964–65 drought, referred to later (chapter 6), prevented reproduction in both the red and the eastern grey kangaroos throughout the harvested area of Queensland for more than a year, and large numbers of adults were observed to die of starvation. The harvest of that year, therefore, of more than one million animals added to a significant natural mortality with no compensation whatever from reproduction, and this must surely have resulted in a large reduction of remaining numbers. Yet kangaroos continued to be visually abundant throughout much of their range, and harvesting continued as usual. Further, despite the large depletion of numbers during 1965, the 1966 harvest was almost one million animals, still with no change in visual abundance, and again in 1967 the total harvest was nearly 900,000. Such were the fears within the industry and the government that these undiminished harvests following so severe a drought might be jeopardizing the survival of both the kangaroo and the industry that a full survey throughout Queensland was undertaken by the then Fauna Conservation branch of the Department of Primary Industries. While the results of this survey were used to justify increases in both population monitoring and industry control, the evidence was clear: kangaroos were still present in sufficient numbers to allow the harvest to continue. Such experiences are the basis of the confidence of both wildlife managers and kangaroo shooters in the resilience of kangaroo populations to current levels of harvesting.

It is thus necessary to look for forces other than changes in kangaroo numbers to explain harvest fluctuations. These are not difficult to locate. The market demand is of course most significant and indeed it was the change in 1959–60 from skins to meat as the main industry product that precipitated the dramatic increase in the harvest at that time. It was much easier for a shooter to prepare a carcass for sale than a skin and hence more animals could be handled by a shooter in a night. Also, because of the easier and less skilful work required, shooters who otherwise took kangaroos as pests without marketing the skins or carcasses were prepared to become involved. Finally, the market for the products had been long underutilized and even when the demand for meat declined in the late 1960s following the discovery of contaminated meat in overseas shipments (as well as a concerted campaign against the local use of the meat by a developing anti kangaroo-shooting lobby), the skin trade remained as the market had been able to adapt to the increased harvest. Moreover, the easier salt preparations of skins allowed the higher daily takes of the carcass trade to apply to the skin-only harvest.

The evidence does not suggest that prices paid to shooters have had any significant influence on the harvest (table 3). While steadily increasing costs, including those of ammunition and petrol, certainly influence a shooter's activities these bear little relationship to eventual harvests; prices are related to supply and demand, and because the industry operates in a competitive marketplace, periods when demand exceeds supply are relatively rare. They occur usually during and after wet weather when kangaroos are difficult to take, but they must also coincide with periods of low supply of competing products. Skins are sold on fairly competitive local and international markets (overseas, the main competition comes from African and Asian goat hides); and the meat market is highly competitive, selling against low-value meats such as horse, buffalo, offal and shin beef. Normally the industry is hard pressed to use the harvest.

The fluctuations about the pre and post 1960 harvests may be attributed largely to the weather (table 3). There is a clear trend, at least before 1973, for harvests to be higher during the drier years, the simple explanation being that during such times kangaroos are more visible and it is thus easier and cheaper to take them; they also congregate at such times near the more permanent sources of food and water. Other reasons are that unemployed rural workers turn to kangaroo shooting to supplement their incomes and the demand for control of numbers of kangaroos is greatest under drought conditions.

Political factors since 1973

The harvests since 1973, however, have been influenced by factors that can only be described as political, and a short review of the history of this period is an appropriate conclusion to this chapter. The late 1960s saw an increasing amount of public and political scrutiny of the industry, largely uninformed although based on genuine concern for the welfare and conservation of the hunted kangaroos. Out of respect for this community concern, the federal government, whose traditional legal involvement in fauna conservation was to control the export of native fauna or products thereof under the *Federal Customs (Export and Import) Act 1901* (later replaced by the *Wildlife Protection (Regulation of Exports and Imports) Act 1982*), instituted a multi-party committee of enquiry into wildlife conservation with particular regard to the interests of the hunted kangaroos. Despite the fact that this committee, after hearing all the evidence available from the pro and anti kangaroo-shooting forces decided that there was no need to use the provisions of this act for the added protection of the hunted kangaroos, the federal government did apply such an export ban in 1973. The effect of this ban on the industry (and federal–state relations) was immediate and by the end of that year the industry, with the loss of some seventy per cent of its market, was in disarray; the rural communities of all affected states were calling for either the lifting of the ban or the reapplication of vermin control legislation of kangaroos. The federal government responded by seeking that the state governments "coordinate" their kangaroo harvesting legislation. In fact, the states had coordinated their activities through the Interstate Fauna Authorities Conference (later the Australian Fauna Authorities Conference and later still the Council of Nature Conservation Ministers or CONCOM) which had met at fairly regular intervals since 1908, with kangaroos high on the agenda since 1936. By requiring that all states set an annual quota and control this through the issue of numbered non-reusable plastic tags to be applied to each kangaroo taken for the trade, the federal government was able to suggest that an uncontrolled situation had at last been brought under control. The public was satisfied; the export ban was lifted in 1975.

The application of the Australian export ban stimulated action in the United States to apply a complementary import ban, by way of placing the harvested kangaroos on their list of threatened fauna. When the Australian export ban was lifted, the complex US legal processes were used by the conservation lobby to ensure that the import ban remained in force for the maximum possible period. Representations by the Australian government secured a temporary lifting of the ban for a trial two-year period in 1981 on the understanding that, if it could be demonstrated that the opening of the American market resulted in an increase in harvest pressure on kangaroos, the ban would be reimposed. Because it did not there was no valid conservation reason for the ban to remain. The ban has now been lifted, but the kangaroo still remains on the US list of threatened fauna, despite representations from the Australian government to have it repealed.

The loss of the North American market resulted in an energetic drive by the industry to secure new local and overseas markets, and the gradual return of the take to pre-1973 levels reflects the success of this effort. The extremely high harvest of 1979 was the conse-

quence of an unusual combination of dry weather following a
succession of good seasons, a high price for kangaroo skins, and an
unusually good overseas market related to a temporary shortage of
domestic animal hides. The 1980 harvest continued high, again
involving drought as well as the anticipation of a continued high
demand; it fell in 1981, which was a year of more normal weather.

During this period of industry revitalization following the export
ban, groups of persons committed to the prevention of kangaroo
harvesting have acquired both numbers and notoriety in the
community. Espousing conservation arguments about the capacities
of populations of wild animals to sustain harvests under the level of
surveillance current in the kangaroo industry, and in an effort to
gain popular support, the ethic behind these groups' activities is that
the killing of animals, especially wild native animals, for profit is
morally wrong. A double standard of morality that allows the decep-
tively inaccurate use of conservation arguments about the likelihood
of extinction to support the entirely unrelated objective of prevent-
ing human use of native animals does not appear yet to be realized.
The certain outcome of their aims, should these be achieved, will be
the infliction of an unnecessary amount of suffering on kangaroos
that will certainly be destroyed as pests by all available means.

The true aim of conservation must surely be the maintenance of
viable populations of all native species, including the kangaroos, in
the presence of man and his activities, allowing the sustainable use
of abundant, successful species for reasonable purposes and the
controlled destruction of those that conflict with man's interests.
The current status and operation of the Australian kangaroo industry
fits well into this aim. Because of the constant constraints of both
local and international competition with its products, the controlling
legislation under which it now operates has not yet been needed to
prevent the industry dictating an unallowable level of harvest, and it
seems unlikely that this will be necessary, at least in the immediate
future.

Chapter 5

Kangaroos as pests

"Middle ground" species

Few matters are more mystifying to wildlife managers in Australia than the contrast between the fervent public interest shown in a few members of the Macropodidae that are either so abundant as to be commercially utilized or so scarce as to be considered in danger of extinction, and the virtually total disinterest in the majority of members of the family.

Perhaps it is because these are mostly of small to medium size and of unremarkable appearance – particularly in the bush. Or perhaps, lacking the emotive and, indeed, identifying issues of commercial harvest and associated charges of cruelty and "mass slaughter" or the threat of imminent extinction unless something drastic is done, it has not been possible for these "middle ground" species to be identified individually in the public mind.

Whatever the reason, these species are no less interesting and no less deserving of public attention and conservation interest than any of the more popular ones. In this chapter they are included as much as possible in a discussion on matters of relevance to the entire family, in the same way as the more popular species have been used in other chapters, and in the process the paucity of knowledge about them will become apparent. This may serve to arouse a greater awareness of and interest in the family overall and, we hope, provide the opportunity for the development of a better perspective both in research effort and public attitude.

Family distribution

Among the more noteworthy features of the kangaroo family is the extent to which the many species have succeeded in occupying the wide variety of habitat types available in Australia. Indeed, they have been so successful that there is scarcely a habitat – natural or modified by man – that does not have at least one macropodid inhabitant; most have more than one. This latter point deserves particular mention. It is in fact virtually impossible to identify any species with either a particular habitat or a locality. This is illustrated by relevant extracts from the fauna surveys of Queensland (which began in 1964 with the objective of locating the vertebrate fauna of the state), and derived maps (table 5, figures 17–19).

So wide and overlapping are the distributions and habitat preferences of the family that they make apparent nonsense of the textbook approach to ecology, which requires that each species fills its ecological niche in an exclusive and identifying way. That the kangaroos do, of course, is undoubtedly true, but the distinctions are far more subtle than the inexperienced student would expect, and it is beyond the scope of this book – and indeed the knowledge of its authors – to delve into and explain them other than in a few obvious instances.

A few species do occupy a large part of their range more or less exclusively. The agile wallaby of the coastal grasslands and adjacent open forests of the tropics, and the red kangaroo of the arid inland come to mind as such species, but the eastern grey kangaroo is well distributed throughout most of the range of the red kangaroo in Queensland, and there are several other species that co-exist with the agile wallaby in parts of its range. It is the rock-wallabies that have the most identifying habitat preference (any rockface or rock-strewn hillside that usually offers cave-type shelter) but even this habitat is shared to some extent by the far less habitat-specific wallaroo. The ubiquitous swamp wallaby, too, occasionally appears on the outskirts of a rock-wallaby colony, confusing even the experienced observer with a similar hop and high carriage of the tail, as well as the remarkable overall similarity (from a distance) to the rock-wallaby species within its range. Originally described from its swampland habitat (and being one of the few members, if not the only member, of the family that seems not to mind wet feet), the swamp wallaby is the most liberal of all in its use of habitat types, being apparently at home in the lightly timbered country of central western Queensland, in the brigalow thickets, and anywhere from the foot to the peak of the highest coastal hill or mountain.

The majority of macropodids are found in the forest grassland habitat so abundant in Australia and there are many places, particularly in coastal and subcoastal eastern Australia, where up to six or

Table 5 Abundance ratings of Macropodidae in Queensland fauna surveys: 1964 to date

Species	District														
	Kilcoy	Warwick	Stanthorpe	Millmerran	Taroom	Booringa	Central Highlands	Lower Burdekin	Townsville	Ingham	Laura	McIlwraith	Weipa	Bulloo	Diamantina
Musk rat-kangaroo	–	–	–	–	–	–	–	–	Scarce?	Common	–	–	–	–	–
Long-nosed potoroo	Uncommon	Uncommon	–	–	–	–	–	–	–	–	–	–	–	–	–
Brush-tailed bettong	–	–	Extinct?	–	Extinct?	–	Extinct?	–	–	–	–	–	–	–	–
Rufous rat-kangaroo	Common	Common	–	Scarce	Common	Common	Common	Common	Common	Common	–	–	–	–	Extinct?
Desert rat-kangaroo	–	–	–	–	–	–	–	–	–	–	–	–	–	–	Extinct?
Spectacled hare-wallaby	–	–	–	–	–	–	Uncommon	Common	–	–	Scarce	–	–	–	–
Bridled nailtail-wallaby	–	–	–	Extinct?	Extinct?	–	Scarce	–	–	–	–	–	–	–	–
Northern nailtail-wallaby	–	–	–	–	–	–	–	Common	–	–	Common	–	–	–	–
Brush-tailed rock-wallaby	–	Abundant	Uncommon	Uncommon	Common	Abundant	Common	–	–	–	–	–	–	–	–
Unadorned rock-wallaby	–	–	–	–	–	–	–	Abundant	Common	–	–	–	–	–	–
Godman's rock-wallaby	–	–	–	–	–	–	–	–	–	–	Uncommon	Scarce	Scarce	–	–
Lumholtz's tree-kangaroo	–	–	–	–	–	–	–	–	–	Uncommon	–	–	–	–	–
Red-legged pademelon	Abundant	Abundant	–	Uncommon	Uncommon	Common	Common	Common	Common	Abundant	Scarce	Uncommon	Scarce	–	–
Red-necked pademelon	Abundant	Abundant	–	Abundant	Abundant	Abundant	–	Abundant	Common	Abundant	–	Common	Abundant	–	–
Swamp wallaby	Abundant	Uncommon	Scarce	Scarce	Common	Common	Common	Common	Scarce	Common	Scarce	Scarce	–	–	–
Agile wallaby	–	–	–	–	–	–	Abundant	Abundant	Abundant	Abundant	Abundant	Common	Abundant	–	–
Black-striped wallaby	Common	Uncommon	Uncommon	Common	Common	Common	Abundant	Common	Common	Common	Common	Common	–	–	–
Red-necked wallaby	Abundant	Abundant	Abundant	Abundant	Abundant	Abundant	Abundant	Abundant	Abundant	Abundant	Uncommon	Uncommon	–	–	–
Whiptail wallaby	Common	Common	Scarce	Scarce	Abundant	Common	Common	Common	Common	Common	Common	Common	–	–	–
Antilopine kangaroo	–	–	–	–	–	–	–	–	–	–	Common	Uncommon	Abundant	–	–
Wallaroo	–	Common	Abundant	Uncommon	Common	Common	Abundant	Common	Common	Common	Uncommon	Scarce	–	Common	Uncommon
Eastern grey kangaroo	Common	Abundant	Abundant	Abundant	Abundant	Abundant	Abundant	Common	Common	Abundant	Common	Uncommon	–	Abundant	–
Red kangaroo	–	–	–	–	–	Common	Scarce	–	–	–	–	–	–	Abundant	Common

Note: "Middle ground" species shown in bold type.

Figure 17 Distribution ranges of rufous rat-kangaroo (top left), spectacled hare-wallaby (top right), northern nailtail-wallaby (bottom left), and red-legged pademelon (northernmost) and red-necked pademelon (southernmost) (bottom right).

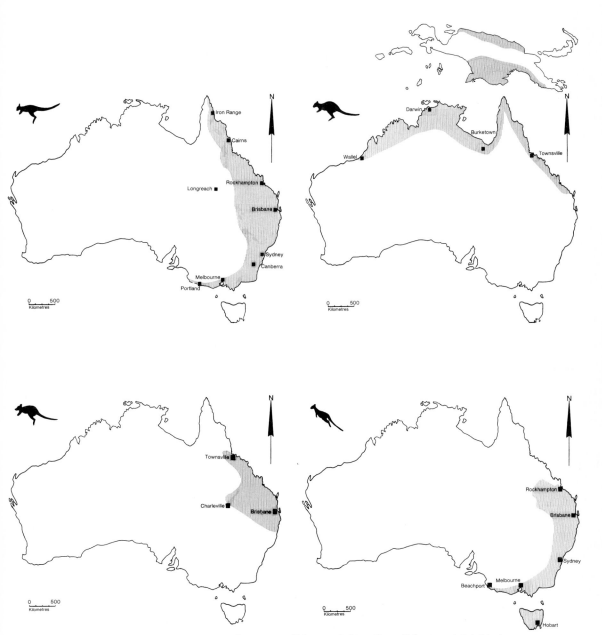

Figure 18 Distribution ranges of swamp wallaby (top left), agile wallaby (top right), black-striped wallaby (bottom left), and (d) red-necked wallaby (bottom right).

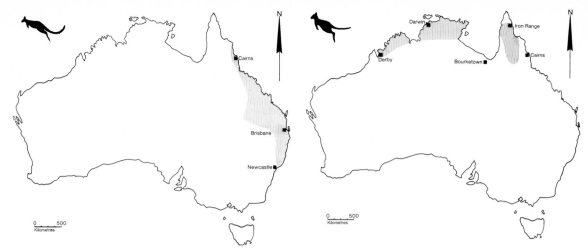

Figure 19 Distribution ranges of whiptail wallaby (left), and antilopine kangaroo (right).

seven species may be observed in an afternoon's walk through the open forest. John Calaby, in his study of the mammals of the Upper Clarence River in northern New South Wales, recorded the red-necked wallaby (surely the most abundant large mammal in eastern Australia), the whiptail wallaby, the black-striped wallaby and the swamp wallaby virtually on the same hillside. In similar situations just north of the New South Wales border, the eastern grey kangaroo and the wallaroo may be added to this list and, if the ground flora includes tussock-forming grasses, one may even step on and flush a rufous rat-kangaroo out of its daytime nest. This last species is so strictly nocturnal that there is practically no other way of encountering it during daylight hours. The group of open forest species changes as one moves north or west in Queensland with, for example, the spectacled hare-wallaby and even the scarce brush-tailed bettong sharing the tussock preference of the rufous rat-kangaroo in the north, with the western grey kangaroo − the "spinifex kangaroo" to those few who have noticed its difference from the eastern grey kangaroo − confusing the issue in the central and southern west. Certainly there are some detailed habitat preferences such as the tussock-nesting habit mentioned above, and the preference for a thick underbrush of wattle or (since European settlement) lantana shown by the black-striped wallaby; even this last little-known but widely distributed and abundant species often mingles with the swamp wallaby and the red-necked wallaby as well as with the eastern grey kangaroo and the wallaroo.

Even the restricting environment of the rainforest is the home of a group of species that occur side by side. Both the red-legged and the red-necked pademelons are frequently found together in the same patches of scrub, and the larger black-striped wallaby is also found in this habitat, often in the vicinity of the pademelons. Such species as the swamp wallaby and the red-necked wallaby rest during the day in the margins of a rainforest adjacent to their more usual open forest habitat, and in these margins is also found the small bandicoot-like potoroo nesting in the thicker undergrowth. The red-necked pademelon does not extend to the northern closed forests, but the black-striped wallaby does, and the unique rat-like musk rat-kangaroo is a common, if infrequently observed, inhabitant of the northern scrubs. Here also are found the remarkable tree-kangaroos, presumed emigrants from New Guinea where the group is represented by a number of other species. Interestingly, the arboreal habitat does not identify the tree-kangaroos, as they share it with the rock-wallabies; the recently discovered Proserpine rock-wallaby was first brought to the notice of zoologists by an interested person who thought that he had discovered a new species of tree-kangaroo! The rock-wallabies do not share the food preference, however, the tree-kangaroos' main food being the foliage of a number of rainforest trees. The only other species that characteristically browses is the swamp wallaby, but this species is equally at home grazing a crop or a pasture – a truly versatile animal.

The broad similarity among these "middle ground" species extends beyond general appearance and geographic distribution. The breeding habits, for example, are not broadly dissimilar yet cover as wide a range as exists for these within the kangaroo family (see table 6).

Pest status

Most of the macropodids find their food in the grasses and forbs of the pasture, and for this reason alone practically every species has been regarded at one time or another as a pest by the rural community. Even a young musk rat-kangaroo – an eater of fallen rainforest tree-fruits and insects in the litter – was once brought in (dead) as an "odd-looking rat" that may have been attacking a cane crop! The justness of this family reputation requires some examination if for no other reason than it is the cause of much friction and increasingly heated argument between the involved rural community and the remote but increasingly protective urban population of Australia.

One example by way of introduction to the subject may be sufficient to illustrate the extent to which the activities of kangaroos are viewed by the individual farmer. In 1979, a grazier from near Goon-

Table 6 A comparison of reproductive periodicities in "middle ground" and other species of Macropodidae based largely on observations in captivity

Species	Sex	Adult size (kg)	Gestation period (days)	Pouch life (months after birth)	Sexual maturity (months after birth)	Interval between birth and subsequent fertilization for quiescent embryo (= post partum oestrus) (days)	Normal interval between successive young (= frequency of births after first birth) (months)	Days between removal/loss of pouch-young and birth from quiescent embryo	Breeding season in northeastern Australia	Life span (years)
Musk rat-kangaroo	♂	0.7	?	5*	12	?	?	?	seasonal (Feb–July)	?
	♀	0.5								
"Middle ground" species:										
Long-nosed potoroo	♂	1.5	35–41	4	12	0–1	4	24–31	throughout year	8+
	♀	1.2								
Rufous rat-kangaroo	♂	3	22–24	4	12	0–1	4	?	throughout year	5+ (captive)
	♂	3.5			10					
Spectacled hare-wallaby	♀	4.5	?	5	13	?	?	?	?	5+ (captive)
	♂	4.3								
Brush-tailed rock-wallaby	♀	5	30–32	7	20	?	7	?	?	11+ (captive)
	♂	4.7			18					
Red-necked pademelon	♂	7	?	6	17–26	7	?	?	continuous (with peaks in autumn & spring)	?
	♀	3.8			20					
Swamp wallaby	♂	18	33–38	8	15	–2 to –7	8	32–34	throughout year	10+
	♀	11								
Agile wallaby	♀	27	29–33	7	12	0–1	7	27–32	throughout year	12+
	♂	14			14					
Black-striped wallaby	♂	16.3	33–35	7	14	0–1	?	?	throughout year	10–15
	♂	11			20					
Red-necked wallaby	♀	25	30–31	9	13	0–1	9	28–29	throughout year (though slight preponderance in summer)	17 (captive)
	♀	14			19					
Whiptail wallaby	♂	26	34–38	9–10	24–36	(?)120–160	10	?	throughout year	12+ (captive)
	♀	29			18–24					
Wallaroo	♂	50	34–35	8–9	>25	0–1	8–9	33–34	continuous	24 (captive)
	♂	23								
Eastern grey kangaroo	♀	54	35–38	10–11	17–28	120–160	12**	35	continuous	24 (captive)
	♂	27								
Red kangaroo	♂	55	33	8	18–24	0–1	8	31	continuous (with preponderance in summer)	20+
	♀	27								

* Normally multiple births.
** Ten (10) if quiescent embryo present.

diwindi in southern inland Queensland assessed amongst his losses to the animals (1) a car destroyed after hitting a kangaroo, (2) the cost of erecting sixteen kilometres of electric fencing to try to protect his wheat crops, with another sixteen kilometres built afterwards to make the first length more effective, (3) the market value of between 1,200 and 1,600 hectares of wheat (twelve to thirty-three per cent of the total crop value) lost to kangaroos, (4) the detrimental effects to livestock caused by kangaroos selecting the green pick and damaging the pasture for stock use, and (5) the subsequent losses on his stock investment.

Three aspects of the pest status of the family require no justification. Collisions between motor vehicles and macropodids are an inescapable fact of Australian life outside the cities, and even within some (as the occasional dead red-necked wallaby, swamp wallaby and even eastern grey kangaroo on the outskirts of Brisbane attest). With the advent of more lightly built vehicles, even a small wallaby can cause expensive damage. Dr David Anderson, the United States zoologist who visited Australia in 1980 to examine at first hand the abundance of kangaroos in Australia and the justness of having the commercially harvested species declared endangered by his government, commented that the extensive use of costly "roo bars" on country vehicles proved something about kangaroo abundance. It is also, one might add, mute testimony to the understandable lack of road sense of the kangaroos.

The second is the damage caused to fences. The ordinary "marsupial netting" erected to keep out kangaroos needs to be constantly maintained – otherwise it serves mainly to identify the tracks by which the animals enter and leave the prohibited areas. The facility with which even the small pademelons tear holes through wire netting is astonishing and, once the entry points are created, repairs are demolished or bypassed as quickly as they are made (plate 13). The common stockproof wire-strand fences, whether barbed or plain, are no barrier at all to any of the kangaroo family, most of them being able to pass between the strands with ease. Sometimes a fence is jumped, however, and occasionally a kangaroo trips by catching its long foot under the top wire and its toe on the second wire on the way over, resulting in the foot being caught firmly between the two wires. Its only possible escape is by demolishing that section of the fence; but more often the animal dies of exhaustion and thirst, though rarely before the two wires, and perhaps the rest of the fence, have been stretched and damaged. The entangled carcass, rather than eliciting sympathy for the animal's dreadful death, more often

(a)

Plate 13 Some effects of macropodids on fences established to control access to rangelands, near Warwick, southern Queensland: (a) repaired and reopened hole; (b) repaired hole and new entry opened up adjacent

(b)

provides the farmer with another reason to abuse the kangaroo family.

The third aspect of the kangaroo's pest status is less widespread but of great significance when and where it applies: this is its competition with stock for drinking water during a drought. There are many rangeland situations where drinking water for stock is provided by the landholder using manufactured watering devices – earth tanks, bores, windmills, troughs, and so on. During drought, there are many situations where the water is insufficient even for the stock, and the additional demand placed on the supply by large numbers of equally thirsty kangaroos is totally unacceptable to the provider of the water.

But is is another aspect – the crop and rangeland damage caused – that arouses the greatest antagonism in the rural community towards the Macropodidae. Such was the attitude towards kangaroos in the late nineteenth century that mass killing of these animals was even regarded as entertainment. Often, eradication was organized on a large scale. On one property in Queensland ("Warroo"), a battue (herding kangaroos towards shooters) continued for six weeks with twelve to fourteen people shooting daily; 20,000 kangaroos were killed during that period. Another property used fourteen shooters and killed an average of 340 kangaroos daily (the maximum was 547); during one drive, 288 kangaroos were shot in about thirty minutes. Some properties (in the Peak Downs and Stanthorpe districts, for example) destroyed between 40,000 and 60,000 kangaroos over a few years, and Carl Lumholtz, the Norwegian explorer, describes how one sheepowner in central Queensland told him about the killing of 64,000 grey kangaroos, spectacled hare-wallabies and black-striped wallabies in the course of eighteen months. It is interesting to note that all these species continue to thrive in the areas where these "massacres" took place.

Extent of crop damage

Unlike predators of stock, such as eagles, crows and dingoes which are also scavengers and have been shown often enough to do at least as much good as harm, the herbivorous marsupials are obvious eaters of crops and competitors of stock for pasture. It is true that the long, soft foot of a kangaroo does far less damage to the soil surface than the sharp, hard hoofs of introduced stock; it is also true that the clean bite of a kangaroo with sharp incisor teeth on both jaws combined with the unique up-and-down scissor action of the lower jaw does far less damage to a plant than the tearing, root-damaging bite of introduced sheep and cattle with incisors only on the lower jaw. However, these advantages are only side issues to the real problem as perceived by the grazier: kangaroos eat pasture, and that pasture is wanted for domestic stock.

The value of crop and pasture loss to kangaroos is a matter so complex that it probably will never be quantified. Even with crops, where a potential value may be placed on an anticipated harvest, it is frequently impossible to value the loss caused by the activities of kangaroos. For example, a crop eaten during a drought, which is a frequent event indeed, may well have failed anyway because of the very drought that forced the kangaroos to graze it, but then the failed crop may have served as stock feed had the kangaroos not consumed it first.

One of the few situations where there has been a genuine attempt to measure crop damage has been in the sugarcane fields of coastal Queensland. Here the damage to cane by the eastern grey kangaroo and a suite of wallabies – the red-necked, the swamp, the black-striped and the whiptail in the south, and the agile (the most important species, replacing the red-necked in the north) – has been measured over many years. In 1959, for example, nearly 57,000 individuals of the five wallaby species were destroyed around Queensland canefields largely as a pest control operation. Climatic conditions throughout the cane belt, with a late-summer wet season of short duration followed by a comparatively dry winter and spring, tend to encourage kangaroos to feed on irrigated young cane or ratoon (regrowth) cane after natural grasses have lost their succulent growth. Damage to young autumn-plant cane becomes apparent during the dry winter months when many tops may be eaten off. This is not always detrimental because the removal of the primary shoot may promote better "stooling", but in some instances the plant is completely removed from the ground and complete loss of the stool results. In cane foliage to 0.5 metre in height, the animals usually bite off the upper, inner leaves and pull out the central spindle, or they attack the lower portion of each cane shoot where it is enclosed in the leaf sheaths; these are bitten through and the inner tissue in the vicinity of and including the growing point is eaten. Continuous and total grazing of an affected area may take place. Kangaroo destruction permits have been issued to affected farms, the numbers killed recorded, and the damage measured. Relevant statistics are given in table 7.

An immediate reaction to these figures, of course, is that the

Table 7 Losses attributed to Macropodidae in sugar cane crops in Queensland: 1948 to 1982

Year (season)	Percentage of total tonnage lost	Percentage of area of total crop damaged	Monetary costs to industry (incl. cost of scalps, netting, subsidies, etc.)*
			($)
1948	0.03	0.27+	11,370
1949	0.03+	0.27+	8,882
1950	0.01+	0.04+	2,548
1951	0.01+	0.01+	2,304
1952	0.08+	0.27+	45,650
1953	0.01	0.10	12,442
1954	0.02+	0.18+	14,414
1955	0.01+	0.12+	11,130
1956	0.01	0.03+	6,872
1957	0.01+	0.03+	8,548+
1958	0.01	0.14	9,796+
1959	0.01+	0.12+	10,390+
1960	0.03	0.15	26,548
1961	0.03	0.30+	26,540
1962	0.03	0.52	16,830
1963	0.04	0.21	46,968
1964	0.01	0.10	11,546
1965	0.05	0.32	54,969
1966	0.06	0.26	73,326
1967	0.03	0.12	38,471
1968	0.01	0.08	21,570
1969	0.04	0.29	46,553
1970	0.01	0.21	14,393
1971	0.01	0.13	12,273
1972	0.02	0.28	34,525
1973	0.02	0.32	27,083**
1974	0.01	0.17	72,300
1975	0.02	0.27	51,871
1976	0.02	0.35	83,167
1977	0.06	0.65	197,538
1978	0.04	0.40	111,691
1979	0.03	0.34	116,110
1980	0.04	0.40	249,100
1981	0.03	0.25	110,000
1982	0.04	0.37	128,400

* In terms of current monetary value.
** The year that payment of bounties ceased.

damage – on average, about 0.03 per cent of the crop – is small compared with its value; but a small amount of damage to an industry can be (and in fact is) a lot to the relatively small number of farmers affected: those with farms adjoining natural vegetation.

Control measures

It is mainly those croplands that adjoin uncleared land that are subject to damage, and when it occurs (which is most frequently in a dry time) it is usually severe. There are two effective solutions, neither of them particularly acceptable. The first is to grow crops unattractive to macropodids. There are few of these – even the prickly safflower may be grazed as a young plant; other factors are important, including the potential value of the crop, and the suitability of the land and of farmer's equipment to produce it. The other solution is fencing, which is often prohibitively expensive and requires continual maintenance. There has been much experimentation with relatively inexpensive electric fences against macropodids in recent years, and most experiments have had the same results. An electric fence is initially an effective deterrent but with time, and especially with the increasing severity of a drought, its effectiveness is lost as the invaders learn to go over it or through it, at high speed and even at low speed, ignoring any shocks. This is not to say, of course, that an effective electric barrier will not be devised. However, it must be noted, the likely effect of the widespread use of a permanently successful electric barrier would probably be disastrous for some species.

Other control methods advocated and attempted include such devices as carbide guns, distractant crops, poisoning (now illegal and always dangerous to non-target species), snaring, shooting, and deterrents such as meatworks fertilizers (shown to be effective in cane for about a month after the application of 224 kilograms per hectare). These measures demonstrate, if nothing else, the seriousness with which the pest problem is regarded by crop farmers. While it is noteworthy that the red-necked wallaby appears to be the only large macropodid that can survive in small areas of forest, extensive habitat clearing for control is simply not practicable and may merely be counterproductive. The tolerance of species of *Bettongia* to fluoroacetate used for poisoning wild dogs has been, in Western Australia, an interesting instance of the conservation value of rural pest control actions.

The payment of bounties has been discredited because of the ineffectiveness of the schemes and the abuses to which they are soon subjected. In the Tully and Ingham areas of northern Queensland, for example, where the sugar-growing areas are bordered by large tracts of forest and scrub lands, some scalps were obtained illicitly from these uncultivated sources. In any event, the efficacy of the induced controls, whatever they might be, have proved unsatisfactory. Table 8 for example, shows the returns that were recorded between 1946 and 1953 in the Mackay area. The slaughter of 28,000 kangaroos over six seasons prior to 1946 had no noticeable effect on either losses or numbers of kangaroos present in later years (table 8).

Table 8 Relationship between bounties paid and scalps recorded in the Mackay area: 1946 to 1953

Season	Bounty value	Number of kangaroos
1946	840	4,032
1947	1,836	8,813
1948	778	3,732
1949	1,154	5,539
1950	974	3,166
1951	974	3,166
1952	3,030	9,847
1953	1,288	4,175
	$10,874	42,470

The killing of almost ten thousand kangaroos in the 1952 season did not prevent losses from reaching high levels the following season.

The best solution of all, of course, is not to plant crops adjacent to uncleared country. Understandably farmers demand that the cleared space be provided on adjacent property rather than on their own land, particularly if the adjacent land is publicly owned (a national park, for example).

The range of species involved in crop damage includes practically the entire family. Bounties were paid even on rock-wallabies by the New South Wales government in the 1800s, an indictment that would hardly be accepted, or at any rate pursued, today. The two pademelon species are well-known invaders of pastures (figure 20) and of unfenced crops grown adjacent to their rainforest cover. The uncommon Lumholtz's tree-kangaroo in northeastern Australia frequents maize crops as well as improved pasture lands. Any farmer generous enough to grow potatoes in the vicinity of a colony of the rufous rat-kangaroo will find that this species, which includes plant roots in its varied diet, will accept the invitation to a nightly feast of tubers. Grain and lucerne crops offer an invitation to all the open forest species, including the eastern grey kangaroo, the wallaroo, the red-necked, whiptail, black-striped and swamp wallabies; the range of the red kangaroos is too far west for most agriculture. Significant damage is normally confined to dry times; the Queensland winter is characteristically dry and most invasions of crops occur during this season. In the unusual event of a wet winter, damage tends to be minimal. During such good times, of course, numbers are likely to build up and cause a greater problem during the next dry period.

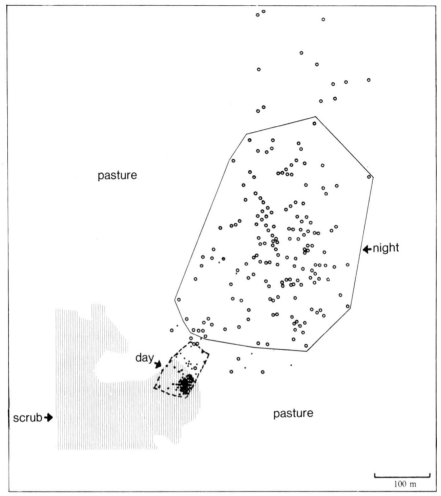

Figure 20   Principal areas of the nocturnal and diurnal ranges of a red-necked pademelon, detected by radio locations (after K.A. Johnson 1980).

Dietary preferences

It is in the rangeland situation, however, that the most extensive, the least measurable, and thus the most contentious conflict occurs. And it is this situation that provides the most frequently used justification for the killing of macropodids, whether for commercial use or simply for pest control. The issue is so complicated that the few studies there are barely touch the fringe of the problem, although there is much inferential material in the observations of landholders, naturalists and scientists that can be drawn on, cautiously, in a review such as this. One such observation relates to the virtual disappearance of the brush-tailed rock-wallaby from the rugged Stanthorpe district of southern Queensland — a district with large areas of apparently suitable habitat that this species once occupied but now occupies only in a few locations. One of the oldest landholders observed that the brush-tailed rock-wallabies "moved out from a property whenever sheep were introduced", the inference being that they objected in some way to the exotic intruders. The more likely interpretation, of course, is that the habitat-specific rock-wallabies were starved out by the much more ubiquitous sheep. This in turn suggests a reliance of the rock-wallabies on the pasture vegetation that was eaten by the sheep.

This conclusion is supported by a detailed study of another species, the yellow-footed rock-wallaby, in western New South Wales. There, a study of food plants eaten by this animal, and several other mammalian herbivores present in its habitat, indicated a marked overlap in dietary preference among them all, particularly during drought and particularly between goats and the rock-wallaby. The scarce status of this previously more common species was reasonably attributed to competition. An interesting and not unexpected finding was that competition appeared to be least between the rock-wallaby and the other native herbivore present, the wallaroo.

Other macropodids, particularly the large ones, are far less limited by a habitat preference than rock-wallabies, and have been much more successful in competing with introduced competitors. The hordes of red kangaroos that are frequently observed to descend on, and demolish, the green pick occurring as the result of an isolated storm in the arid inland are merely demonstrating their adaptation to the habitat, but in the process they are also in direct and obvious conflict with the landholder's equally hungry (but less astute) stock. In an interesting relevant study, in the Forty-Mile Scrub National Park near Mt Garnet in northern Queensland, exclusion plots were set up to keep (a) domestic stock (cattle), and (b) both cattle and the locally common black-striped wallaby, from the native pasture. The result (figure 21 and plate 14) demonstrated beyond any doubt that during the dry time of 1982 this wallaby had the same effect on the pasture as did a mixture of wallabies and cattle.

The level of competition is understandably much less in a good season when, normally, there is an abundance of food for all the herbivores present including — to the surprise of most people — the native invertebrates, particularly termites. The role of these insects

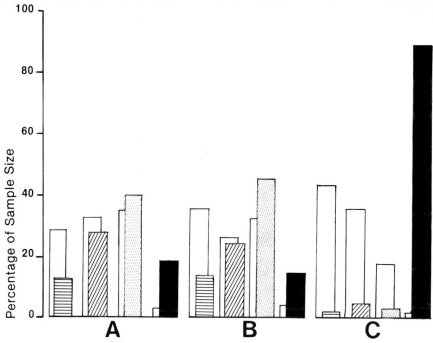

Figure 21 Results of pasture measurements in areas of Forty-Mile Scrub National Park, northern Queensland, where cattle and black-striped wallabies occurred (A), where cattle were excluded (B), and where cattle and wallabies were excluded (C). Open histograms: April 1980 controls; other histograms: March 1982 readings of numbers of vigorous grass clumps (solid), pedestalled grass clumps (cross-hachured), partly dead grass clumps (hachured), grass clumps with few green tufts (horizontally lined).

Plate 14 Exclusion trials in progress at Forty-Mile Scrub National Park, Queensland, 1982, showing pastures outside and inside fencing which excluded cattle and black-striped wallabies during a dry period (C.M. Weaver)

in pasture losses, particularly in cleared country in which termite numbers have been greatly increased, is an important consideration. But such detailed studies as have been made of the food preferences of the macropodids and stock have mostly been made in good times. And despite the fact that relevant data are notoriously difficult to acquire — analysis of either stomach contents or faeces rely on techniques that are painfully tedious and inevitably inaccurate because of differences in the availability and identifiability of different plant parts following mastication and digestion — results have been produced that indicate that sheep, red kangaroos, eastern grey kangaroos and wallaroos all prefer different components of the pasture. This does not mean that each species eats different plants from the others, but rather that there are species-specific variations in the quantity of each plant species taken, indicating that preferences exist (figure 22). Thus red kangaroos were found in one study to use the mulga-perennials community of their arid habitat (ground wattle woodlands with a shrub and perennial grass under-storey) during good foliage conditions and moved to the drought refuge open communities when forage conditions deteriorated. Cattle in the same area, on the other hand, were found to use open communities during good foliage condition and tended to move to the mulga communities and the hills when drought began. Thus interaction between the two species was minimal except during drought when red kangaroos concentrated on the open communities and some cattle continued to feed there.

Elsewhere, it was concluded that red kangaroos, wallaroos and sheep selected grasses and forbs when these were readily available. When pasture deteriorated, however, sheep selected mainly saltbushes (flat-leaved chenopods) whereas kangaroos selected mostly grasses, with varying amounts of flat- and round-leaved chenopods (old-man saltbushes and roly polys). Wallaroos were the most selective, eating grasses when these were present even at low levels. Potential overlap in diet between kangaroos and sheep was greatest under good pasture conditions and least under deteriorating conditions.

Another study compared the "last bite" — the (easily identified) contents of the mouth of shot eastern grey kangaroos — with the measured composition of the pasture (table 9). The study indicated that this species grazed the pasture "as it came" — there was no real preference for any species indicated, even though the pasture contained some thirty per cent of such disliked plants to sheep as the wire grasses (*Aristida* species). This is not really unexpected for a

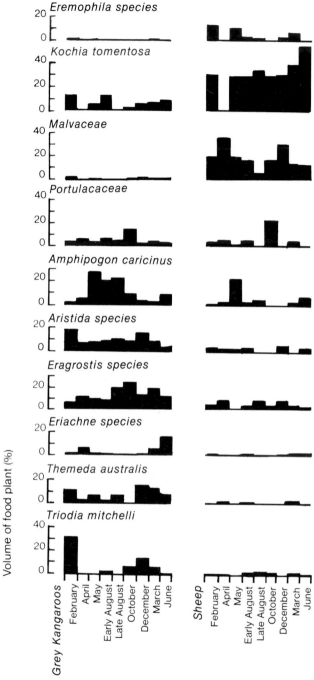

Figure 22 Volumes of ten major food plant species eaten by grey kangaroos and sheep at nine samplings near Cunnamulla, southwestern Queensland: 1967 to 1968 (after Griffiths et al. 1974).

Table 9 Frequencies of plant species in pastures using a point quadrant and in the mouths of eastern grey kangaroos, Greymare–Durikai area (near Warwick), Qld: 1962 to 1963

Plant species	Pasture		Kangaroos	
	Number of occurrences	Percentage of total occurrences	Number of occurrences	Percentage of total occurrences
Grasses:				
*Aristida** species	192	30.0	65	32.5
Arundinella nepalensis	n.r.**		0	
Bothriochloa decipiens	138	21.2	36	18.0
Chloris acicularis	n.r.		0	
Chloris divaricata	13	2.0	2	1.0
Cymbopogon refractus	6	0.9	0	
Danthonia purpurascens	26	4.0	11	5.5
Dichanthium humilius	n.r.		1	0.5
Dichelachne micrantha	n.r.		0	
Digitaria brownei	2	0.3	0	
Digitaria tenuissima	2	0.3	2	1.0
Echinopogon ovatus	3	0.5	3	1.5
Eleusine tristachya	n.r.		0	
Enneapogon gracilis	2	0.3	0	
Eragrostis leptostachya	107	16.5	35	17.5
Eragrostis elongata	3	0.5	0	
Eulalia fulva	n.r.		0	
Leptochloa debilis	n.r.		0	
Microlaena stipoides	4	0.6	5	2.5
Panicum effusum	13	2.0	2	1.0
Paspalidium gracile	7	1.0	5	2.5
Paspalidium radiatum	16	2.5	1	0.5
Paspalum dilatatum	10	1.5	3	1.5
Sporobolus elongatus	5	0.8	2	1.0
Stipa setacea	7	1.0	4	2.0
Stipa verticillata	n.r.		0	
Themeda australis	n.r.		0	
Tripogon loliiformis	n.r.		1	0.5
Other monocotyledons:				
Cyperus sp.	9	1.4	0	
Dianella sp.	5	0.8	2	1.0
Fimbristylis dichotoma	2	0.3	1	0.5
Lomandra sp.	1	0.2	0	
Susyrinchium micranthum	n.r.		1	0.5
Indet.	n.r.		1	0.5
Dicotyledons:				
Bidens pilosa	1	0.2	2	1.0
Dichondra repens	15	2.3	0	
Euphorbia drummondii	2	0.3	0	
Goodenia hederacea	15	2.3	2	1.0
Glycine tabacina	20	3.1	4	2.0
Helipterum australe	2	0.3	1	0.5
Medicago minima	3	0.5	1	0.5
Solanum sp.	1	0.2	0	
Solenogyne bellioides	9	1.4	2	1.0
Wahlenbergia sp.	1	0.2	3	1.5
Indet.	n.r.		1	0.5
Ferns:				
Cheilanthes sieberi	5	0.8	1	0.5

* Principally *A. vagans* and *A. caput-medusae.*
** Not recorded by quadrant.

native animal in its own country, even if the composition of its pasture has been drastically altered (which it has) by considerable overgrazing by introduced stock; the eastern grey kangaroo is a successful survivor in this situation and the capacity to eat any plant that is available must surely rank as an important relevant character. Nor does it necessarily conflict with the studies reported above, as a distinct preference for different species by both sheep and the other kangaroos, with no such preference by the eastern grey kangaroo, would still allow these results.

A third study of this species in southern Queensland (by G. J. E. Hill) demonstrated a preference for grasses at their most succulent stage when these were available, with movements of animals in and out of cover related to the availability of pasture in its most attractive condition. Such a preference might reasonably be expected to apply to all the macropodids, and, for that matter, to all herbivorous mammals.

The evident success of the larger macropodids in the presence of introduced stock undoubtedly is based, at least in part, on this adaptation to the native vegetation, and two of the earlier studies of the interaction between stock and kangaroos have invoked it to explain increases in kangaroo numbers at the apparent expense of stock numbers. A study by Dr E. H. M. Ealey in the Pilbara region of Western Australia during the 1950s resulted in the conclusion that a recent substantial increase in numbers of the local wallaroo (euro) was not the cause of an equally substantial decline in sheep numbers, but that both changes were attributable to an earlier period of over-grazing by grossly excessive numbers of sheep. The sheep were unable to maintain themselves on the degraded pastures created by this overgrazing and were therefore declining, while the euros, which were far better adapted to their native environment and its vegetation, were able both to survive and to increase in the changed situation.

Similarly Dr A. E. Newsome, studying red kangaroos in central Australia in the early 1960s, suggested that an increase in kangaroo numbers alleged by the local graziers may well have been caused by cattle changing the structure of the pasture to one preferred by the kangaroos, thus increasing their capacity to survive during drought.

Whatever the final outcome of research into kangaroo/stock competition, the much simpler evaluation of it (by the grazier quoted earlier in this chapter) that for every macropodid removed a grazier would be able to graze its equivalent in sheep or cattle is clearly only partly true despite the appeal of its simplicity. While it would surely be correct in the crop/improved pasture situation where the vegetation has been grown specifically for its attractiveness to mammalian herbivores, in rangelands with different histories of overgrazing and consequent degradation in terms of stock-preferred species, the part of a sheep-day gained by the removal of each kangaroo, if any, would necessarily vary according to the level of degradation. Nevertheless, the concept of a sheep-day (the amount of pasture a sheep grazes in one day) as a yardstick in a project to examine competition has considerable potential, and may represent a simpler way of examining the extremely complex equation that is at present being developed by students of the subject.

The most useful deduction from this work, of course, is that a suitable stocking rate for a mixture of native and introduced herbivores would provide maximum productivity, in terms of animal protein, from the pasture. Such an integration of cattle and game ranching in South Africa is prescribed as the optimum form of land use there (see, for example, Professor B.H. Walker, 1976).

It might be added that only a study that produced a different conclusion would raise any challenge. Even the combination of sheep and cattle is well known to be more productive on practically any pasture than either species alone, and there is every reason to expect that any combination of grazing species, whether exotic or native, would be the same. The more relevant question is how some economic use may be made of a mixture of native and exotic herbivores, and this must raise the frequently asked question of the potential of kangaroo farming. Ignoring the inescapable fact that virtually every rangeland grazier in Australia is a kangaroo farmer whether he wants to be or not, the question relates to the concept of conventional farming, and the answer at the moment includes far more disadvantages than benefits. Perhaps there is somewhere a farmer who is able to devise a way of adding the problem of managing a wild animal (other than leaving it to a commercial shooter as occurs at present) to the already significant burden of managing domestic stock, and who can alter the public attitude to the use of kangaroo meat for something other than cheap pet food, although this seems unlikely.

Numbers, mobility, and social behaviour

The components of the pest problem are of course far more than mere food preferences. Other relevant factors are quantities eaten and the numbers of animals present, this last raising also the questions of mobility and social behaviour. All are contentious and little studied issues. The once commonly repeated belief that a kangaroo eats as much as nine (or four, or three) sheep is obviously wrong, but the work needed to determine the facts is a major undertaking. In one study comparing food intakes of eastern grey kangaroos and wether sheep (several groups of these), the animals were held on enclosed crops of grazing oats for specified periods and the quantities available before and after were carefully measured. The results allowed the conclusion that a thirty-two kilogram kangaroo consumed half as much as a forty-five kilogram sheep, but there were fairly obvious differences – unmeasured because of the crudity of the technique – between the amounts eaten by growing animals, full-grown males and females carrying pouch-young. The same sort of differences occur in sheep, of course. Laboratory studies have indicated that sheep are better able to digest coarse plant material than red kangaroos despite the fact that the digestive processes of both species are similar (including the ruminant-like use of microbial nitrogen by the kangaroos) and that basal metabolic rates, and hence digestible food needs, are significantly less (by about twenty-five per cent) for kangaroos. The complexities of the subject, particularly involving nutritional needs during growth and lactation, however, have not yet been studied.

The highly contentious question of actual numbers of the larger kangaroos is discussed elsewhere in this book. Nobody has attempted a large-scale count of any of the less popular species. The numbers of some of these, such as the agile and the red-necked wallabies, are obviously huge. But numbers alone do not necessarily create a problem; mobility and social behaviour are modifying factors influencing the significance of a species in conflict with man. Thus the loose social organization of the red kangaroo and its preparedness to act as a nomad – an obvious advantage to an inhabitant of its arid and semi-arid environment where attachment to a particular locality may be suicidal – combine to allow a substantial increase in numbers during prolonged good seasons and, as explained in chapter 3, the sudden appearance of large numbers ("plagues") on small areas of good grazing during a drought. The rock-wallabies, on the other hand, with an attachment to a precisely defined habitat, have an extremely strict social organization, including well-defined adult territories, that prevents any significant increase in numbers. A small but readily observed colony has been under surveillance in the Warwick district for many years (see figure 23); it has maintained,

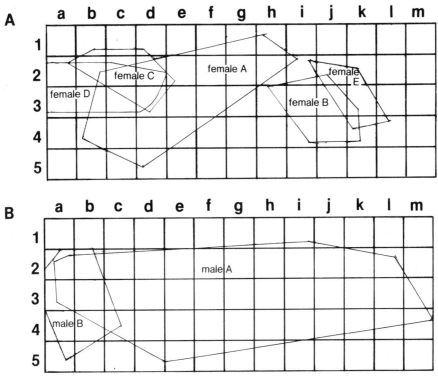

Figure 23 Example of diurnal home ranges of female and male brush-tailed rock-wallabies (A and B, respectively) in summer on a small rocky outcrop at Emuvale near Warwick, southeastern Queensland. The eight-metre grid indicates the limits of the area involved (after Scholz 1980.) (Winter ranges were different but of a similar pattern.)

during good years and bad, an adult population varying from five to seven by the simple expedient of violently evicting young soon after weaning. In captivity, this behaviour also means that weaned young may be killed by the adults if they are unable to escape from the enclosure. Such species, because of their strict population-limiting behaviour, lack the capacity to cause any real problem even to crops in their immediate vicinity.

The majority of the Macropodidae, however, fit between these two behavioural extremes, as indeed does the red kangaroo in the less arid parts of its range. Most species may be described as gregarious with some, such as the whiptail wallaby, more obviously so than others. The relationships involved appear to be simple, essentially mother–young (until weaning) and short-term male–female (during oestrus), and lacking the complexity of relationships found in the herd-forming ungulates of other countries. Most observed groups other than mother–young and male–female are more or less transient and aggregations appear to be based on ecological factors such as food, water, shelter and, above all, the weather, rather than on positive social responses. Individuals of most species appear to be fairly tolerant of another member of the same species in the general vicinity. There is evidence that dominance hierarchies occur in those species that have been studied, and indeed there is every reason to expect these in all species. They serve essentially to allow large numbers to co-exist relatively peacefully within the same range, but at the same time exerting subtle pressure on the young to emigrate in search of suitable, unoccupied habitat.

What these things mean in terms of the present discussion is that numbers of most macropodids will increase in good seasons without overt social behaviour acting to control numbers (as has been observed in rock-wallabies); and if emigration – the resort of subadult animals noted above – is restricted by a fence or some other form of physical barrier, such as an expanse of cleared land, extremely large numbers can build up without much intra-specific conflict (table 10). The appearance and effects of these large numbers when they invade crops and open rangelands during dry times are the basis of most complaints about macropodids by the rural community.

Long migrations do not seem to occur in any species other than the red kangaroo, and even in this species (as discussed in an earlier chapter) most observed "migrations" are only movements of short to medium distances that result in temporarily high concentrations followed by dispersal. The majority of species appear to be essentially sedentary, finding their food in the immediate vicinity of their birthplaces. It is a common experience, for example, to observe numbers of the eastern grey kangaroo or the red-necked wallaby grazing in a crop and similar numbers grazing in adjacent poorly grassed forest; and it is not at all unusual to find one or more species of macropodid apparently starving to death in a locally drought-stricken area within easy hopping distance of good pasture.

Another aspect of kangaroo behaviour highly relevant to the damage problem is the timing of their activities. Macropodids are predominantly crepuscular and nocturnal. The rufous rat-kangaroo, as already noted, is strictly nocturnal, never appearing in daylight unless disturbed, and the potoroo similarly appears to avoid daylight. The great majority of species, however, are active during the period from late afternoon to early morning, when the farmer is not normally about. During the day, kangaroos usually remain lying or sitting – in the shade in summer, in the sun in winter – with brief inter-

Table 10 Social organization and other habits and features of the "middle ground" species of Macropodidae in relation to their perception as agricultural and pastoral pests

Species	Body size (larger rather than smaller)	Continuous breeder (rather than seasonal)	Overtly unaggressive (rather than aggressive)	Widespread habitat preference incl. altered habitat (rather than restricted natural types)	Aggregated at times (rather than mostly solitary)	Crepuscular/nocturnal (rather than diurnal)	Grazer (rather than browser)	Diet of grasses (rather than other plants)	Recorded as pests
Rufous rat-kangaroo	X	✓	X	intermed.	X	✓	✓	✓	✓
Spectacled hare-wallaby	X	✓*	X*	intermed.	X	✓	✓	✓	X
Northern nailtail-wallaby	X	?	?	intermed.	intermed.	✓			X
Brush-tailed rock-wallaby	X	✓	X	X	✓	✓	intermed.	intermed.	✓
Unadorned rock-wallaby	X	✓	X	X		✓	intermed.	intermed.	X
Red-legged pademelon	X	?	✓	X	intermed.	✓		intermed.	X
Red-necked pademelon	X	✓	✓	✓	intermed.	intermed.	X	intermed.	✓
Swamp wallaby	✓	✓	X	✓	intermed.	✓	intermed.	✓	✓
Agile wallaby	✓	✓	intermed.	✓	✓	✓	✓	✓	✓
Black-striped wallaby	✓	✓	✓	✓	intermed.	✓	✓	✓	✓
Red-necked wallaby	✓	✓	intermed.	✓	intermed.	✓	✓	✓	✓
Whiptail wallaby	✓	✓	✓	intermed.	✓	intermed.	✓	✓	✓
Antilopine kangaroo	✓	X	✓	✓	✓	✓	✓	✓	X

* Intermediate.
** Species observed in captivity.

mittent periods of grooming. Towards sunset – earlier in winter, later in summer – they become more active and begin to graze, locally at first and then moving towards the main grazing area for the night, returning to the resting site after daylight (figure 24). Many factors influence this pattern, however: wind particularly inhibits movements outside cover, for example, as does heavy rain, although light rain is of little consequence. But their nocturnal habits create problems in detection and assessment of the effectiveness of control measures, as well as interfering with research programmes to investigate the natural history of the animals!

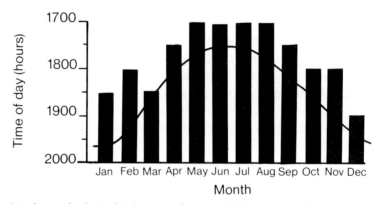

Figure 24 Seasonal relationship between the time of day red-necked pademelons fed on pasture (bars) and the time of sunset (line) (after K.A. Johnson 1980).

An overall review of the alleged pest status of the Macropodidae must result in acceptance of the fact that while the beliefs are based on realities, the problem is extremely complex and that its quantification (particularly in rangelands) requires a massive input of research. In the meantime, it is unrealistic to expect the rural community to change either its traditional attitude or its response to its perceived problem. It should be appreciated that as long ago as 1923, the secretary of the United Graziers' Assocation of Queensland accepted that "the prevention of the extinction of these native animals is a most laudable object to keep in view" (Longman, 1923). The answer must lie in some form of conservation management based on as much knowledge as is available at the time, with a preparedness to adjust and adapt procedures as more information is acquired.

Agricultural development in Queensland kangaroo habitat

In view of the place of Queensland in the distribution of so many species, it is interesting to note the major agricultural and livestock developments that are occurring in this kangaroo habitat.

Sugar cane. This crop dominates the agricultural scene in coastal northeastern Australia where ninety-five per cent of the total output is produced. It has been a major factor in land development in the high rainfall areas formerly covered with dense closed forest. Because the crop requires heavy rainfall when temperatures are favourable for plant development, the area suited for cane growing is restricted to the narrow 1,600 kilometre strip between the Great Dividing Range and the coastline. This belt is not continuous, comprising a series of compact districts that are mainly areas of river alluvium where soils (of a wide variety of types) and climate are favourable. In the 1980 seasons, 366,000 hectares of land were cultivated for sugar cane – a thirty per cent increase in the decade and an elevenfold increase since the turn of the century.

Grain crops. Grain and seed crops occupy more than 1.5 million hectares. The major grain and seed crops are divided into winter-growing and summer-growing crops – the winter crops being wheat, barley, oats, linseed, canary seed, and safflower; and the summer crops sorghum, maize, millet, sunflower, soybean, and navy beans. Two crops of rice can be grown each year. Wheat production – the largest grain crop, with nearly two million tonnes grown annually – is centred on the open plains of the central and western Darling Downs. Sorghum is the main summer grain crop. Buoyant export prices and the development of high-yielding hybrid varieties in recent years have resulted in a three-hundredfold increase over the last four decades in annual plantings to over 500,000 hectares for the sorghum crop. The potential for further land development of agricultural cultivation is estimated to be fivefold.

Livestock. This endeavour in Queensland has been developed at three levels of intensity. The extensive sheep and open-range beef cattle industries are found throughout the inland. The semi-intensive beef and dairy industries are centred along the coastal and sub-coastal districts and near the centres of population. The south-eastern corner of the state caters for the more intensive pig and poultry industries because supplies of grain as well as the markets are closer. Livestock numbers (1983 figures) are around 9 million beef cattle, 370,000 dairy cattle, 12.2 million sheep, and 550,000 pigs. The beef cattle industry is the most widespread, on nearly 22,000 landholdings, under a wide range of climatic conditions. Most cattle are still bred and fattened on native pastures that are unimproved. The provision of more water impoundments can markedly upgrade the cattle-carrying capacity of the land and there is a marked increase in effort of recent years to provide these. More than ninety per cent of sheep are Merino and are maintained primarily for wool production; one-half of these are run on the open downs country of the inland. In this area (the Queensland pastoral zone of 537,000 kilometres within the dog fence), the native grasses form the basis of vegetation; virtually no improved pasture is sown except in the gidgee scrubs in the central west where large areas have been cleared and sown to buffel grass. In other areas of Queensland, sheep are run on native and unimproved pastures.

Throughout northeastern Australia rural development is being actively promoted by such means as major irrigation schemes, road and land development, and pasture improvement. Rural holdings now represent about ninety per cent of Queensland.

There can only be speculation on the consequences of projected changes, should they occur. Agriculture and kangaroos are essentially incompatible, but at the same time it must be acknowledged that the establishment of reserves is usually concurrent with land development. Perhaps the most important requirement is for constant supervision of the effects of changes, as they occur, on the wildlife, with appropriate recommendations for solutions to problems perceived by what may be anticipated to be an increasingly sympathetic community. It is to be hoped that increasing public interest and expanding conservation effort in relation to species that are still abundant will ensure that desperate solutions such as that to save the bridled nailtail-wallaby (discussed in chapter 2) will not be needed.

Managing a slaughter of a national symbol. . .

Roo numbers down, not up

JIM NICHOLS (C-M, November 25) obviously has some information on kangaroo numbers not exposed to the Australian National Parks and Wildlife Service.

Kangaroo programme

BRISBANE. — The Australian Council of Conservation Ministers wants to ensure all kangaroo species are preserved but at the...

'Roos in drought

ROO FIGURE WRONG CLA

AUSTRALIAN cons tionists in Washi claim the Fraser Go ment released inflate formation on kang numbers to sway U.S islators towards com cial kangaroo culling

Roo numbers high despite cull quota

CANBERRA — The kangaroo population remained abundant despite the drought and culling quotas for more than three million kangaroos issued by the Federal Government this year,

'False' roo figure

THE FACTS BEHIND THE KANGAROO SLAUGHTER

Kangaroo numbers

ROMA — Queensland jumping with kang and according to estimates there a

WILDLIFE

New count meth could determine kangaroos' futu

FEELINGS NOT FACTS

WHEN it comes to a propaganda battle the kangaroo and its supporters have a decided advantage over those wh seek to control its numbers

'Roo survival

THE intelligentsia in this country have long considered that Europeans should have only settled those areas immediately around Melbourne and Sydney. The rest of the country would have made a splendid fauna and Aboriginal reserve.

Unknown disease kills roos

By environment reporter BILL ORD

A MYSTERY disease is killing thousands red kangaroos in far western Queensland an New South Wales.

A sick kangaroo and post-morte dead ones have been flown ical tests, but atte

Computer 'roo contr

COMPUTER science is being used to help take the guesswork out kangaroo management in Queensland.

Service helps 'roo

STAFF of the Queensland National Parks and Wildlife Serv protection for all wildlife, the National Parks Mini said.

Raising joeys no easy task — ask Dr Spear

Get roo facts righ

SO the worldwide Greenpeace Movement leader, Dr Patrick a Canadian, wants to stop of kan-

vince metropolitan residents, total and abysmal ignorance of situat Moore and F

Ne New uni to monit kangaro

BRIEFLY.

'ROOS MOVE

The kangaroo problem Hughenden's aero ome has eased, thanks to cent heavy rainfalls in e area.

The 'roos nearly caused als of accidents to er.

Roos hop to it

SYDNEY.— Australian animals changed their mating habits this year to cope with drought, fire and flood, the New South Wales National Parks and Wildlife Service reported.

The service's annual report said red k he Kinchega National Park near I howed how Australian fauna had ada Many red kangaroos in the park d er. But all females had mated with first autumn rains in April, 198 veeks.

A look at roos

The National Farmers United States has invited d media to look at the Australian kangaroo situation.

This follows reports in leading newspapers attacking Australia's kangaroo culling prog-

'Roo numbers 'will be halved this year'

THE kangaroo population will be halved by the end of the year unless overseas markets for their products can be closed, according to a conser-

"The legal kill quota for 1984 will be just over two million for the three species of kangaroo — reds, eastern and western greys — a drop of one mil-

kangaroo populatio

THE Federal Govern s set up a unit to mo 'angaroo populations i tates.

The eight-person unit is

Roo information wrong

KANGAROO MANAGEMENT DEFENDED

Information on roos 'inaccurate'

SYDNEY (AAP) — The Federal Government used false informatic

mental organisations are now putting

Roo claim challenged

Roo numbers on the increase

Graziers in southern Queensland have asked the United Graziers Association to step up their efforts in

The Federal Member for Maranoa, Mr. I eron, believes State and Territory wildlife authoriti are managing the kangaroo population in a responsib manner.

Chapter 6

Biology for management

Introduction

Research into the biology and ecology of the kangaroos in Queensland began in the late 1950s following a field review of the kangaroo industry. The way for research was paved by the proclamation in 1954 of *The Fauna Conservation Act of 1952*, which placed all the kangaroos (and most other native fauna) under government protection; this permitted the taking of several commercially valuable species under a system of regulations requiring permits, payment of royalties, and record of harvest by species and numbers. For the first time, the taking of kangaroos was considered as the harvesting of a renewable resource rather than the destruction of vermin – an activity that required regulation which in turn demanded a knowledge of the animals' biology on the part of the regulating authority – as well as a means for continuous assessment of the population status of the exploited species.

That the necessary knowledge was not available at the time was as much a reflection of the great abundance of the harvested kangaroos as it was of the disinterest of Australians generally (including much of the scientific community) in the native mammals. Even as recently as 1951, Ellis Troughton of the Australian Museum in Sydney was able to lament the lack of biological knowledge about them and call urgently for a biological survey of Australia's fauna while "there was still time to study at least the majority of the known species".

It is not true, of course, to say that the fauna unique to Australia, including the kangaroos, had not been studied by biologists. The interest generated in Europe by the discovery of a continent where a large proportion of the mammal inhabitants were marsupials was considerable; in the century following European settlement the marsupials were the subject of active and extensive study in the fields of taxonomy (classifying and naming) and anatomy, which were the main interests of zoologists of the day. Observations of lives and habits were left largely to zookeepers and amateur naturalists; much of the information available to Troughton at the time he wrote was, as he recognized, essentially superficial, anecdotal, and even of doubtful validity. It was certainly totally inadequate as a basis for any sort of management of a commercially exploited but protected animal. For only one species, the eastern grey kangaroo, was a gestation period (of thirty-eight days) recorded in the literature, and this was based on a single record made in the London Zoo in 1854. Even this observation became of doubtful value when in 1908 two confusing observations (of red kangaroos) were made in the Philadelphia Zoo (USA); two animals gave birth, one at three months and the other at eleven months after the death of the only possible male parent! Such a wide range of gestation periods gave rise to much interest and speculation, and until 1954, when Professor G. B. Sharman discovered the cause of the variations and made sense of such observations (described later in the chapter), nobody knew what to make of them. Similarly, and most surprisingly, there was no published record of the duration of the pouch life of even a single kangaroo, and it was commonly believed (most people still do believe) that the pouch life was only two or three months, and that kangaroos had several young each year.

Despite the lack of knowledge, it would be unrealistic to say that harvesting should not have been permitted until more was known. The fact was that the large kangaroos had been taken with virtually no control; indeed governments actually had paid for their destruction for more than one hundred years yet the animals were still manifestly abundant. The necessity for the introduction of regulations, however, could hardly be argued against, and when they came into force the government had to accept the responsibility for finding out what was really happening. The legislation also gave the government the right, and provided for the opportunity, to restrict harvesting should it be considered necessary at any future time.

Early research in Queensland

When research work began in Queensland, studies of the biology of kangaroos had already been under way for some years in the University of Western Australia where the urgency of the need had been recognized and acted upon; and scientific institutions in other parts of Australia were beginning to move into the enormous research field that had been ignored for so long.

The species selected for major study in Queensland was the eastern grey kangaroo, one of the most abundant species in Australia, with a range from northern Queensland to Tasmania, and also the principal species taken for commercial purposes. Virtually nothing was known of its biology and ecology when studies commenced; the sum of available knowledge was the gestation period referred to above, that it lived in Queensland in large numbers, and that the harvest rate (after many decades of apparent stability) was just beginning to increase as a consequence of a change from hunting only for skins to taking whole carcasses. The eastern grey kangaroo had remained abundant despite European man's alteration of its environment and concerted efforts to reduce its numbers, but it had to be accepted that such a situation might not last. To wait until the species was in apparent trouble might well have been to wait until it was too late. Thus field studies of the eastern grey kangaroo, and indeed of most other species as well, began while apparently normal, successful and healthy populations existed throughout its recognized range. During the subsequent twenty-five years, the eastern grey kangaroo has become one of the most studied native animals in Australia. It need scarcely be said, of course, that there is still far more to know about it than is known, but at the same time a sound basis is now available for management of wild populations of this commercially harvested species. This chapter brings together relevant research results about the eastern grey kangaroo from all available sources; it includes also comparative data on some other species.

Research in Queensland has been aimed essentially at understanding the effects of harvesting on populations. This has necessitated basic studies of distribution and habitat preferences as well as of reproductive biology, social organization, and population age structure (including juvenile survival) under all environmental conditions; age structure has necessitated the development of methods of age determination. The objective has been not only to understand (and, if possible, measure) the relationship between the kangaroo and its environment, but also to provide a basis for monitoring the status of its population at any time. The idea was that the population status – whether increasing, stable, or declining – may be determined at any time by the measurement of a number (as few as possible) of key, readily measurable parameters. The problem of determining absolute numbers, determined by some form of census, has not as yet been attempted by Queensland authorities and the reasons for this are discussed in chapter 7.

The first Queensland studies began at St George, one of the oldest centres of kangaroo harvesting and an area of great abundance of the species, with considerable numbers of the red kangaroo also present. Here, the objective was to become familiar with the animals in their habitat, to get that "feel" for the animals — where they lived, when and how they moved about, what they ate, how they reacted to wind and rain, cold and heat, day and night — that could later be used to devise practical research projects.

Those early days did indeed provide the basis for all future work. There was an obvious need to discount many simple beliefs based on casual observations by the rural community that, when examined, could not possibly be true. One example was that when kangaroos became highly visible ("in plague proportions" is the statement loved alike by graziers and journalists) it was assumed they had "moved in from the west", yet any person driving as far west as possible could and would never find the kangaroo-free territory the animals had vacated. Then, when they all disappeared again, it was understood they had all been "shot out" over their entire range. And, when they reappeared again (usually coinciding with dry, cold weather), they had "bred up" like rabbits.

The superficiality of these explanations soon became apparent. The questions were legion. To find the answers required much more than walking around in the bush. The research work was moved in 1960 to Warwick, where there were yard and laboratory facilities, where captive animals could be studied, and where extensive populations of many macropodids (including the eastern grey kangaroo) were available for study in the surrounding forests and farmlands. Here work began on the basic details of the lives of the eastern grey kangaroo and the dozen or so other local species.

Captive colonies of kangaroos were established beginning with hand-reared pouch-young of ages later determined by appropriate measurements of their own offspring. These were used to provide methods of age determination and basic details of reproduction such as gestation period, duration of pouch life and age at sexual maturity. These are matters basic to the understanding and interpretation of field-collected data, both those taken from professional shooters and those collected by research staff.

Age determination

Age determination of young, growing animals is fairly straight-forward, involving simple measurements such as weight (which is probably the most inaccurate, and used only when there is no other readily measurable feature) and lengths of suitable body parts, the pouch-young of kangaroos offering many to choose from. Queensland studies have used lengths of the tail and hind feet, which in the eastern grey kangaroo increase from some 7 millimetres to 570 millimetres, and from 4 millimetres to 250 millimetres, respectively, during the first year of life. This represents an average weekly growth rate of 11 millimetres for the tail, and this may be used as a guide to provide an approximate age for a young eastern grey kangaroo. Surprisingly, the same rule (most easily remembered as "a centimetre a week") gives a useful approximation of age for the pouch-young of all the medium to large macropodids. For more accurate estimation of age, of course, graphs based on the measurements of many pouch-young are constructed; tables 11 and 12 are derived from such graphs.

Body parts' lengths other than those of the tail and the hind feet that have proved useful are of the tibia (shinbone), the forearm, and the head (according to one southern Australian study, the head provided the most accurate measure of age). Another rough guide to age is the timing of developmental stages of the young (table 13).

The sexual dimorphism of the adults commences after pouch life; both sexes are born at the same size and grow at the same rate while in the pouch, although in one study of the agile wallaby (a tropical species) in captivity in Canberra, pouch life was abnormally long and males grew faster than females. However, this was probably an artefact of the environment.

The main field use of estimated ages of pouch-young is the determination of dates of birth, from which such matters as breeding seasons, and stoppages of reproduction caused by environmental conditions such as drought, may be established.

It is the age determination of the adult, however, that is of major value to the wildlife manager and that presents the greatest problem. Most attempts to find the age of a mammal begin with the teeth. Everyone knows that the age of a horse may be told from its teeth, although not many people know how to do it; fortunately, the kangaroos, too, have a number of dental characters that have proved to be of considerable value.

In all animals with teeth there are two basic processes, eruption

Table 11 Ages of various species of Macropodidae estimated from length of tail of pouch-young. The last age given approximates the end of pouch life.

Length (cm)	Age (days)								
	Long-nosed potoroo	Rufous rat-kangaroo	Unadorned rock-wallaby	Agile wallaby	Red-necked wallaby	Whiptail wallaby	Wallaroo	Eastern grey kangaroo	Red kangaroo
1	16	8	10	10	7	0	9	7	8
2	29	19	24	23	25	24	26	22	21
3	41	29	35	34	42	35	38	34	31
4	52	39	45	43	52	45	48	45	41
5	63	47	55	52	62	58	57	55	51
10	103	87	101	93	109	98	98	97	90
15	112	96	128	122	146	135	125	135	120
20			144	144	172	159	146	166	140
25			184	161	195	175	166	196	155
30				176	214	191	181	221	170
35				189	230	207	197	235	185
40				200	248	224	213	250	195
45					288	242	232	271	210
50						252	257	293	225
51						255	263	301	230
52						265	269	311	
53						275			
54									
55									
56									
57									

Table 12 Ages of various species of Macropodidae estimated from mean length of hind feet of pouch-young. The last age given approximates the end of pouch life.

Length (cm)	Age (days)								
	Long-nosed potoroo	Rufous rat-kangaroo	Unadorned rock-wallaby	Agile wallaby	Red-necked wallaby	Whiptail wallaby	Wallaroo	Eastern grey kangaroo	Red kangaroo
1	30	19	28	22	25	25	24	25	20
2	52	41	51	47	55	49	43	44	41
3	73	54	74	66	75	71	61	62	57
4	86	67	91	81	94	88	79	77	69
5	99	75	106	96	108	104	92	90	81
6	112	83	118	106	122	117	103	102	93
7		107	180	136	170	158	138	143	125
14		139		150	210	193	166	179	153
16				200	235	213	181	197	167
17					253	224	191	206	174
18					272	241	202	215	181
19						256	225	234	195
20						271	244	245	205
21							266	257	218
22								271	242
23								295	
24									
25									

Table 13 Timing of significant events of pouch-young development in the eastern grey kangaroo

Event	Minimum observed age (days)
Sex distinguishable	8
Tips of ears free	9
Papillae of facial vibrissae evident	28
Vibrissae visible to unassisted eye	67
Eyelashes visible to unassisted eye	100
Eyes open	154
Pelage (fur) visible on head to unassisted eye	165
Pelage visible all over body to unassisted eye	175
Colour of pelage definite	200
Tips of first incisors through gum	277
Permanently out of pouch	300

and wear, that are age-related, the former ceasing to be useful (as in man) after the attainment of adulthood when all the teeth are normally erupted. Wear tends to be area-specific particularly for grazing animals, with greater rates of wear occurring in localities with the more abrasive soils and plants. Kangaroos, however, have an additional age-dependent dental character called molar progression – a forward movement of the cheek teeth in the jaws relative to other parts of the head (see figure 25). The incisors move too, but the movement is not readily measurable.

Tooth progression occurs more or less in all mammals; in man it is known an "mesial drift" and is frequently taken advantage of by orthodontists to correct dental problems in children. But only in a few other animal groups besides the kangaroos, notably elephants and sea-cows, does it occur in a significant enough fashion to be used as a measure of age.

Both eruption rate and molar progression have been used to estimate the age of kangaroos by many scientists, and different ways of measuring these characters have been devised. Eruption rate is more useful in kangaroos than in most animals because the last tooth in the molar row is not fully erupted until the animal is middle-aged – in the eastern grey kangaroo at about six years – but molar progression has proved to be of even more value because it continues throughout life. In fact, it is one of the most easily used and accurate measures of age available for any mammal. There is the possibility that it is influenced by the rate of tooth wear such that a greater rate of wear accelerates progression slightly; this is not currently considered to be significant enough to affect field use.

There are two ways of measuring molar progression. The way employed by the earliest workers involved determination of the

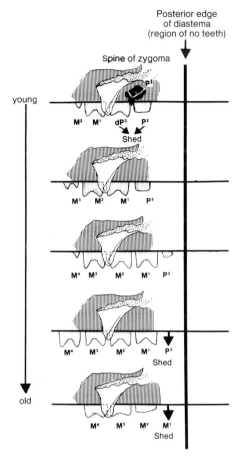

Figure 25   Diagrammatic representation of a series of lateral views of part of the upper jaw of the eastern grey kangaroo to show eruption replacement and the forward progression of the molar row of teeth with increasing age. The naming of the teeth is in accordance with the following system, which is one of several available: P^2 and P^3 are the unreplaced premolars; dP^3 is the deciduous premolar replaced by P^3; M^{1-4} are the unreplaced molars; (occasionally a fifth molar, M^5 occurs).

extent to which the molar row had progressed past the zygomatic process which is a bony projection of the zygoma (cheekbone) that partly obscures the molar tooth behind it when the skull is viewed from the side (figure 25). The advantage of this method is that it may be used fairly readily on a living animal: the disadvantages are that it is crude and imprecise and that different age-determining formulae are needed for each sex because the tip of the zygomatic process generally twists forward in females and backward in males (figure 26) and becomes increasingly forward and backward in these sexes, respectively, with age.

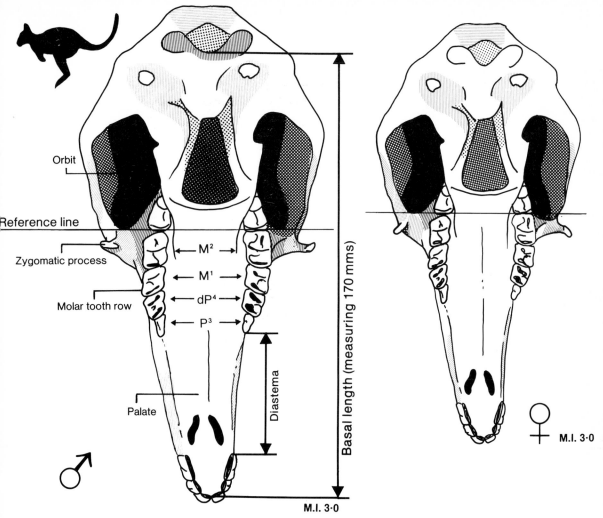

Figure 26 Relevant parts of the upper skull of a male (♂) wallaroo and a female (♀) wallaroo with reference line for molar index (MI) and the measurement of basal length for discriminating sex (see table 14). (Note the sex difference in both size of skull and projection of zygomatic process.)

The second method used is to employ a reference line drawn across the anterior rims of the two orbits, with the cranium held in palatal view and the tooth row held at right angles to the viewer (figure 26). Using a suitable sighting device, the number of teeth anterior to the line, and for the molar beneath the line the proportion of it anterior to the line, may be measured with considerable accuracy. Accuracy is one of the advantages of the second method as also is its independence of sex. The disadvantages are the care needed in taking the measurements and the necessity for x-ray equipment if the animals are living. One study of the agile wallaby did suggest a sex difference in molar progression for this species and called for a review of data in those species where differences were not recognized; so far, no one has responded to this challenge other than to suggest that in that study the males may have been held under the x-ray camera at a different angle from the females.

In both techniques (that is, zygomatic process and a line across the orbits) the measurement of progression is expressed as an index, termed molar index (abbreviated to MI), consisting of a whole number representing the number of molars anterior to the reference point, and a fraction representing the extent to which the molar under the reference is anterior to it. For the second technique, this fraction is simply expressed as a decimal, calculated to either 0.05 or 0.1 of the total tooth length.

Indices of molar progression taken from animals of known age have allowed the relationship between age and molar index to be calculated: it is logarithmic, and formulae have been constructed for many species enabling age to be calculated directly from the index. Table 14 is derived from the formulae for the eastern grey kangaroo and a number of other species. It should perhaps be observed that the molar index is of no apparent value in the rat-kangaroos (the Potoroinae).

Table 14 Molar indices of eastern grey kangaroo, red kangaroo, wallaroo, red-necked wallaby and agile wallaby at one-year intervals from one to twenty years.

Age (years)	Molar index				
	Eastern grey kangaroo	Red kangaroo	Wallaroo	Red-necked wallaby	Agile wallaby
1	0.36	0.93	0.76	0.88	1.13
2	1.39	1.77	1.61	1.69	2.01
3	2.0	2.26	2.12	2.16	2.51
4	2.42	2.61	2.43	2.50	2.88
5	2.75	2.88	2.76	2.79	3.16
6	3.01	3.10	2.99	2.97	3.39
7	3.24	3.29	3.18	3.16	3.58
8	3.44	3.45	3.34	3.31	3.75
9	3.61	3.59	3.49	3.45	3.90
10	3.77	3.72	3.62	3.57	4.03
11	3.91	3.83	3.74	3.68	4.15
12	4.04	3.94	3.85	3.78	4.26
13	4.16	4.03	3.95	3.88	4.36
14	4.27	4.12	4.04	3.97	4.46
15	4.37	4.21	4.13	4.05	4.55
16	4.47	4.29	4.21	4.12	4.63
17	4.56	4.36	4.28	4.19	4.70
18	4.64	4.43	4.35	4.26	4.78
19	4.72	4.49	4.42	4.33	4.84
20	4.80	4.56	4.49	4.39	4.91
95% confidence limits (approx.)	±0.2	±0.3	±0.3	±0.25	±0.3

It must be noted that supernumerary and unerupted teeth are potential sources of error in the use of these age-determining methods; the incidence of these confusing abnormalities in some of the species mentioned in table 14 have included, for example, fifth molars in five per cent of eastern grey kangaroo skulls, in ten per cent of red kangaroo skulls, in three per cent of wallaroo skulls, and in one per cent of red-necked wallabies examined. These represent a real source of error that must be accepted in data secured by oral examinations.

Virtually all the ageing methods used in kangaroos for both pouch-young and adults have been taken from known-age captive animals, on the not unreasonable assumption that growth rates in field-collected young and first generation animals born to unselected wild-caught parents are unlikely to vary significantly from those of wild animals. Of the few opportunities that have ever arisen to allow the formulae to be checked using data from the field, one of the most valuable occurred following the 1964–65 drought in inland Queensland, referred to in more detail later in this chapter; this occasion provided confirmatory data for the eastern grey kangaroo. In a study area between Mitchell and Bollon during that drought, it was positively established that no young born between September 1964 and November 1965 survived the drought, and also that most adult females gave birth to young during January 1966 following the break of the drought in November 1965. This allowed for a field study of both the growth of pouch-young and the relationship between molar index and age by the simple expedient in the former instance of calculating the ages of all young taken in 1966, and in the latter by measuring the molar index of all kangaroos taken subsequent to the drought breaking. The reasoning behind these proposals was, for pouch-young, that firstly no young should be older than an estimated age that indicated a birth date before one mean gestation period (37 days) after the drought broke, and secondly that, because the great majority (if not all) of the adult females came into oestrus within a few days of the drought breaking, the mean estimated date of birth of samples of the first post-drought young taken at monthly intervals for ten months (the duration of pouch-life) should be about the same. For the older animals, it was postulated that as the estimated ages of those born before the drought and those born after it would be separated by fourteen months, no eastern grey kangaroo would be expected with a molar index indicating a date of birth within that fourteen-month period until such time as the confidence limits of the ages estimated from the molar index overlapped (from the formula this would occur some 5.5 years later, in March 1970).

Both propositions were fully supported by the data collected, involving thousands of kangaroos taken by professional shooters, giving a remarkable authentication of the means of age determination of both pouch-young, and of adults up to 6.7 years old. In fact, even 10 years later it was still apparent from the age distribution of adults taken by professional kangaroo shooters throughout Queensland that reproduction had ceased during that period in 1964–65.

The uses to which the ageing techniques for adults are put are indicated in the remainder of this book. One indirect use is in the determination of the sex from an isolated skull. Although, as mentioned above, there is a sex difference in the structure of the zygomatic process of many species, the distinction is not absolute, and a more accurate distinction is possible based on the fact that in most species of Macropodinae, a male is larger than a female of the same age (figure 27).

Thus it has been possible to construct discriminant functions for many species – it would be possible for the majority – that allow the sex of a skull to be determined from two simple measurements: basal head length and molar index. Species for which these functions have been established are the eastern grey kangaroo, the red kangaroo, and the wallaroo (table 15), all species which are harvested commercially.

Studies of captive animals also were needed to determine the bases of reproduction (gestation period, pouch life, and so on) which in

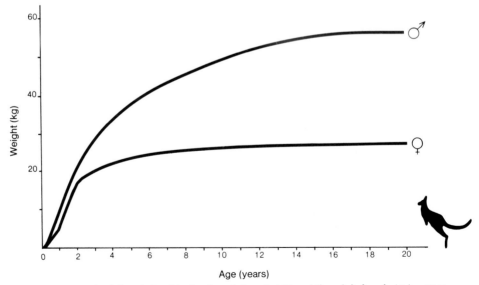

Figure 27 Age/weight relationship for the adult male (♂) and the adult female (♀) eastern grey kangaroo.

Table 15 Discriminant values of molar index for eastern grey kangaroo skulls, red kangaroo skulls, and wallaroo skulls of particular basal lengths

Basal length (millimetres)	Molar index		
	Eastern grey kangaroo	Red kangaroo	Wallaroo
131			1.73
132			1.82
133			1.91
134			2.00
135			2.09
136			1.18
137			2.27
138			2.36
139			2.45
140		1.75	2.54
141		1.84	2.64
142		1.93	2.73
143		2.01	2.82
144		2.10	2.91
145		2.19	3.00
146	1.72	2.28	3.09
147	1.82	2.37	3.18
148	1.92	2.46	3.27
149	2.01	2.55	3.36
150	2.11	2.64	3.45
151	2.21	2.73	3.55
152	2.31	2.82	3.64
153	2.40	2.91	3.73
154	2.50	3.00	3.82
155	2.60	3.09	3.91
156	2.70	3.18	4.00
157	2.80	3.27	4.09
158	2.89	3.36	4.18
159	2.99	3.45	4.27
160	3.09	3.54	4.36
161	3.19	3.63	4.46
162	3.29	3.72	4.55
163	3.38	3.81	
164	3.48	3.90	
165	3.58	3.99	
166	3.68	4.08	
167	3.77	4.17	
168	3.87	4.26	
169	3.97	4.35	
170	4.07	4.44	
171	4.16	4.53	
172	4.26		
173	4.36		
174	4.46		
175	4.55		

Note: Skulls with molar indices above a given value are females; those below are males.

1960 were unknown matters for the majority of macropodids. The mystery of marsupial birth had, of course, been solved long since, although there are still many people including bushmen who cannot believe that so small and poorly developed a creature can make the fifteen to twenty centimetre journey from its mother's birth opening to pouch unaided. An interesting observation is that the majority of macropodids which have been seen giving birth have been sitting with the tail forward between the hinds legs; the known exceptions are the grey kangaroos and the wallaroo, which give birth while standing.

Reproduction

From a combination of data taken directly from captive animals and, where appropriate, derived from wild-caught kangaroos using the ageing methods described above, the details of the life histories of the eastern grey kangaroo and most other species of kangaroos have now been revealed. Such data for the eastern grey kangaroo include a gestation period of 35 to 38 days and a pouch life of 300 to 320 days; this latter is the longest of any marsupial, significantly longer than the 235 days for the red kangaroo and a far cry indeed from the two to three months commonly believed to be its duration by the rural community. Sexual maturity is reached in both sexes of the eastern grey kangaroo at about two years, although females have been found with newborn young in the pouch at the early age of eighteen months. During drought, the initiation of reproduction is delayed in young animals until the drought breaks — the oldest female recorded in first pregnancy being twenty-eight months. Although males are sexually mature as young as twenty months, under field conditions involving competition with mature adults they are not normally effective in reproduction under three years of age.

After eviction of a pouch-young at the average age of 310 days, the female eastern grey kangaroo usually comes into oestrus one to two weeks later and gives birth at about one year after the brith of its first young. These and other life history "statistics" for those species for which these are now known are given for comparison in table 6 (chapter 5).

The long intervals between successive young in kangaroos generally, and in the eastern grey kangaroo in particular, come as a surprise to most people, including members of the rural community, who because of the obvious abundance of kangaroos and the apparent resilience of these animals to hunting pressure, have come to believe that kangaroos must have several young every year. Perhaps there are more kangaroos around than even the most pessimistic grazier fears, or the most optimistic conservationist hopes!

Under normal conditions, a high rate of failure (fifty per cent) to rear young to independence has been found. This loss does not appear to be seasonal because females that have lost young have been collected at all times of the year when weather and pasture conditions could not reasonably be expected to cause such a seasonal loss. Reasons for death of young are difficult to determine with certainty, but separation of mother from dependent juveniles, leaving them exposed to predation and starvation, is involved. Such separation may occur as the result of a chase by a predator, when the female kangaroo characteristically drops any large pouch-young if the chase is at all extended; and it has been observed among captive animals, at least, that some young leaving the pouch for the first time (normally at seven months of age) are too small to be able to get back in. This may occur in the field, and indeed some data collected in 1966 from the drought-affected area referred to earlier indicated that significant pouch-young losses did begin at about seven months (figure 28).

Some researchers have considered that adequacy of nutrition in the female is a significant factor in survival of late pouch-young and dependent juveniles of the red kangaroo; and there are undoubtedly drought times when this affects the eastern grey kangaroo, although this species characteristically inhabits a less harsh environment than the red kangaroo. Also, both the red and the eastern grey kangaroos suckle their young from outside the pouch for some months following eviction and there appears to be a significant reliance on the mother's milk for some time. This dependence may well be exaggerated during times of nutritional stress.

The quiescent embryo

The most interesting feature of reproduction in the macropodids as a family, however, lies in the delayed (or quiescent) embryo, discovered in 1954 by Professor G.B. Sharman in the quokka of Western Australia, which made sense (at last!) of the hugely variable gestation periods recorded by mystified zookeepers as far back as 1908. In his study of the quokka, one of the smallest macropodids, he discovered that the female normally mated and conceived within one day of giving birth, and the resulting conceptus developed only to an early

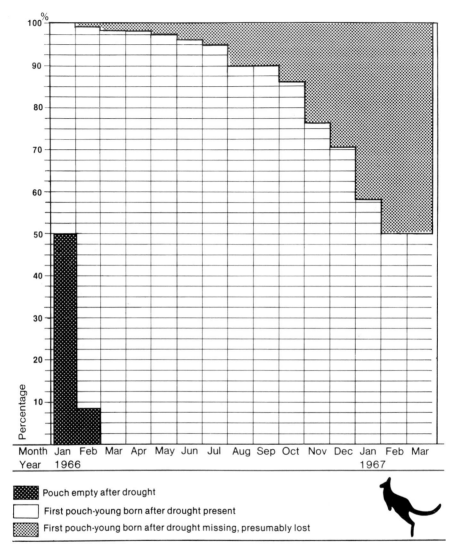

Figure 28   Survival of pouch-young born to adult female eastern grey kangaroos in January and February 1966, following the breaking of the 1964/1965 drought in southern Queensland.

(embryonic) stage − a blastocyst of about one hundred cells − and then went into a state of quiescence broken only when the young occupying the pouch died prematurely following which the birth occurred about a normal gestation period after loss of young. The existence of this mechanism was soon found to occur in the red kangaroo and (in due course) most other macropodids; in these species, the embryo was able to survive the entire pouch life of the first young and be born at the time of its eviction. Naturally, it was expected to occur in the eastern grey kangaroo too but, surprisingly, for many years no quiescent embryo was ever found in the uterus of any field-collected female with young; nor was post-partum oestrus (the fertile period immediately after a birth when mating and conception resulting in the quiescent embryo normally occur) observed in captivity; nor was another young ever born on the day of eviction of the pouch-young. Instead, the female eastern grey kangaroo typically came into oestrus a week or more after either premature loss or eviction of the pouch-young, and gave birth thirty-five to thirty-eight days later. After several years of such observations it was assumed that the eastern grey kangaroo did not have quiescent embryos, and they were no longer sought in field-collected females. Then, unexpectedly, in 1968 an observation in the yards at Warwick aroused new questions. A female eastern grey kangaroo with a 120-day-old pouch-young mated, and on the day of eviction of her young (at 310 days old) a new young was born. Soon afterwards, several others did the same, all mating with pouch-young about the same age (100–160 days); when the pouch-young of some of these were removed prematurely, in each instance a new young was born some 35 days later without another mating.

Previously unexamined field-collected reproductive systems taken over the previous few years (and merely stored) were carefully inspected, and quiescent embryos were found; one was even subsequently collected (in 1970) in advanced pregnancy with a 120-day pouch-young – evidently the delaying mechanism had broken down. The eastern grey kangaroo apparently had its own system, but under what circumstances?

At this point, it is necessary to discuss the questions raised by the existence of quiescent embryos. The matter is something of an enigma. The "normal" situation, as first described in the quokka and subsequently found to occur in many species, is fairly straightforward, even though different reasons are offered for its occurrence in the several species. For whatever reason, females of the majority of members of the family Macropodidae experience a post-partum oestrus with the resulting embryo entering a period of quiescence, broken either by loss of the first young or by the approaching eviction of the first young from the pouch. This reactivation is generally explained on the basis of some experimental results as being dependent on a cessation of, or reduction in, lactation. It was established by a series of removals and replacements of red kangaroo pouch-young (they were kept in the pouch of another lactating female for the period of absence) that a five or six day absence was needed to "trigger" the reactivation; this period nearly, but not quite, coincided with cessation of lactation. Once reactivation had commenced, however, return of the young and revival of lactation did not stop its development. If a conception does not occur at the post-partum oestrus, the red kangaroo (at least) comes into oestrus about one gestation period in time before the resident pouch-young is due to be evicted, and the second birth then occurs at the usual time. In the eastern grey kangaroo, apart from the late start, the occurrence of this quiescent embryo appears to work the same way. The basic (and as yet unanswered) question is why it happens at all in the eastern grey kangaroo or, indeed, any of the others. A ready explanation is that it saves a female from having to find or be found by a male after eviction or loss of the pouch-young, but this is not particularly convincing. After all, she has to find or be found by a male sometime; admittedly, having two chances − at the beginning and at the end of pouch life − must be seen as an advantage. The situation where males have not been available to attend to females in oestrus, however, has yet to be observed in the field.

Perhaps the best clue to one explanation is provided by the behaviour of the female red kangaroo in a drought. After a short period of severe drought − two to three months − the milk supply to a pouch-young large enough to be a significant drain on her system is cut off. The young then dies in the pouch and is replaced thirty to thirty-one days later by the previously quiescent embryo. The mother may then come into oestrus as usual and conceive another embryo which becomes quiescent. Should the drought continue this "infanticide" may be repeated, up to several times in some individuals.

As drought progresses, the breeding programme ceases altogether and does not restart until after sufficient rain falls to break the drought. But should the drought break during this infancticide/birth cycle, the female red kangaroo has breeding already under way, has maintained her condition as much as possible, and has gained time in providing a young to take advantage of the good conditions following the rain, conditions that often enough last for too short a time anyway. This mechanism theoretically is available to the other species that can have quiescent embryos. Whether they use it or not has not been adequately demonstrated, but in a characteristically drought-prone country like Australia any species with this capacity would have probably needed to use it many times in the history of its kind.

The field evidence of quiescent embryos in eastern grey kangaroos, however, has required another explanation, and one that fits only that species, although recently collected data suggest that the whiptail wallaby has the same system (see table 6); and the same explanation is valid. On the few occasions where quiescent embryos were found in eastern grey kangaroos in the field, these involved a high percentage of the females, and all occurrences were found following winter months that had experienced significant rainfall. These females were then able to (and did) give birth to a second young at the time of eviction of the first young – at ten months old – instead of coming into oestrus during the fortnight after eviction and giving birth at the more usual interval of twelve months. This represented a significant increase (16.6 per cent) in the reproductive rate and at a time following winter rainfall when reasonable end-of-winter conditions might be expected, thus allowing the species to gain an advantage by producing more young; the fact is significant for management decisions.

It is interesting to note that the infanticide/birth-from-a-quiescent-embryo cycle has not been observed in this species during drought. Indeed, in the study of eastern grey kangaroos during a prolonged drought referred to previously beginning in September 1964 and lasting until December 1965, females in a study area on the pastoral property named "Abbieglassie" (between Mitchell and Bollon) attempted to retain their pouch-young up to eviction age, and certainly until both mothers and pouch-young were in such poor condition by drought-induced starvation that lactation apparently ceased and the pouch young died. These females (or, at least, those that survived) did not come into oestrus again until the drought broke. The data on which these observations were made are summarized in table 16, in which information is presented so as to make the progress of the effect of the drought on reproduction and pouch-young survival easy to follow. The data reveal the disappearance of the older young beginning after about eight months of drought (in April/May, 1965), the slight (but unsuccessful) return to breeding following two light showers of rain each in June and July, and the almost total return to normal reproduction following drought-breaking rain (163 millimetres) that fell between 29 November and 14 December 1965.

Consideration of the responses to drought allows the suggestion that the eastern grey kangaroo, being more coastal in distribution, is adapted not to long droughts but to short ones, its reproductive mechanism programmed to take every advantage of good seasons, and to survive the normally short droughts of coastal and subcoastal regions. In contrast, reproduction of the red kangaroo of the arid

Table 16 Monthly reproduction and survival of pouch-young in the eastern grey kangaroo, "Abbieglassie" study area: February 1965 to January 1966
All data are expressed as percentages

Month	Non-reproducing		Reproducing, with young born:		
	Expected*	Observed	on or before March 1965**		after March 1965
			Expected	Observed	Observed
February } March }	6.0	9.0	94.0	91.0	0
April	0	n.d.	81.0	n.d.	n.d.
May	0	86.5	74.0	11.5	2.0
June	5.0	100.0	68.0	0	0
July	8.0	84.0	65.0	8.0	8.0
August	7.0	93.0	59.0	0	7.0
September	8.0	100.0	55.0	0	0
October	9.0	100.0	52.0	0	0
November	8.0	100.0	40.0	0	0***
December	7.0	n.d.	23.0	n.d.	n.d.
January	0	0	18.0	0	100.0†

   * Based on reproductive data collected from area, 1959–64.
  ** March 1965 is used because it was during this month that deaths of pouch-young commenced.
 *** One young born November 1965 collected January 1966; no other eastern grey kangaroo with a birth date attributable to this month was ever collected subsequently.
   † Mean calculated birth date of all young was 16 January 1966; mean date of return to oestrus was ten days after first rain (29 November 1965).

inland is programmed for droughts to be long (which they usually are) and to take maximum advantage of good conditions, which are often, if not usually, shortlived. The quiescent embryo is thus put to quite different – even opposite – uses in these two species.

Severe drought, of course, affects all species similarly in a broad sense: the early effect is death of pouch-young, followed by death of recently weaned young and the aged, followed by cessation of reproductive activity, and followed finally by death of all remaining age groups.

During the more normal years – if there can be said to be such periods in inland Australia – the eastern grey kangaroo has been shown to be something of a seasonal breeder. From the estimated ages of pouch-young collected over many years, it has been established that the young are born (five weeks after conception) in all months of the year, with a peak during the summer months (October to January) and a low in mid-winter. Because there is nearly a year from conception to eviction from the pouch, this timing provides for the majority of young to be "tipped out" and new ones to be born during the most favourable period of the year.

Social organization

Social organization has substantial implications for management of kangaroos, particularly in respect of such dependent relationships as mother–young and male–female during oestrus, and also in respect of the effects of harvesting on these relationships. The subject has been addressed superficially in a number of studies including some of the eastern grey kangaroo; it remains as a potentially fruitful, if difficult, field to understand. Such matters as group size and the sex and age of group members have been examined over many years; these data are relatively easily gathered and even though the relationships involved are more often guessed at rather than known, they are of value in management controls.

The more subtle interrelationships that must surely be involved, however, are the ways in which groups interact, in the ways hierarchies are established to allow the co-existence of large numbers of groups and individuals to exist in the same general area. This latter includes in those times when kangaroos form much larger groups than normal – in drought, for instance; far more detailed study of such times than has been yet done is needed.

The eastern grey kangaroo is usually conceded to be a gregarious species, as are the red kangaroo, whiptail wallaby and many others (see table 10 in chapter 5). Other species, such as some of the rock-wallabies, are obviously quite intolerant of individuals in their immediate vicinity, yet their environmental preferences dictate that large numbers live in close proximity. Other species again, such as the red-necked wallaby, are generally seen as solitary animals although it is apparent that the members of this species occupying the same parcel of land (home range?) have a system of mutual recognition and regard.*

The eastern grey kangaroo is probably typical of most of the overtly gregarious species in that the commonest grouping is of two animals: the most frequent interrelationship being between a mother and its young, the next most common between a male and a female. Larger groups appear to be loose aggregations of females and their young, with the adult males moving from one group to another presumably looking for females in or near oestrus. Subadult males are frequently

* Professor Heini Hediger (in 1950) pointed out that, to mammals, it is not so much an occupied area which is important as a number of points of interest connected by an elaborate network of paths, along which the territory inhabitant travels according to a more or less strict daily, seasonal, or otherwise determined routine. To draw through the outer points of this network and call this the boundary of the home range would be a purely abstract procedure. Neighbouring individuals may even use the same paths.

found alone or in small groups of other subadults, and aged males are usually solitary individuals. The majority of unaccompanied kangaroos, however, are females. There is no evidence of accumulation of "harems" by adult males, nor is there any evidence of permanent pairing.

The implications of these habits for management are obvious. A dependent young, orphaned by having its mother shot, is a reasonably certain casualty as well, although fostering has been observed, rarely, in captivity and may occur, with even greater rarity, in the field; the shooting of a male in the company of a female in oestrus simply leaves the female free for another male and one is unlikely to be far away. Overall, the disturbance and breaking up of larger groups by shooting is not likely to have any significant effect.

The social organization of the other gregarious species is not much different from that of the eastern grey kangaroo, certainly not in its implications for management. The evicted pouch young, for example of the agile wallaby, have an extremely short period of dependence on the mother; in the red-necked wallaby it is less than one week, with a consequent reduction in the significance to the population of the loss of a mother by shooting, or by non-human predation.

Predation and disease

In common with all herbivores, the macropodids represent a food source for a group of predators. Undoubtedly, in earlier times, carnivorous marsupials (such as the native cats) preyed on smaller macropodids (such as the bettongs); nowadays these species prefer rabbits, which are more abundant than their native prey. The larger marsupial carnivores such as the thylacine and the so called marsupial-lion (*Thylacaleo*) undoubtedly preyed on the larger species but, on the mainland at least, this was before the advent of man. Now, introduced carnivores are common and attack the larger species. The dingo is undoubtedly the most significant of these; indeed, it is widely accepted by the rural community that there is an inverse relationship between the abundance of dingoes and of kangaroos, and there is a vast body of inferential material that bears this out. Thus on the "sheep side" of the dog fence that winds its way from Queensland to South Australia where dingo control programmes are a constant feature of the pastoral industry (see chapter 3), macropodids are abundant and themselves the subject of control programmes. On the other side, which is largely the province of cattle-raising pastoralists, dingoes are common and kangaroos, generally speaking, are not. In South Australia particularly, "north of the dog fence" is virtually synonymous with "kangaroos are scarce", while "south of the dog fence" means the opposite. The situation is not so clear in Queensland, although the greater part of the kangaroo industry is located within the protection of the fence; one study offered the presence of an abundance of dingoes as the most likely reason for the relative scarcity of red kangaroos in Queensland's southwest region. In one of the few studies in which the activities of dingoes have actually been observed (in northwestern New South Wales), the rate at which a group of five dingoes ambushed young kangaroos at a waterhole was both wasteful and sufficient to prevent adult recruitment to an average-density red kangaroo population. The adult kangaroos were rarely attacked, and adult males essentially ignored the dingoes; it is well known that an adult male kangaroo, at least, is more than a match for a dog.

The significant role of the dingo as a predator of the black-striped wallaby and the bridled nailtail-wallaby in the central Queensland reserve established for the latter species has been noted in chapter 2. There are many instances, too, of virtual disappearance of the two pademelon species from the small remaining patches of closed forest left as enclaves when large areas have been cleared for agriculture or forestry: such disappearances may reasonably be attributed to dingo predation.

The corollary, involving dramatic increases in kangaroo numbers following concerted dingo control campaigns, is described in innumerable anecdotes from the pastoral areas of Australia and, in the light of the foregoing, there is every reason to believe them. There can be little doubt that the dingo, in many areas at least, is a significant influence on the abundance of macropodids.

Compared with the dingo, the other predators of macropodids are minor. They include the introduced fox and cat which have been accorded roles in the disappearance of the smaller marsupials that, in the absence of any real evidence, have certainly been grossly overrated; the wedge-tailed eagle is able to kill young of the larger species and will also attack adults. Several reptiles, in particular the amethystine python of the north Queensland rainforests and the carpet snake of the forests of eastern Australia, have been known to capture the young of the smaller macropodids including the pademelons and rock-wallabies. None of these predators, however, can be considered reasonably as having the capacity to affect numbers of the prey species in any significant way. In any event, it is important, but not easy, to distinguish between a predatory role and mere scavenging of already dead kangaroos that may be taking place.

Parasites and disease, like predation, are also barely understood influences on the macropodid populations. Many of the large array of external and internal parasites – which include the hippoboscid flies, nasal bot flies, lice, ticks, fleas, stomach and intestinal round-worms and tapeworms – are not yet named. In fact, little is known about the effects they have on their macropodid hosts apart from such general observations as the following: lice and ticks seem to have obviously deleterious effects only during times of environment-al stress, particularly drought; enormous numbers of nematodes are usual in macropodid stomachs without any obviously deleterious effects; almost all adult kangaroos have tapeworms in their bile ducts. The only deaths attributed directly to parasites that have been observed in Queensland studies are from hydatids – the inter-mediate stage of the dog tapeworm – which not uncommonly block the lungs of the rock-wallabies and the pademelons.

The relationship between hydatids and the dingo is currently under review by research workers at the Animal Research Institute, Queensland Department of Primary Industries: it appears to involve a strain of this universal parasite which is specific to the dingo and the Macropodidae. It is also important to note here that none of the other parasites of macropodids appears to be shared with domestic stock.

Probably the best known parasite of kangaroos is the kneeworm, so called because of its usual location in the connective tissue immediately underneath the skin of the knee in a number of macro-podids including the commercially utilized species. Its notoriety relates to accidental inclusion of these worms in packaged meat which has resulted in its condemnation by overseas purchasers, despite the fact that there is no possibility of human infection from such a source. This worm is one of the few for which a life history has been described; Dr David Spratt established that the larval stages are released by the adults in the knees, then enter the blood and are ingested by blood-sucking march flies, in which they develop to an infective stage. Infection occurs when a march fly with these infec-tive larvae bites a kangaroo. As for the other parasites, there is no evidence that animals other than macropodids can be infected.

The diseases of macropodids are even more poorly known and less understood than parasites. Coccidiosis, a disease best known in domestic chickens but to which most vertebrates appear subject, affects macropodids and a number of species of this protozoan peculiar to the kangaroo family have been identified. The disease can be fatal, although the only positively identified instances of death have been among captive animals; this occurred usually following wet weather, and nearly always involved recently evicted pouch-young, although older animals previously unexposed to the disease have been known to succumb. The only documentary field evidence of fatalities involving coccidiosis was in grey kangaroos. Large numbers were congregated on small islands created by rising floodwaters, and deaths of some of the juveniles present were attributed to a coccidiosis outbreak. Contributing factors were overcrowding, food shortage, damp conditions, and, possibly, feed supplementation.

Another disease best known from captive animals is "lumpy jaw", the infected animal developing a substantial deforming growth of either upper or lower jaw, sometimes both, and which is frequently fatal. Many attempts to identify the causal organism have been made over the years; the most recent (Samuel, 1983) suggests that *Fusobacterium necrophorum* is the cause, infection probably occurring through injuries inside the mouth. There is a substantial field occurrence of this condition in red-necked wallabies at least in the Warwick district, where as many as ten per cent of adult animals have been found infected in some years. The only other field occurrences recorded in the Queensland kangaroo research programme have been, rarely, in eastern grey kangaroos.

The two most spectacular diseases that affect kangaroos have so far eluded positive identification of their cause. One is a condition known as "pock", which appears to affect mainly red kangaroos, and frequently occurs over a wide area. The condition is discovered only after an individual has been shot and skinned, when the inside of the skin is found to be marked with small blood spots about five millimetres in diameter; if the skin is tanned these spots fall out, rendering the skin useless. There is no evidence of any other effect on the diseased animal.

The other disease, however, is commonly fatal, usually dramatically so. Again the red kangaroo appears to be the major victim, although affected eastern grey kangaroos and wallaroos have been found and it is reasonable to expect that other macropodids in immediate areas also would be involved. Invariably associated with the aftermath of a flood and the presence of large numbers of sandflies breeding in the evaporating rivers of the inland – events that occur at about ten-year intervals in the inland river basins – it involves the death of a significant number of the kangaroo community, usually over a large area. There are two groups of symptoms: one involves animals that become emaciated and swollen (oedematous), particularly around the head, prior to death; the other is in animals that are not emaciated when they succumb. In the latter case, an affected animal seems to be partly blind, loses the locomotive capacity of the hindlimbs and collapses, dying after one or two days of futile scratching at the ground with the forelegs; in the process, it wears around itself a characteristic circular, saucer-like depression. There may be more than one condition involved, although the common belief is that harassment by sandflies is alone responsible, and this may be true for those that become emaciated. Other suggestions include poisoning from unfamiliar plants that may grow after a flood, or the transmission of a virus-like disease by the sandflies. Identification of an acceptable cause, however, has so far eluded researchers and despite veterinary examination of affected animals the cause (or causes) still are not positively identified.

Chapter 7

Conservation

Introduction

The term conservation is used far more often than it is understood. Certainly most perceptions of conservation include the idea of protection of some kind of asset. But how much protection and whether and to what extent a particular asset may be used are matters in which the majority of interested people are not personally involved; those who are rarely reach agreement about the answers.

In this book, no attempt is made to coerce readers to accept a particular point of view. Rather, the way conservation of the kangaroo family in Queensland has been approached is presented with particular reference to the commercially harvested species, and contained in this the reader will discover an approach to wildlife conservation that has proved workable to date. This accepts an Australia-wide concern for kangaroo conservation currently embodied in the stated objectives on this subject of the Council for Nature Conservation Ministers:

1. To maintain populations of the designated species of Macropodidae over their natural ranges
2. To contain the deleterious effects of kangaroos on other land management priorities.

That all the species of kangaroos recorded for Queensland were still present when the conservation legislation was proclaimed in 1954 was certainly because of the persistence of the species themselves. The fact that they have all continued to the present, in the face of extensive change to the environment, includes at least an element of sound management.

For the majority of kangaroo species, the protection afforded by legislation that makes them the property of the state, combined with their manifest capacity to persist in the presence of man and his activities, appears adequate to ensure survival at least into the immediate future. For those species described in chapter 2, which appear to be threatened with extinction without more positive measures to provide for their protection, reserves have been established solely for their preservation. It is the commercial species for which the particular attention of the government is demanded by the Australian community, and the need for the conservative management of these species has provided the basis for a major study of the principles of the population dynamics of these wild animals.

It is the ambition of today's manager of any population of wild animals to base management on a knowledge of the size of population, as well as how this reacts to the environmental influences to which it is subjected. That this is still a dream, at least as far as the kangaroos are concerned, certainly does not mean that harvesting should not continue until it is.

Wild animals have been taken by man ever since he had the capacity and the reason to do so, and while it is true that some harvested species have become extinct, most have not; certainly the kangaroos have thrived even despite deliberate and far-reaching attempts at extermination. But the attitudes of today do require that the major deficiencies of knowledge about actual abundance and distributions relative to available habitat be overcome, and that inadequacies be compensated for in the meantime.

These are controversial subjects still in their infancy as far as zoological research is concerned. Clearly related to these topics is the issue of when and why kangaroos are seen and not seen by observers, presently the greatest single cause of the misconceptions about their abundance.

The problem of visibility

Characteristically, kangaroos are secretive and nocturnal, and although there are times when they may be seen by travellers on major roads during daylight hours, such observations are the exception rather than the rule; they are correlated usually with some abnormal combination of circumstances that may apply only for a day. It is the recollections of such atypical events that cause the same travellers on subsequent trips to the area when conditions may be more usual, to think that kangaroos have been "shot out". Similarly, the reverse order of observation leads to assertions that the animals now abound in plague proportions.

The normal pattern of visibility during the day is related to resting and feeding movements; the daily feeding movements commence in late afternoon and continue during the first half of the night. There is usually a lull in activity during the early hours of the morning followed by further movement and final return to daylight resting areas some two to three hours after sunrise, when kangaroos become extremely difficult to locate. Day to day changes in visibility are related to weather patterns – on windy days and nights kangaroos are rarely seen, whereas after a heavy storm they are remarkably active and obvious, even in daylight and often for a few hours. Seasonal variations in visibility are generally marked. During a rainy season and for weeks or sometimes months afterwards kangaroos remain in cover and are normally difficult if not impossible to see at any time of the day or night, even if present in quite large numbers. After the grass produced by the rain has dried out, or has been "hayed off" by frost, or when the pasture has been eaten down by native or domestic stock, kangaroos become increasingly visible; towards the end of a greatly extended drought kangaroos tend to move about and be easily observed at all times of the day. Because of this increasing visibility, during a dry time it is often alleged that kangaroos have "moved in from the west" when in fact large numbers have always been present but have been difficult to view. These points are illustrated by the numbers of kangaroos taken per night during collections by a research team, where the relationship between numbers taken and rainfall is obvious (figure 29).

Visibility has a direct and most significant effect on any study that depends on field observations of kangaroos for measuring their abundance or their use of habitat. To avoid this problem Dr Greg Hill used the distribution of droppings (faecal pellets) to measure habitat utilization. This, however, introduces new problems such as the influence of the defaecating pattern (in particular how well it conforms to habitat use), the durability of droppings in different weather conditions, and the time taken for them to be dissipated or eaten by dung beetles or termites. Dr Hill's work in southern Queensland has confirmed the general observation others have made over the years that tree and shrub cover, particularly shelter growing to about kangaroo head-height, is extremely important to the eastern grey kangaroo; grazing areas are preferentially related to their proximity to the best cover. The most important eastern grey kangaroo habitat therefore is where open grassland and suitable tree cover are contiguous, and an area with a mosaic of cleared and uncleared patches is ideal for this species. The sheep grazing country of

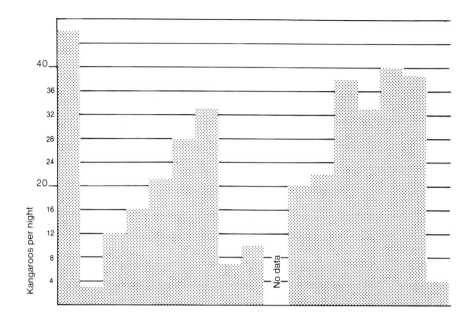

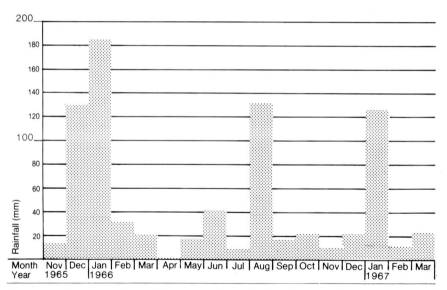

Figure 29 Average numbers of kangaroos taken each night for research purposes compared with monthly rainfall, "Abbieglassie" study area near Mitchell, western Queensland: November 1965 to March 1967.

central-southern Queensland conforms to that pattern, and predictably the greatest concentrations of eastern grey kangaroos occur throughout that region. Unfortunately, the counting of faecal pellets has not been refined to the point where it might be used to estimate actual numbers, and in the light of similar studies on other animals the possibility of such refinement seems remote.

All attempts to estimate numbers of kangaroos have depended on sighting by observers, whether on the ground or from the air, and as yet (in recognition of the visibility problem) no person engaged in counting kangaroos has been prepared to state unequivocally that the population sizes so determined are indeed accurate. The patchiness in distribution induced by the habitat preference, the preference for timbered rather than open areas, and the tremendous variation in the exercise of this preference caused by the weather, all combine to make both aerial and ground counts over huge areas and involving indisputably enormous numbers of individuals highly suspect, particularly during seasons favourable to eastern grey kangaroos.

Much has been done by Dr Graeme Caughley to refine observational techniques and analytical procedures of aerial counts, with the result that there is a high level of precision (that is, repeatability) in counts taken using his method. However, those who undertake such counts still regard them as an index rather than as absolute counts indicating possible trends rather than actual changes. This is largely on account of the necessity for correction factors which Dr Caughley has derived for the different habitat types in which kangaroos are found. They represent the figures by which the numbers seen must be multiplied to compensate for individuals present but not observed. His factor for the type of habitat most preferred by the eastern grey kangaroo, and which constitutes most of the habitat of this species probably in Australia and certainly in Queensland, is quite high (2.53) although certainly questionable, giving lower estimates than are real during favourable habitat conditions. Thus Dr Hill, who used aerial counts in attempts to quantify his studies based on counts of faecal pellets, found that the numbers of eastern grey kangaroos in a study area exceeding 100,000 square kilometres in southern Queensland nearly trebled between November 1978 and August 1979: the first count was in a favourable season and the second was in a drought. However, it is probable, if not certain, that the population had in fact barely altered: there had been insufficient time for the females to have reared young to independence, and the area was too large to suggest immigration. Such results support the proposal that the aerial index is not really of abundance but rather of visibility.

There is much work to be done before the problems associated with population estimations by actual counting are resolved and this must surely involve the development of correction factors based on the measurement of suitable (as yet undefined) environmental parameters. Further, numbers alone represent an uncertain basis for management because not only is it necessary to understand how populations change in response to both adverse pressures and favourable influences but also the sex and age ratios are imperative to such predictions and are not resolved by counts.

Collecting and using harvest data

While allowing that aerial census techniques may well be used at some time in the future, the current management of the exploited kangaroos in Queensland does not rely on these. Instead, a number of parameters of the harvest are monitored and from the data so collected the status of the several species is inferred. Those measures, and the way they have been and are being used, are explained at some length later in the chapter. By way of introduction to this discussion a number of facts about the populations of these species are re-presented, all of them having been enlarged upon in earlier chapters.

The harvested kangaroos occur in millions, occupy millions of square kilometres of the most abundant habitat types in Australia (open forest and grassland), and have been harvested annually in hundreds of thousands (even millions) for more than a century. They are superbly adapted to the climatic vagaries of Australia, their country of origin. In addition, they have been able to benefit substantially from the kind of rangeland management practices throughout the greater part of their habitat by Europeans, which involves increasing the availability of pasture and surface water and control of the only significant predator, the dingo.

The success of the larger kangaroos in the current Australian environment has resulted in their being regarded with ample, if not precisely definable, justification as pests by the rural community, with the inevitable demand by affected landholders for the right to exercise control of numbers. The fact that a dead kangaroo is a saleable item, providing meat and skins, has allowed the development of a kangaroo industry involving substantial investment in plant, equipment, and property by shooters, dealers, and processors to take advantage of the commercial opportunities provided by this demand for control. The industry has come to exist in its own right to exploit a renewable resource, not merely to serve the control functions.

An important question at this point is to what extent an industry exploiting as a renewable resource an animal regarded as a pest, and using that pest status as the reason for its existence, can satisfy the demands of landholders who want their problem solved. The answer lies firstly in the extent to which the animals are in fact regarded as pests, a subject discussed earlier in this book, and secondly in the way that harvesting occurs. The truth is that kangaroos are seen, generally, as serious enough pests to require short-term reduction of numbers preferably in specified areas, but not as serious as to require extermination. Thus the crop farmer is happy if the majority of invaders are "chased off" the crop by judiciously timed shooting forays that destroy only a percentage of the offenders, even though he or she knows that those destroyed will be replaced in due course by breeding or immigration. Similarly, the grazier is satisfied to have the shooter concentrate greatest efforts in those paddocks that are being spelled from stock grazing, which are of course those to which kangaroos characteristically gravitate and thus are of greatest reward to the shooter. All landholders cherish the hope that continued shooting, as carried out by the commercial industry, results in keeping overall numbers below what is theoretically possible from reproductive rates and food availability; and this may be true at times or in places, certainly during droughts. However, the majority are perceptive enough to realize, and pragmatic enough to accept, that the industry as at present organized and constrained by government legislation essentially meets only short-term needs. The problem will remain indefinitely.

This industry investment, because of its size and limited applicability to other uses, constrains the industry to operate conservatively towards its source of income, and virtually forces it to cooperate with the government authority which exists to pursue the same objectives in respect of kangaroo populations as the industry: survival of the harvested species.

Since 1954, when the legal status of kangaroos in Queensland was changed (by act of Parliament) from being vermin to that of protected species for which a controlled open season might be declared, the interaction between the industry and the exploited species has been under constant and increasingly complex review. Relevant data collected nowadays include:

- number of shooters operating, where they shoot, and the numbers taken, according to species
- number and location of dealers, and their operations in terms of shooters with whom they deal, and the numbers of kangaroos, according to species, that pass through their hands
- samples from professional shooters throughout the area of commercial harvest that allow analysis of the species and sex and age of their take, particularly to detect any changes in those parameters
- observation by field staff of distribution and visual abundance of all harvested species throughout their ranges, and unbiased samples by research staff from both harvested and unharvested populations.

The reasoning behind these collections of data is simple and relevant to the straightforward needs of management of such abundant animals. It includes the logical belief that commercial shooters will never knowingly endanger their own livelihood by conscious over-harvesting, and the certainty – based on much experience – that commercial harvesting becomes uneconomic, and therefore stops, long before a hunted kangaroo species disappears from an area. It involves recognition of the fact that there are large parts of the territory of each species that are never harvested, and large parts of even the harvested areas that are inaccessible to shooters. It also includes acceptance of the responsibility of the government as the permitting authority to be aware of how harvesting is affecting populations, and the need to be in a position to detect adverse trends attributable to harvesting so that appropriate controlling action may be taken as quickly as possible after they begin.

Probably the most useful segment of these data relates to the annual harvest. It must be acknowledged, of course, that the first harvest of any species proves no more than that the number taken was in fact present prior to the harvest, as likewise does a dramatic increase in the harvest such as happened in Queensland during the 1960s. Both may prove to be disastrous. Once records are available for many years, however, and especially if these have been taken over a wide range of environmental conditions that have been appropriately recorded, they serve as an invaluable reference and basis for subsequent management decisions. Such figures have been taken in Queensland since 1954, embracing a wide range of environmental circumstances as well as commercial and government-caused pressures on both kangaroos and the industry.

The sex and age distribution of the take is a measure of shooter selectivity, and as such is essentially a form of catch–effort data. Catch–effort analysis is a universally accepted technique for measuring the effects of hunting an abundant species, with particular application to fisheries. Such an approach has obvious application to the abundant kangaroos, including the fact that as low-value animals they are not worth harvesting in small numbers. It is appropriate to point out here that it is generally (and probably correctly) believed that the numbers of kangaroos outside the border dog fence in South Australia are kept low by dingoes and are too small to allow harvesting even to be contemplated; but even in that situation there is no suggestion that they are endangered.

The relationship of the sex–age composition of the take to kangaroo abundance is a measure of the availability of the preferred classes (largest size) which, like aerial counts, is significantly affected by visibility. The advantage of these data over aerial survey information, however, is that they may be (and are) taken at far more frequent intervals, and there is immediate opportunity to investigate any apparent change that cannot be attributed directly to the weather.

Species distribution from shooters' records and from direct observations by research or ranger personnel are of considerable importance to the understanding of the status of an exploited species. When an animal disappears from a significant part of its known range, an explanation is necessary; to date, no such changes have been observed in the exploited species of kangaroos. The only relevant observation is an apparent westward extension of the continuous distribution range of the eastern grey kangaroo; this is under what may best be described as low-level surveillance. To date it does not appear to involve overt competition with the red kangaroo; this species still extends as far eastward into the range of the eastern grey kangaroo as it always has. The subject is marked for future detailed investigation.

The reasoning behind the monitoring procedure used is therefore basically simple. It does, however, involve an understanding of a complex set of factors operating in the field as well as the development of a little-explored approach to the theory of population dynamics of wild animals. According to this theory, a population of wild animals is defined as the total of adults (that is, breeders); this is seen as a relatively stable entity numerically, particularly in the longer-lived, slower-breeding species which includes the kangaroos, but with considerable potential for variation in age composition. Variations in the size of such a population are undoubtedly related to environmental conditions – "highs" and "lows" must be governed by "good" and "bad" conditions, respectively – but it is clear that under natural conditions populations regulate their numbers within narrow limits, and far below what is theoretically possible from reproductive rates and food availability. ("Plagues", particularly of some rodents, are exceptions that prove this rule.)

The Australian environment, of course, is well known for its alternation of drought and flood, and the kangaroos are adapted to these climatic extremes. It is a severe drought indeed that results in a significant death rate of adults; similarly, while a succession of good seasons must result in a higher than normal survival of juveniles with consequent increases in the breeding population, increases in numbers to the potential "carrying capacity" of the pasture are mostly checked long before this is reached.

While the mechanisms of this regulation are not yet understood, the social interactions between adults and independent juveniles are manifestly involved, and survival of juveniles is seen as a variable directly related to the adult death rate. Under normal conditions juveniles survive only in sufficient numbers to replace adults that die, and the excess (which is normally large) is expendable, but also available to replace adults taken under a harvesting programme. Thus, in this theory, the reproductive rate of a species (whether intrinsic or actual), which is the usual parameter considered in population studies, is meaningful only as basis for determining the juvenile survival rate (that is, the rate at which juveniles survive to enter the adult population); this is seen as a key statistic for any population, and from it a great deal of information about the population may be deduced.

The age composition of the population is regarded as a direct consequence of the interactions between adult death rate and juvenile survival rate and because this is an obtainable statistic from many populations, certainly of the larger kangaroos, it is considered reasonable that this theory can be thoroughly tested using population simulation techniques as detailed below, and comparing results with data from known populations.

The age–sex data are collected for the monitoring programme on the assumption that these may be manipulated statistically to provide a realistic indication of the age composition of the populations from which they are taken, and thus may be used as a measure of the level of overharvest or underharvest. As mentioned above, the reasoning is simple, involving recognition that shooters are as selective for large animals as the size of the population allows them to be, and that in an underexploited population they will be able to stay selective indefinitely. Recognizing that the oldest animals are the largest and that a male at any age is larger than a female, a shooter's selectivity is measurable in terms relevant to the foregoing theory of population dynamics; and the monitoring data, if correctly treated, may be used to provide a precise measure of the individual's harvesting level. There are many confounding factors, however, in the field situation, involving visibility problems related to the weather, effects of long-term drought on reproduction and survival, and thus on the age composition of the shooter's sample.

A corollary is that the number of kangaroos present in an unharvested population at any time is in fact the number that the environment has determined should be present, so this is the population level that in the absence of any other constraints, conservation effort should strive to maintain. If, however, other constraints are accepted, such as the need to keep numbers down in order to reduce damage to rural enterprises, a basis is available for measuring their likely effects. This is an important consideration indeed, because despite the extensive community interest in kangaroo conservation, there is in fact no established basis on which any interested group is able to define the number of kangaroos that should be seen as desirable, apart from those few persons who would have all kangaroos exterminated or all preserved. Merely to propose, as some do, that kangaroos should be allowed to reproduce without restraint is to call for a change not in the number that will be present, but in the age structure. Once the environment is saturated, more adults will survive into old age at the expense of juveniles. To demand an abundance below saturation — the wish of the rural community — would necessitate an overharvest sustained throughout an appropriate period followed by a carefully controlled harvest rate to match the rate at which weaned young are produced. This would, incidentally, require harvest surveillance to an extent that is not yet possible, even though it may be justifiable on some grounds.

Adherence to this theory to date has allowed a regular broad assessment of whether the harvest rate has been one of overexploitation or underexploitation. In many of the years since 1968, kangaroo heads have been collected from professional shooters representing various exploited areas of Queensland. These have provided the information for both monthly and yearly sex and age distributions of the harvest. There has been no evidence to date of overexploitation on a statewide basis, as would be indicated by an increasing percentage of females and younger animals in the harvest. Data since 1978,

Table 17 Sex and age composition of harvested macropodids in Queensland: 1978 to 1983

Eastern grey kangaroo				Red kangaroo					Wallaroo			
♂	10+ yrs	4-9 yrs	<4 yrs	♂	10+ yrs	4-9 yrs	<4 yrs	Year	♂	10+ yrs	4-9 yrs	<4 yrs
%	%	%	%	%	%	%	%		%	%	%	%
82	7	58	35	76	10	53	37	1978	96	13	75	12
81	7	60	33	82	9	64	27	1979	93	16	65	20
88	9	73	18	74	10	63	27	1980	94	14	70	16
76	7	66	27	76	13	58	29	1981	92	23	64	13
73	9	75	16	72	14	45	21	1982	98	19	71	10
75	9	64	27	78	18	66	16	1983	97	16	75	9

for which continuous records are available, are presented in table 17.

A logical extension of the reasoning behind this programme, given that body weight is age- and sex-related in a known way, is that carcass weights of the harvested animals may also be used in the same kind of analysis. When the relative ease of acquiring this information from practically the entire whole-carcass segment of the industry is compared with the logistical difficulty of securing the age–sex data from a small sample of the harvest, the advantage of using dealer-supplied weights is immediately obvious. With the current availability of electronic data processing to handle the enormous amount of information involved, these data are soon to be required from the industry. The population model described in the following pages is expected to provide a sound basis to allow the sex–age monitoring to be substituted ultimately by data on carcass weight. It will be necessary, of course, that appropriate field sampling of the actual age and sex composition of both the harvest and the residual population continue in key areas.

A simulation model of monitoring procedures

In 1981, the Reserve Bank of Australia (Rural Credits Development Fund) agreed to underwrite a three year study of these monitoring procedures using a simulation model of the eastern grey kangaroo population. The objectives of this project were:

1. To establish principally for the eastern grey kangaroo the definitions of underharvest or overharvest in relation to the composition of the professional shooters' take
2. To institute a field monitoring programme to provide appropriate data for both objective (1), above, and the continual monitoring of the eastern grey kangaroo population.

Data available as a basis for this study included:

- the basic biological information of the animals themselves (reproductive rates, etc.), all readily available
- a considerable amount of data on pouch-young survival under normal and drought conditions, as well as a study of the effects of drought on reproduction
- some years (about ten) of randomly collected samples taken from a population exploited only for the purpose of taking the samples. Sex, age and date of collection of every specimen collected are available, together with considerable data on kangaroo availability under varying weather conditions
- one year's data, recorded similarly to last item, above, from a heavily exploited population, with a lesser amount for several subsequent years
- several years' data, recorded similarly, from a heavily exploited population together with a large number of shooters' samples from the same population taken at the same time
- consecutive monthly shooters' samples from a total of thirty localities (including the one mentioned in last item, above), ranging from several months (the majority) to many years.

For the benefit of this project, collection of data representing exploited areas, both randomly collected and professional shooters' samples, have been increased. In particular, the locality of "Abbieglassie", the property involved in the collection of data in the second last item listed above, has been sampled more intensively.

The simulation model consists of an age- and sex-structured population of eastern grey kangaroos as detailed below. Subjected to natural mortality, reproduction, maturation into older age groups and different harvest strategies, the final population age structure together with the corresponding simulated harvest is compared with the similar data available from exploited populations.

Within the model the population structure consists of the following stages.

Pouch-young. This stage lasts approximately nine to eleven months after birth.

Young-at-foot. Following the pouch stage, joey is evicted from pouch but continues to suckle for approximately six months.

Independent males and females — subadults. Young are no longer dependent on mother but have not yet reached sexual maturity.

Adult (pre-breeding) females. Independent females have matured into the adult population but have not yet begun to breed.

Pouch-young and young-at-foot exist only as parameters of the adult female breeding population. There is no evidence of sex-differentiated mortality for these two stages, and therefore dependent young mature to independent status in the ratio of one male to one female.

Independent males and females are considered as a "resource" for the adult population. An individual matures into the adult sector only when a "space" due to adult mortality exists. The population remains equal to the initial number (assuming a constant environment) except when adult death exceeds production of weaned young. A refinement to be introduced later consists of an environmental index. This would allow more independents than were needed for replacement of adults to mature into the adult population during times of optimum habitat conditions. Subadults in the independent stage are fifteen to twenty-four months old. Replacement of adults can occur in one of two ways: random replacement – independents are chosen randomly with no regard for age or sex; and alike replacement – individuals are replaced by independents of the same sex (regardless of age).

If a juvenile has not matured to the adult population within this age (fifteen to twenty-four months), it is regarded as "excess" and ceases to exist. This corresponds to the theory that subadult deaths occur (from a variety of causes) to the extent needed to maintain a relatively stable adult population.

The "deficit" represents the number of adult deaths exceeding the number of independents available for replacement. This continually changes as more independents become available for replacement. The "excess" is regarded as an index of population wellbeing. A state of overharvest would imply a zero excess and a growing deficit.

Male independents mature directly into the male sector of the adult population. Female independents mature into a female pre-breeding adult array until their first pregnancy, when they move into the female sector of the adult population. The simulated adult population is thus a breeding population and is structured in yearly age groups for each sex.

Program details

The program of the simulation model is in FORTRAN language, using the structured design, top-down approach as explained by E. Yourdon and L. L. Constantine in their book *Structured Design* (1979). This approach modularizes the design, enabling separate writing and testing of the component modules – essential for a program this size. There are eight component modules, one control module and seven independent submodules representing survival, maturity, reproduction, harvest, replacement, update, and validation.

The submodules and their roles are identified and described on the following pages.

Validation

1. For first time period only, inputs:
   length of simulation
   drought figures
   all population data.
   Formulates all arrays.

2. Validates these arrays for obvious numerical inaccuracies.

Validate is called by the control module at start of simulation, and after each cycle to check that array values are within reasonable boundaries.

Survival

1. For first time period only, inputs:
   survival rates (corresponding to natural mortality)
   upper age limit for adults.
   Calculates changes to survival rates due to drought.
2. Calculates survival of all groups within the population.
3. Updates the records of pouch, dependent, independent and adult death caused by natural mortality.

Estimates of survival for pouch- and dependent young are available from an observed population of females, all of which gave birth within one month of a drought breaking.

Adult survival rates were calculated from annual shot samples, using the minimum variance unbiased estimator (MVUE) described by D.G. Chapman and D.S. Robson in 1960. The assumptions required for this analysis are a stationary population (that is, a stable age distribution and constant population size) and, above some minimum age, an annual survival rate constant over age and time. This implies a geometric age distribution. Biases in the survival estimates will occur if the population is not stationary. It will be assumed that in the absence of external pressures (for example, harvesting) and extremes in natural conditions, the adult population maintains a reasonably stationary level.

In 1965, the drought which affected the area including Mitchell in central Queensland was responsible for the death of many adult members of the population; one result of this was unusually large numbers of two- and three-year-olds in the following years, 1966 and 1967. The assumption that the age distribution is stationary is therefore invalidated and calculation of survival rates is affected for many years by the passage of these large year classes through the population age structure.

Reproduction

1. For the first time period only, inputs:
   reproduction rates.
   Changes reproduction rates to zero during a drought.
2. Calculates percentage of adult (breeding) females pregnant.
3. Calculates percentage of pre-breeding females pregnant and transfers these to the adult (breeding) female group.
4. Updates record of pregnancies per month of year, and pregnancies per age.

Female eastern grey kangaroos begin reproducing at an average age of twenty-two months. Age structure data enable the percentage of females which begin reporduction at each age between sixteen and twenty-seven months to be known, and also the percentage of females breeding in each month of the year.

A female kangaroo comes into oestrus (lasts 1 day), then either conceives or continues in oestrous cycle — that is, it waits forty days then comes into oestrus again. If it conceives, gestation lasts an average thirty-seven days, and a young is born and remains in pouch for a period of nine to eleven months. The female evicts its young from the pouch and within the next four to twenty-five days, comes into oestrus. If the young dies while in the pouch, the female comes into oestrus again also between four and twenty-five days later. Under normal conditions a female gives birth to one young a year.

Delayed embryos occur rarely in eastern grey kangaroos, but when these do they occur in almost all females for that particular year. In this situation, after giving birth a female comes into oestrus 120 days later and conceives. After nine to eleven months, the young is evicted from the pouch and the female gives birth to the delayed embryo the same day. If the pouch-young dies, a delayed embryo is born 35 days later.

Figure 30 shows the daily breeding-state transitions possible for the adult females, where the first half of the word specifies the number of dependent juveniles the female has, according to the following

BARR: no juvenile
POUCH: one pouch-young
DEPEND: one young-at-foot
P&D: two juveniles, one pouch-young, one young-at-foot

The second half of the word represents the state of reproduction the female is currently in, according to the following

PREOEST: time until (and including) next oestrus if pouch-young has died (4–25 days)
NBR: not breeding due pouch-young
GEST: gestation (37 days)
WAIT: time until (and including) next oestrus if did not conceive at previous one, (40 days)

Example: DEPEND-GEST, a female who has a young-at-foot and is pregnant.

Under drought conditions females cease breeding, but within two months of the drought breaking approximately ninety-eight per cent of the breeding females are pregnant or with pouch-young.

Maturation
1. For the first time period only, inputs:
   maturity rates of
   pouch-young to young-at-foot
   young-at-foot to independent.
2. Calculates percentage of pouch-young and young-at-foot maturing.
3. Updates record of maturing dependent juveniles.

Pouch-young mature to young-at-foot between nine and eleven months old. Young-at-foot mature to independence between fifteen and seventeen months old.

Harvest
1. For the first time period only, inputs:
   social organization data
   harvest strategy.
2. Calculates social organization of the population.
3. Harvests the population according to the strategy selected.
4. Updates records of adults and independents shot.

The harvest strategy used must reflect the selectivity of professional shooters. At any level of exploitation several confounding factors affect this selectivity and hence must be accounted for by the harvest strategy. These factors are environmental conditions; social organization; and the economic state of the kangaroo industry.

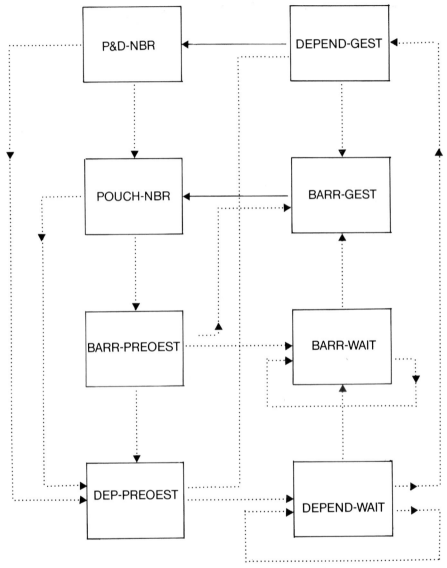

Figure 30 Model of the stages in the reproductive cycle of the female eastern grey kangaroo, excluding the feature of delayed embryos. (See text for explanation of terms.)

Environmental conditions. Two distinct effects – availability and abundance – result from short- and long-term environmental conditions, respectively. In the short term, the availability of kangaroos is affected by windy nights, poor visibility due to rain or vegetation, and an abundance of food. This results in fluctuations in the age structure of daily harvests, which are assumed neither to interfere with nor to conceal any overall trend that could be occurring. Long-term environmental conditions such as drought can seriously affect the population age structure. During a drought increased mortality, especially within the older population, together with a cessation of reproduction can create large gaps in the natural age structure. Subsequent harvests are affected for many years. Although quantitative information on changes in demographic rates during a drought is not available, the simulation model allows a wide range of possibilities to be explored.

Social organization. Eastern grey kangaroos are gregarious animals, usually found in mobs with numbers ranging from a few to some dozens. The selection strategy chosen by a professional shooter is based on his perception of kangaroo abundance; this is determined by the rate of encounter and composition of these social groups in addition to any prior knowledge of the area. A study in 1966 on social organization of the eastern grey kangaroo found that the family group of a female and her most recent young is the basic unit of organization. With the data presented on group composition, a method for arranging a population into social groups was formed. Before harvesting, the harvest submodule using this method organizes the population into groups and by utilizing various encounter rates and harvest methods (discussed later) determines the harvest strategy.

Currently, only one member per group can be harvested as the disturbance created by shooting a group member increases the difficulty for shooting another. If necessary, this restriction in the model can be removed later. Large mobs (population size greater than three) are almost certainly feeding groups and are loosely cohesive collections of smaller groups. They are treated as such by the simulation model, so the one-harvested-per-group rule applies to the smaller component groups.

These social groups can also affect the selectivity of shooters by influencing their perception of an animal's size. An example of this is when a doe and her young-at-foot are mistaken for a buck and doe, resulting in the smaller female being shot unintentionally. It is assumed in the model that this effect on selectivity by the social groups would have a negligible effect on the harvest structure over a period of time.

Economic state of the kangaroo industry.   Large fluctuations in the numbers of professional shooters operating and kangaroos harvested are a result of changes in meat and skin prices. Demand for these products is affected by factors such as increased sales tax on pet food and the opening or closing of export markets.

Lower prices force many professional shooters to cease operating; those who remain might need to become less selective and possibly increase the time spent harvesting in order to make an adequate return. The harvest submodule incorporates this economic factor into the method of harvesting and subsequent selection strategy.

For the purpose of determining an animal's desirability for harvest and the subsequent economic return to the shooter, each population member not only belongs to a particular type of social group, but also to one of six weight groups; in order of decreasing average weight, these are:

> adult male, aged three or older
> adult female, aged three or older
> adult male, aged two
> adult female, aged two
> subadult male, aged one
> subadult female, aged one

The average weight of each group was determined from a comparison of male and female weight-per-age graphs presented in 1964 (figure 27). Overlap between these weight groups does occur, but for simplification the model assumes the average group weight for each group member, and therefore the sequence of decreasing weight groups, corresponds to the decreasing desirability of the members for harvest. Average group weights are variable; different rates of weight loss in each weight group during droughts are possible; and a minimum allowable weight group for harvesting can be specified if desired.

There are three alternative methods of harvesting possible during the simulation. These are a set annual rate of return; a maximized economic return; and a sustained economic return. Each method is restricted by the encounter rate (number of social groups encountered per time period), total time spent harvesting, and the minimum allowable weight group (if applicable). These restrictions in conjunction with the method of harvesting chosen determines the selectivity index (SI) for each weight group. When a group encountered contains an animal belonging to a weight group with the SI set to one, this member will always be harvested.

Set annual rate of return: Annual rates of return are input for each year of the simulation. Starting with the heaviest weight group, the SI is set to one until the number of animals corresponding to the specified annual rate of harvest can be taken within the three restrictions. If this is not possible, the options available are to increase the time spent harvesting; to decrease the minimum allowable weight group; or to continue as is, accepting a smaller annual rate of harvest and economic return.

Maximized economic return: This method depends on the age and social structure of the population and is independent of the time spent harvesting. Selectivity indices are set to one, starting with the heaviest group until the situation is reached where setting the next group's SI to one produces a decrease in the expected return; thus economic return is maximized. However, if the maximum return drops below a specified minimum allowable return value which corresponds to a shooter's accepted living standard, the options available include the three from the set annual rate of return method as well as a fourth: lowering the minimum return value. This corresponds to the situation where a shooter attempts always to get the maximum possible return for time, as long as it exceeds the return that provides a reasonable standard of living.

Sustained economic return: Selectivity indices are set to one until the calculated expected return just exceeds a specified value of return. Economic return is not necessarily maximized over the time; this corresponds to a shooter desiring only to maintain a particular living standard.

Any combination of the three methods can be used during a simulation run to study the effect on subsequent harvests and population age structures.

   Without doubt, the greatest limitation of the model is the assumption of a constant environment. An index of the environmental conditions would enable the size of the adult group within the population to be adjusted according to current environmental conditions by allowing more or fewer subadults than required to compensate for adult death to enter the adult group. The difficulty in determining an index to account for all the environmental aspects that affect population levels and can be readily measured are obvious. Yet, without this environmental index, the simulation model cannot be used alone as a monitoring device.

When modelling a system (regardless of whether the system is bio-logical or mechanical), the success or failure of the model to achieve the desired objectives does not affect the usefulness of the exercise for demonstrating areas of the system where the information available is inadequate. There are three such areas for the eastern grey kangaroo population model:

1. Survival of young-at-foot. Adequate data are available to estimate survival for pouch-young up to thirteen months of age; no data on survival are available beyond this age. There is a notable difference in the simulation model results if the high mortality which precedes thirteen months of age is assumed to continue for the entire young-at-foot stage or, alternatively, if a levelling off of this mortality is assumed.

2. Pregnancy rate of females. Although breeding occurs throughout the year, there is a preferred season during the wetter months of summer during which the majority of females breed. This implies that a higher likelihood of pregnancy exists during these months when compared with the drier months. There is little information available to enable estimates of these different pregnancy rates to be made. Consequently over- or under-production of young is possible.

3. Effect of drought on demographic parameters. Changes to parameters such as survival, reproduction, weight loss, and maturation as a consequence of drought are not able to be quantitatively assessed using the available information.

The uncertainty of the estimates of these parameters particulary those affected by 1 and 2, above, have resulted in the simulated population age structures as outputted by the model differing from those obtained through the data on unselectively shot population samples. The main difference is in production of weaned young or juveniles. Estimates of these parameters are being varied until a combination is found which recognizes the simulated age structures resembling as closely as possible those obtained from data.

Catch-effort analysis

A complete monitoring programme for the harvested eastern grey kangaroo population will require an alternative method to be used in association with the simulation model. One such possibility is through catch–effort analysis.

Catch-effort is a definitive zoological term, particularly applied to fisheries, in which the size of a heavily exploited animal population is estimated from catch data and related harvest effort information. This method has been refined through studies of fish and small mammals since 1914, and is particularly appropriate for estimating the sizes of commercially exploited populations where these sizes are too large to make mark-recapture feasible and where habitat types make direct counting methods economically impracticable. In the past, catch-effort analysis has concentrated on the change in total catch numbers for a unit of effort; with kangaroo harvests, it is more appropriate to contemplate and analyse change in economic value rather than actual quantity of harvest. (The relative economic values of different sex and age groups within the population depend on their relative weights.)

The catch-effort analysis would require detailed data on the catch:

- number per night per shooter
- sex and age distribution
- corresponding weights

and the effort −

- number of shooters per night
- time spent shooting per night
- equipment including vehicles used.

These data are readily obtainable from chillers' record books. However, these apply to "meat" shooters only, because they are required to place their carcasses in chillers within a prescribed time. Obtaining similar data on professional "skin" shooters is more difficult because these are not restricted (as are the meat shooters) to work within range of the chiller boxes. Data on a sample of these skin shooters can be obtained with the cooperation of those having access to nearby chillers, and then extrapolated to estimate the total effect of skin shooters.

W.D. Dupont in 1976 developed a stochastic catch-effort analysis which enables estimates of population sizes with asymptotic error bounds and predictions of subsequent catches to be made for current levels of effort. Using these estimates of population size and subsequent catch, the ability of the population to maintain a stable level of adults and age structure can be measured, in terms of the abundance of the subadult resource, by the simulation model.

A monitoring programme for the harvested eastern grey kangaroos would need to provide continual measurement of the population so that changes in population levels and stability could be detected quickly; if necessary, harvests could then be adjusted accordingly. The addition of catch–effort analysis to the current simulation studies will provide just such a monitoring programme.

This book, and the long-term record it seeks to present dispassionately, has travelled full circle. It began with an apology for the absence of such a record for the continent's most characteristic and most exploited native animal. It concludes with the admission that there is still much to be learnt about the commonest of these species if the awesome task of conserving them is to be taken seriously.

The role of wildlife managers is not an easy one in any circumstance; the more is it so when the social responsibility is so great. They must act in the full light of public scrutiny without adequate knowledge of the facts (see figure 31). Moreover, in Queensland at least, they must act over an immense area of relatively inaccessible countryside without any prospect of funds sufficient to meet the demands of the tasks.

The book has covered an extended path. Its beginning sits in a fossil record of gigantic species long since extinct, and in a later Aboriginal history of exploitation no less impressive. Its course lies through a range of extant species so diverse and so widespread in their habits that few Europeans still have grasped the magnitude of the conservation problems these might pose: few people yet can recognize all of the species involved, let alone the subtle changes taking place to their habitats.

The modern Australian history – written over only two centuries – concerns largely a westernized society with traditions and customs ill-suited to a land so different as to be populated by kangaroos. These, far better adapted than domestic forms, readily withstand the extremes of a natural environment that regularly tests all the ingenuity of man for his own survival.

The harsh and mostly unproductive landscape has created a pioneering, exploitative attitude that still prevails across its largest face – an attitude that has absorbed the killing of some terrestrial native animals on a monumental scale. Yet there has emerged concurrently some order in this activity, to provide a measure of harvest and the first tool in the hands of the wildlife manager. This person, often less familiar with kangaroos than the professional shooter, can at best hope merely to modify disturbance by slow and methodical means.

Australian Rock Wallaby Survey

QUESTIONNAIRE

Please tick where appropriate)

1. Have you sighted rock wallabies on your property:

   (a) regularly? (i.e. at least every month) ☐

   (b) once or twice a year ☐

   (c) occasionally over the last five years ☐

   (d) not for at least five years ☐

   (e) never, but know them to occur
       in the district ☐

       If so, where and when...........................
       ....

   (f) never heard of them in the district ☐

2. If you have rock wallabies on your property, on what kind of country do you see them?
   ....

3. Would the area be accessible by vehicle?
   ....

4. What would your estimate of their numbers be?
   ....

5. Have numbers fluctuated in recent years?
   ....

6. Are they more common at certain times of the year?
   ....

7. Would you allow a biologist to visit your property to examine the colony?
   ....

8. What other kangaroos and wallabies do you see on your property?
   ....
   ....

9. Rock wallaby locations known to you:
   ....
   ....
   ....
   ....
   ....
   ....
   ....
   ....
   ....
   ....

10. Any additional comments:
    ....
    ....
    ....
    ....
    ....
    ....
    ....
    ....
    ....
    ....

Name: _____

Address: _____

_____

Phone Number: _____

Please detach and return this questionnaire as quickly as you can to:

**Professor Geoff Sharman,
School of Biological Sciences,
Macquarie University,
North Ryde NSW 2113.**

Thank you for your co-operation.

Figure 31 Questionnaire from the Australian Rock-Wallaby Survey commenced in 1983 by the School of Biological Sciences, Macquarie University in association with the Queensland National Parks and Wildlife Service.

The rural community outlook still prevailing is that the kangaroo is a threat to productive use of the countryside. Until very recent times, this view was to label the kangaroo family as vermin; it must not be underestimated how strong the force of opinion still is in this direction. Continuing development of agricultural lands in coastal areas, with more and more demand for cost efficiency, keeps the pest status of the family in view of the largest rural population.

Yet here, too, lies the wildlife manager's opportunity to influence the course of conservation. For in these coastal lands occur the most fascinating species of the Macropodidae – the unusual, the scarce, the picturesque, the unexpected and the intriguing – safe from the farmers' or the shooters' direct attentions. They serve as the source of inspiration from which a greater orderliness of land use must surely prevail.

It is not the place of the wildlife manager to moralize about shooting native fauna. It is a fact that harvesting creates and justifies those opportunities for management that would not otherwise exist. And so long as shooting does not exceed the limits for survival of those few species involved, the opportunity must be taken to draw on the interest in the family Macropodidae as a whole to ensure that a sound course of conservation action for all time is implemented.

Post Script

Since the manuscript "The Kangaroo Keepers" went to press, the population model for the eastern grey kangaroo (see chapter 7) has been constructed, which allows the effects of various levels of simulated harvesting on the key parameters of sex and age ratios to be determined. As well, areas of inadequacy in existing knowledge have been identified: in particular, these cover population sampling methods and the effects of droughts on survival rates.

The computer simulation study has now shown that the harvest sex ratio (that is, the percentage of females in the harvest) taken by a professional shooter actively selecting for the largest available animals *is* a reliable index of the state of under- or over-harvest. Measured in conjunction with properly defined environmental conditions, harvest sex ratios obtained over a series of years can in fact indicate (i) the extent of net population losses (which may result from reduced reproduction, natural deaths and harvests), and (ii) when the population has reached a signal point. This latter is when the harvest is 50 per cent female, and the population is reduced to about one-half its original size. Other indicators of a population approaching the signal point are (i) when the harvest by a shooter selecting for the largest animals comprises only 1 per cent – 2 per cent males aged 10 or more years, (ii) when the harvests consist of approximately equal proportions of males aged 1-3 years and 4-9 years; and (iii) when professional shooters are operating at the maximum practicable level of effort.

From this signal point, the population enters a critical phase when rate of population decline accelerates significantly to extermination. The decline can be reversed if appropriate action is then taken to reduce harvesting. If corrective action is not taken, the period to extinction can be predicted from the model.

Results have been shown to be independent of possible errors in estimation of the basic demographic parameters (survival rates, reproduction and maturation rates) and of certain assumptions made in the model regarding the operation of professional shooters.

While some field work remains to be done to test these hypotheses, they do provide a valuable basis for interim monitoring and managing eastern grey kangaroo populations using information readily available from the kangaroo industry. The extension of the model to other harvested species is expected to be a simple matter of substituting the relevant biological data.

Bibliography

Abbreviations used in Bibliography

Amer. J. Physiol.	*American Journal of Physiology*
Ann. Rev. Ecology and System.	*Annual Review of Ecology and Systematics*
Animal Behav.	*Animal Behaviour*
Archaeol. & Phys. Anthrop. in Oceania	*Archaeology and Physical Anthropology in Oceania*
Aust. J. Ecol.	*Australian Journal of Ecology*
Aust. J. Sci.	*Australian Journal of Science*
Aust. J. Zool.	*Australian Journal of Zoology*
Aust. Mammal.	*Australian Mammalogy*
Aust. Mammal Soc. Bull.	*Australian Mammal Society Bulletin*
Aust. Wildl. Res.	*Australian Wildlife Research*
Aust. Zool.	*Australian Zoologist*
Biol. Conserv.	*Biological Conservation*
Bull. Amer. Mus. Nat.	*Bulletin of the American Museum of Natural History*
Bull. Zool. Nomencl.	*Bulletin of Zoological Nomenclature*
Cane Growers' Quart. Bull.	*Cane Growers' Quarterly Bulletin*
CSIRO Div. Wildl. Res. Tech. Pap.	*CSIRO Division of Wildlife Research Technical Paper*
CSIRO Wildl. Res.	*CSIRO Wildlife Research*
Dental Mag. and Oral Topics	*Dental Magazine and Oral Topics*
Environ. Management	*Environmental Management*
Int. J. Parasit.	*International Journal for Parasitology*
Int. Zoo Yb	*International Zoo Yearbook*
J. Appl. Ecol.	*Journal of Applied Ecology*
J. Appl. Physiol.	*Journal of Applied Physiology*
J. Aust. Anim. Tech. Assn	*Journal of the Australian Animal Technicians' Association*
J. R. Soc. W. Aust.	*Journal of the Royal Society of Western Australia*

J. Zool. Lond.	*Journal of Zoology (London)*
Mammal.	*Journal of Mammalogy*
Mammal Rev.	*Mammal Review*
Mem. Qd Mus.	*Memoirs of the Queensland Museum*
N. Qd Nat.	*North Queensland Naturalist*
Proc. Ann. Sympos. of CQ sub-branch of Aust. Inst. Agric. Sci.	*Proceedings of the Annual Symposium of the Central Queensland sub-branch of the Australian Institute of Agricultural Science*
Proc. Ecol. Soc. Aust.	*Proceedings of the Ecological Society of Australia*
Proc. Grassl. Soc. S. Afr.	*Proceedings of the Grassland Society of South Africa*
Proc. Linn. Soc. NSW	*Proceedings of the Linnaean Society of New South Wales*
Proc. NZ Geog. Conf.	*Proceedings of the New Zealand Geographical Conference*
Proc. R. Soc. Qd	*Proceedings of the Royal Society of Queensland*
Proc. Zool. Soc. Lond.	*Proceedings of the Zoological Society of London*
Qd Agric. J.	*Queensland Agricultural Journal*
Qd J. Agric. Sci.	*Queensland Journal of Agricultural Science*
Qd J. Agric. Anim. Sci.	*Queensland Journal of Agricultural and Animal Sciences*
Sauegetierkd Mitt.	*Sauegetierkundliche Mitteilungen*
Sci. Amer.	*Scientific American*
Trans. N. Amer. and Nat. Resources Conf.	*Transactions of the North American Wildlife and Natural Resources Conference*
Trans. Philos. Soc. NSW	*Transactions of the Philosophical Society of New South Wales*
Trans. R. Soc. S. Aust.	*Transactions of the Royal Society of South Australia*
Trans. & Proc. & Rep. Phil. Soc. Adelaide	*Transactions and Proceedings and Reports of the Adelaide Philosophical Society*
Trop. Grassl.	*Tropical Grasslands*
Vet. Microbiol.	*Veterinary Microbiology*
Vict. Nat.	*Victorian Naturalist*
Wildl. in Aust.	*Wildlife in Australia*
Zool. Anz.	*Zoologischer Anzeiger*
Zool. Jahrb.	*Zoologische Jahrbuecher Abteilung fuer Allgemeine Zoologie und Physiologie der Tiere*

Abott, I. 1980. Aboriginal man as an exterminator of wallaby and kangaroo populations on islands around Australia. *Oecologia* 44; 347-54.

Amos, P.J. 1982. The potoroo in Queensland. *Qd Agric. J.* 108: 5-6.

_____. in press. Reproduction in the potoroo (*Potorous tridactylus tridactylus* Kerr), in captivity, with age estimation of pouch young and molar eruption and progression. *Qd J. Agric. Anim. Sci.*

Anderson, D.R. 1980. Information on management programs for red, eastern grey, and western grey kangaroos in relation to the US Endangered Species Act. Unpub. report, Utah State University, Logan.

Archer, M. 1981. Review of the origins and radiations of Australian mammals. In *Biogeography and ecology in Australia,* ed. A. Keast, 1435-88. The Hague: W. Junk.

Archer, M., and A. Bartholomai. 1978. Tertiary mammals of Australia: A synoptic review. *Alcheringa* 2: 1-19.

Archer, M., and S. Quirk, eds. 1983. *Prehistoric animals of Australia.* Sydney: Aust. Museum.

Australia, Parliament, House of Representatives Select Committee on Wildlife Conservation. 1971. *Conservation and Commercial Exploitation of Kangaroos.* Canberra: AGPS.

Australian Information Service. 1974. *Kangaroos.* Canberra: AGPS.

Barker, I.K., K.E. Harrigan, and J.K. Dempster. 1972. Coccidiosis in wild grey kangaroos. *Int. J. Parasit.* 2: 187-92.

Barker, S.C. 1982. Ecology, behaviour and social organization of the plain rock-wallaby, *Petrogale inornata assimilis* (Macropodinae). Unpub. B.Sc. (Hons) thesis, James Cook University of North Queensland, Townsville.

Bartholomai, A. 1972. Aspects of the evolution of the Australian marsupials. Presidential address. *Proc. R. Soc. Qd* 82: v-xviii.

_____. 1975. The genus *Macropus* Shaw (Marsupialia: Macropodidae) in the Upper Cainozoic deposits of Queensland. *Mem. Qd Mus.* 17: 195-235.

_____. 1978. The fossil kangaroos. *Aust. Mammal.* 2: 15-22.

Bayliss, P. 1980. Kangaroos, plants and weather in the semi-arid. Unpub. M.Sc. thesis, University of Sydney, Sydney.

Beaglehole, J.C., ed. 1962. *The Endeavour journal of Sir Joseph Banks 1768–1771.* 2 vols. Sydney: Trustees, Public Library and Angus & Robertson.

Bell, H.M. 1973. The ecology of three macropod marsupial species in an area of open forest and savannah woodland in north Queensland, Australia. *Mammalia* 37: 527-44.

Bell, R.H.V. 1971. A grazing ecosystem in the Serengeti. *Sci. Amer.* 225: 86-93

Beveridge, I. 1982. A taxonomic revision of the Pharyngostrongylinae (Nematoda: Strongyloidea) from macropod marsupials. *Aust. J. Zool. Supp. Ser.* no. 83: 1-150.

Beveridge, I., and J.H. Arundel. 1979. Helminth parasites of grey kangaroos, *Macropus giganteus* Shaw and *Macropus fuliginosus* (Desmarest) in eastern Australia. *Aust. Wildl. Res.* 6: 69-77.

Bolton, B. L., A. E. Newsome, and J. C. Merchant. 1982. Reproduction in the agile wallaby *Macropus agilis* (Gould) in the tropical lowlands of the Northern Territory: Opportunism in a seasonal environment. *Aust. J. Ecol.* 7: 261-77.

Breeden, S., and K. Breeden. 1966. *The life of the kangaroo.* Sydney: Angus & Robertson.

_____, and _____. 1970. *Tropical Queensland.* In *Natural history of Australia series.* Sydney: William Collins.

Briscoe, D. A., J. H. Calaby, R. L. Close, G. M. Maynes, C. E. Murtagh, and G. B. Sharman. 1982. Isolation, introgression and genetic variation in rock-wallabies. In *Species at risk: Research in Australia,* ed. R. H. Groves and W. D. L. Ride, 73-87. Canberra: Aust. Academy of Science.

Burbidge, A. A., ed. 1977. *The status of kangaroos and wallabies in Australia. Report on the working group on macropod habitat of the standing committee of the Council of Nature Conservation Ministers.* Canberra: AGPS.

Calaby, J. H. 1966. Mammals of the Upper Richmond and Clarence Rivers, New South Wales. *CSIRO Div. Wildl. Res. Tech. Pap.* 10: 1-55.

_____. 1968. Observations on the teeth of marsupials, especially kangaroos. *Dental Mag. & Oral Topics* 85: 23, 26-27.

_____. 1971. Man, fauna and climate in Aboriginal Australia. In *Aboriginal man and environment in Australia,* ed. D. J. Mulvaney and J. Golson, 80-93. Canberra: Australian National University Press.

_____. 1971. The current status of Australian Macropodidae. *Aust. Zool.* 16: 17-31.

Calaby, J. H., and W. E. Poole. 1971. Keeping kangaroos in captivity. *Int. Zoo Yb* 11: 5-12.

Caughley, G. 1964. Density and dispersion of two species of kangaroos in relation to habitat. *Aust. J. Zool.* 12: 238-49.

_____. 1964. Social organization and daily activity of the red kangaroo and the grey kangaroo. *Mammal.* 45: 429-36.

_____. 1977. *Analysis of vertebrate populations.* London: Wiley.

Caughley, G., and G. C. Grigg. 1982. Numbers and distribution of kangaroos in the Queensland pastoral zone. *Aust. Wildl. Res.* 9: 365-71.

Caughley, G., G. C. Grigg, J. Caughley, and G. J. E. Hill. 1980. Does dingo predation control the densities of kangaroos and emus? *Aust. Wildl. Res.* 7: 1-12.

Chapman, D. G., and D. S. Robson. 1960. The analysis of a catch curve. *Biometrics* 16: 354-68.

Chapman, L. S. 1960. Wallaby deterrents. *Cane Growers' Quart. Bull.* 24: 47-48.

Clay, T. 1981. A report on a collection of lice (Boopidae: Phthiraptera) on *Petrogale* rock wallabies. *Proc. Linn. Soc. NSW* 105: 65-78.

Close, R. 1983. Rock wallabies. Unpub. report to 38th Annual Conference of International Union of Directors of Zoological Gardens, Melbourne Zoo, Melbourne.

Collett, R. 1887. On a collection of mammals from central and northern Queensland. *Zool. Jahrb.* 2: 829-940.

Conway, W.G. 1979. Where we go from here. *Int. Zoo Yb* 20: 184-89.

Cooke, B.N. 1979. Field observations of the behaviour of the macropod marsupial *Thylogale stigmatica* (Gould). Unpub. M.Sc. thesis, University of Queensland, St Lucia.

Corbet, G.B., and J.E. Hill. 1980. *A world list of mammalian species.* London: British Museum of Natural History.

Coulson, G.J. 1977. Social behaviour of eastern grey kangaroos, *Macropus giganteus,* and western grey kangaroos, *Macropus fuliginosus. Aust. Mammal Soc. Bull.* 3: 10.

Croft, D.B. 1981. Behaviour of red kangaroos, *Macropus rufus* (Desmarest, 1822) in northwestern New South Wales, Australia. *Aust. Mammal.* 4: 5-58.

_____. 1981. Social behaviour of the euro, *Macropus robustus,* in the Australian arid zone. *Aust. Wildl. Res.* 8: 13-50.

_____. 1982. Some observations on the behaviour of the antilopine wallaroo *Macropus antilopinus* (Marsupialia: Macropodidae). *Aust. Mammal.* 5: 5-13.

Crossman, D.G., and D.S. Reimer. In press. Mammals, birds, reptiles and amphibians of the Taroom Shire, central Queensland. *Qd. J. Agric. Anim. Sci.*

Dawson, T.J. 1972. Thermoregulation in Australian desert kangaroos. In *Comparative physiology of desert animals,* ed. G.M.O. Malory, 133-46. London: Zoological Society of London.

Dawson, T.J., and M.J.S. Denny. 1969. A bioclimatological comparison of the summer day microenvironments of two species of arid zone kangaroos. *Ecology* 50: 328-32.

_____, and _____. 1969. Seasonal variation in the plasma and urine electrolyte concentration of the arid zone kangaroos *Megaleia rufa* and *Macropus robustus. Aust. J. Zool.* 17: 777-84.

Dawson, T.J., M.J.S. Denny, E.M. Russell, and B.A. Ellis. 1975. Water usage and diet preference of free ranging kangaroos, sheep and feral goats in the Australian arid zone during summer. *J. Zool. Lond.* 177: 1-23.

Dawson, T.J., and B.A. Ellis. 1979. Comparison of the diets of yellow-footed rock-wallabies and sympatric herbivores in western New South Wales. Aust. Wildl. Res. 6: 245-54.

De Blase, A.F., and R.E. Martin. 1974. *A manual of mammalogy with keys to the families of the world.* Iowa: W.C. Brown Co.

Denny, M.J.S. 1973. Water relations in arid zone macropodids. Unpub. Ph.D. thesis, University of New South Wales, Sydney.

_____. 1975. The effects of dehydration on the body water distribution of kangaroos. *Aust. Mammal.* 1: 409-10.

———. 1979. Ground versus aerial counts. In *Aerial surveys of fauna populations*. Special publication 1, Australian National Parks and Wildlife Service, 25-37. Canberra: AGPS.

———. 1981. Kangaroos: A historical perspective. In *Kangaroos and other macropods of New South Wales*, ed. C. Haigh, 36-45. Sydney: New South Wales National Parks and Wildlife Service.

———. 1981. Management programs for macropods. In *Wildlife management in the 80's*, ed. T. Riney, 264-72. Proceedings of Conference of the Field and Game Federation of Australia and the Graduate School of Environmental Science, Monash University, Melbourne.

———. 1982. Adaptations of the red kangaroo and euro (Macropodidae) to aridity. In *Evolution of the flora and fauna of arid Australia*, ed. W.R. Barker and P.M.J. Greenslade, 179-83. Adelaide: Peacock Publications.

———. 1983. Animals: Native and feral. In *What future for Australia's arid lands?* ed. J. Messer and G. Mosley, 19-25. Melbourne: Australian Conservation Foundation.

Denny, M.J.S., and T.J. Dawson. 1972. Water metabolism of kangaroos. *Aust. Mammal.* 1: 66-67.

———, and ———. 1975. Comparative metabolism of tritiated water by macropodid marsupials. *Amer. J. Physiol.* 228: 1794-99.

———, and ———. 1975. Effects of dehydration on body water distribution in desert kangaroos. *Amer. J. Physiol.* 229: 251-54.

———, and ———. 1977. Kidney structure and function of desert kangaroos. *J. Appl. Physiol.* 42: 636-42.

Devanny, J. 1951. *Travels in North Queensland.* London: Jarrolds.

Dudzinski, M.L., W.A. Low, W.J. Muller, and B.S. Low. 1982. Joint use of habitat by red kangaroos and shorthorn cattle in arid central Australia. *Aust. J. Ecol.* 7: 69-74.

Du Pont, W.D. 1976. A stochastic method for estimating animal abundance from catch–effort data. Unpub. Ph.D. thesis, Johns Hopkins University, Baltimore.

Dwyer, P.D. 1972. Social organization of a population of rock wallabies, *Petrogale inornata. Aust. Mammal.* 1: 72.

Dwyer, P.D., M. Hockings, and J. Willmer. 1979. Mammals of Cooloola and Beerwah. *Proc. R. Soc. Qd* 90: 65-84.

Ealey, E.H.M. 1967. Ecology of the euro, *Macropus robustus* (Gould), in north-western Australia. 1. The environment and changes in euro and sheep populations. *CSIRO Wildl. Res.* 12: 9-25.

———. 1967. Ecology of the euro, *Macropus robustus* (Gould), in north-western Australia. 2. Behaviour, movements and drinking patterns. *CSIRO Wildl. Res.* 12: 27-51.

———. 1967. Ecology of the euro, *Macropus robustus* (Gould), in north-western Australia. 4. Age and growth. *CSIRO Wildl. Res.* 12: 67-80.

Ealey, E.H.M., and A.R. Main. 1967. Ecology of the euro, *Macropus robus-*

tus (Gould), in north-western Australia. 3. Seasonal changes in nutrition. *CSIRO Wildl. Res.* 12: 53-65.

Edwards, G.P., and E.H.M. Ealey. 1975. Aspects of the ecology of the swamp wallaby *Wallabia bicolor* Marsupialia Macropodidae. *Aust. Mammal.* 1: 307-17.

Ellis, B.A., E.M. Russell, T.J. Dawson, and C.J.F. Harrop. 1977. Seasonal changes in diet preferences of free-ranging red Kangaroos, euros and sheep in western New South Wales, Australia. *Aust. Wildl. Res.* 4: 127-44.

Finlayson, H.H. 1931. On mammals of the Dawson Valley, Queensland. Part one. *Trans. R. Soc. S. Aust.* 55: 67-89.

_____. 1932. *Caloprymnus campestris*: Its recurrence and characters. *Trans. R. Soc. S. Aust.* 56: 146-67.

_____. 1935. *The Red Centre.* Sydney: Angus & Robertson.

Floyd, R.B. 1980. Density of *Wallabia bicolor* (Desmarest) (Marsupialia: Macropodidae) in eucalypt plantations of different ages. *Aust. Wild. Res.* 7: 333-37.

Frith, H.J. 1964. Mobility of the red kangaroo. *CSIRO Wildl. Res.* 9: 1-19.

_____. 1973. *Wildlife conservation.* Sydney: Angus & Robertson.

Frith, H.J., and J.H. Calaby. 1969. *Kangaroos.* Sydney: F.W. Cheshire.

Ganslosser, U. 1980. An annotated bibliography of social behaviour in kangaroos (Macropodidae). *Sauegetierkd Mitt.* 28: 138-48.

_____. 1982. Social structure and communication in marsupials. *Zool. Anz.* 209: 294-310.

George, G.G. 1982. Tree kangaroos *Dendrolagus* spp.: Their management in captivity. In *The management of Australian mammals in captivity* ed. D.D. Evans, 102-7. Healesville: Australian Mammal Society.

Gilbert, J. 1844–45. Diary of the journey of exploration of Ludwig Leichhardt and party from Jimbour to Port Essington (1844–45). 2 vols. Unpub. report, Mitchell Library, Sydney.

Gill, E.D. 1955. The problem of extinction with special reference to Australian marsupials. *Evolution* 9: 87-92.

Goodwin, H.A., and C.W. Holloway, eds. 1978. *Red Data Book.* Vol. 1 *Mammalia.* Morges: IUCN.

Gordon, G., and B.C. Lawrie. 1980. The rediscovery of the bridled nail-tailed wallaby (*Onychogalea fraenata* [Gould]) (Marsupialia: Macropodidae) in Queensland. *Aust Wildl. Res.* 7: 339-45.

Gordon, G., D.G. McGreevy, and B.C. Lawrie. 1978. The yellow-footed rock-wallaby *Petrogale xanthopus* Gray (Macropodidae) in Queensland. *Aust. Wildl. Res.* 5: 295-97.

Gould, J. 1973. *Kangaroos: With modern commentaries by Joan M. Dixon.* South Melbourne: Macmillan.

Grady, L., and N. Duplaix. 1980. The harvest of northeastern furbearers, past and present. Unpub. report, Traffic (USA) [newsletter].

Greenaway, S. 1954. Some notes on the wallaby pest. Report of minutes and proceedings of Cane Pest and Disease Control Boards' Conference, Mackay, 29 April 1954, p. 25. Brisbane: Bureau of Sugar Experiment Stations.

Griffiths, M., and R. Barker. 1966. The plants eaten by sheep and by kangaroos grazing together in a paddock in south-western Queensland. *CSIRO Wildl. Res.* 11: 145-67.

Griffiths, M., R. Barker, and L. Maclean. 1974. Further observations on the plants eaten by kangaroos and sheep grazing together in a paddock in south-western Queensland. *Aust. Wild. Res.* 1: 27-43.

Hediger, H. 1950. *Wild animals in captivity.* London: Butterworths.

Hill, G.J.E. 1978. Preliminary assessment of defecation patterns for the eastern grey kangaroo (*Macropus giganteus*). *Aust. Zool.* 19: 291-99.

_____. 1979. Application of LANDSAT to habitat analysis for the grey kangaroo. *Proc. NZ Geog. Conf. (49th ANZAAS)* 10: 293-96.

_____. 1981. A study of grey kangaroo density using pellet counts. *Aust. Wildl. Res.* 8: 237-43.

_____. 1981. A study of habitat preferences of the grey kangaroo. *Aust. Wildl. Res.* 8: 245-54.

_____. 1981. Grey kangaroo survey in southern inland Queensland. *Qd Agric. J.* 107: 330-31.

_____. 1982. Seasonal movement patterns of the eastern grey kangaroo in southern Queensland. *Aust. Wildl. Res.* 9: 373-87.

Hopwood, P.R., M. Hilmi, and R.M. Butterfield. 1976. A comparative study of the carcass composition of kangaroos and sheep. *Aust. J. Zool.* 24: 1-6.

Horne, R.R. 1975. Wallaby browsing in eucalypt plantations. In *Agriculture, forestry and wildlife: Conflict or co-existence?* ed. P.J. Jarman, 80-100. Armidale: University of New England.

Horton, D.R. 1981. Faunal remains from the Early Man Shelter. In *Early Man in North Queensland: Art and archaeology in the Laura area. Terra Australis 6.*, ed. A. Rosenfeld, D. Horton, and J. Winter, 35-44. Canberra: Australian National University Press.

Inglis, J. 1880. *Our Australian cousins.* London: Macmillan.

Iredale, T., and E.LeG. Troughton. 1934. *A check list of the mammals recorded from Australia.* Sydney: Australian Museum.

Jarman, P.J., and M.J.S. Denny. 1975. Red kangaroos and land use along the New South Wales, Queensland and South Australian borders. In *Agriculture, forestry and wildlife: Conflict or co-existence?* ed. P.J. Jarman, 55-67. Armidale: University of New England.

Jarman, P.J., and K.A. Johnson. 1977. Exotic mammals, indigenous mammals and land use. *Proc. Ecol. Soc. Aust.* 10: 146-66.

Jewell, P.A., and S. Holt, eds. 1981. *Problems in management of locally abundant wild mammals.* New York: Academic Press.

Johnson, C.N. 1983. Variations in group size and composition in red and western grey kangaroos, *Macropus rufus* and *Macropus fuliginosus.* *Aust. Wildl. Res.* 10: 25-32.

Johnson, C.N., and P.G. Bayliss. 1981. Habitat selection by sex, age and reproductive class in the red kangaroo, *Macropus rufus,* in western New South Wales, Australia. *Aust. Wildl. Res.* 8: 465-74.

Johnson, K.A. 1975. Aspects of macropod problems on the Dorrigo Plateau. In *Agriculture, forestry and wildlife: Conflict or co-existence?* ed. P.J. Jarman, 39-45. Armidale: University of New England.

_____. 1977. Ecology and management of the red-necked pademelon, *Thylogale thetis,* on the Dorrigo Plateau of northern New South Wales. Unpub. Ph.D. thesis, University of New England, Armidale.

_____. 1980. Spatial and temporal use of habitat by the red-necked pademelon, *Thylogale thetis* (Marsupialia: Macropodidae). *Aust. Wildl. Res.* 7: 157-66.

Johnson, K.A., and P.J. Jarman. 1975. Records of wildlife as pests in the Armidale district, 1812–1975. In *Agriculture, forestry and wildlife: Conflict or co-existence?* ed. P.J. Jarman, 26-32. Armidale: University of New England.

Johnson, P.M. 1978. Husbandry of the rufous rat-kangaroo *Aepyprymnus rufescens* and brush-tailed rock wallaby *Petrogale penicillata* in captivity. *Int. Zoo Yb* 18: 156-57.

_____. 1978. Studies of Macropodidae in Queensland. 9. Reproduction of the rufous rat-kangaroo (*Aepyprymnus rufescens* [Gray]) in captivity with age estimation of pouch young. *Qd. J. Agric. Anim. Sci.* 35: 69-72.

_____. 1978. The brush-tailed rock wallaby in Queensland. *Qd. Agric. J.* 104: 397-99.

_____. 1979. Reproduction in the plain rock-wallaby, *Petrogale penicillata inornata* Gould, in captivity, with age estimation of the pouch-young. *Aust. Wildl. Res.* 6: 1-4.

_____. 1980. Field observations on group compositions in the agile wallaby *Macropus agilis* (Gould) (Marsupialia: Macropodidae). *Aust. Wildl. Res.* 7: 327-31.

_____. 1980. Observations of the behaviour of the rufous rat-kangaroo, *Aepyprymnus rufescens* (Gray), in captivity. *Aust. Wildl. Res.* 7: 347-57.

_____. 1981. The rearing of marsupial pouch young by foster mothers of different species. *Int. Zoo Yb* 21: 173-76.

Johnson, P.M., and T.R. Aaskov. 1980. A record of an albino rufous rat kangaroo (*Aepyprymnus rufescens*). *N. Qd Nat.* 45: 2.

Johnson, P.M., and I.R. Bradshaw. 1977. Rufous rat-kangaroo in Queensland. *Qd Agric. J.* 103: 181-83.

Johnson, P.M., and A.T. Haffenden. 1980. Husbandry of the spectacled hare-wallaby *Lagorchestes conspicillatus* in captivity. *Int. Zoo Yb* 20: 253-54.

Johnson, P.M., A.T. Haffenden, and J. Denison. 1983. Husbandry of the musky rat-kangaroo in captivity. *J. Aust. Anim. Tech. Assn.* 8: 1-8.

Johnson, P.M., and R. Strahan. 1982. A further description of the musky rat kangaroo *Hypsiprymnodon moschatus* Ramsay, 1876 (Marsupialia, Potoridae), with notes on its biology. *Aust. Zool.* 21: 27-46.

Johnson, R.W. 1964. *Ecology and control of brigalow in Queensland.* Brisbane: Queensland Department of Primary Industries.

Johnson, R.W., and G. Gordon. 1981. The impact of development on flora and fauna. *Proc. Ann. Sympos. of CQ sub-branch of Aust. Inst. Agric. Sci.* 2: 7 pp.

Jones, R. 1968. The geographical background to the arrival of man in Australia and Tasmania. *Archaeol. & Phys. Anthrop. in Oceania* 3: 186-215.

Kaufmann, J.H. 1974. Habitat use and social organization of nine sympatric species of macropodid marsupials. *Mammal.* 55: 66-80.

_____. 1974. Social ethology of the whiptail wallaby, *Macropus parryi,* in northeastern New South Wales. *Anim. Behav.* 22: 281-369.

_____. 1975. Field observations of the social behaviour of the eastern grey kangaroo, *Macropus giganteus. Anim. Behav.* 23: 214-21.

King, D.R., A.J. Oliver, and R.J. Mead. 1981. *Bettongia* and fluoroacetate: A role for 1080 in fauna management. *Aust. Wildl. Res.* 8: 529-36.

Kirkpatrick, T.H. 1963. A note on the dental eruption of some Macropodinae, with particular reference to Captain Cook's kangaroo. *Qd J. Agric. Sci.* 20: 539-41.

_____. 1964. Molar progression and macropod age. *Qd J. Agric. Sci.* 21: 163-65.

_____. 1964. Rock wallabies around Warwick. *Wildlife* 1: 32-33.

_____. 1964. Some aspects of the biology and ecology of the grey kangaroo (*Macropus major* Shaw). Unpub. M.Sc. thesis, University of Queensland, Brisbane.

_____. 1965. Studies of Macropodidae in Queensland. 1. Food preferences of the grey kangaroo (*Macropus major* Shaw). *Qd J. Agric. Anim. Sci.* 22: 89-93.

_____. 1965. Studies of Macropodidae in Queensland. 2. Age estimation in the grey kangaroo, the red kangaroo, the eastern wallaroo and the red-necked wallaby, with notes on dental abnormalities. *Qd J. Agric. Anim. Sci.* 22: 301-17.

_____. 1965. Studies of Macropodidae in Queensland. 3. Reproduction in the grey kangaroo (*Macropus major*) in southern Queensland. *Qd J. Agric. Anim. Sci.* 22: 319-28.

_____. 1966. Mammals, birds and reptiles of the Warwick district, Queensland. 1. Introduction and mammals. *Qd J. Agric. Anim. Sci.* 23: 591-98.

_____. 1966. Studies of Macropodidae in Queensland. 4. Social organization of the grey kangaroo (*Macropus giganteus*). *Qd J. Agric. Anim. Sci.* 23: 317-22.

_____. 1967. Studies of Macropodidae in Queensland. 6. Sex determination of adult skulls of the grey kangaroo and the red kangaroo. *Qd J. Agric. Anim. Sci.* 24: 131-33.

_____. 1967. The grey kangaroo in Queensland. *Qd Agric. J.* 93: 550-52.

_____. 1967. The red kangaroo in Queensland. *Qld Agric. J.* 93: 484-86.

_____. 1968. Mammals, birds and reptiles of the Warwick district, Queensland. 3. Reptiles and general conclusions. *Qd J. Agric. Anim. Sci.* 25: 235-41.

_____. 1968. Studies on the wallaroo. *Qd. Agric. J.* 94: 362-65.

_____. 1969. The dentition of the marsupial family Macropodidae with particular reference to tooth development in the grey kangaroo *Macropus giganteus* (Shaw). Unpub. Ph.D. thesis, University of Queensland, Brisbane.

_____. 1970. Studies of Macropodidae in Queensland. 8. Age estimation in the red kangaroo (*Megaleia rufa* [Desmarest]). *Qd J. Agric. Anim. Sci.* 27: 461-62.

_____. 1970. The agile wallaby in Queensland. *Qd Agric. J.* 96: 169-70.

_____. 1970. The swamp wallaby in Queensland. *Qd Agric. J.* 96: 335-36.

_____. 1974. Kangaroo harvesting and survival. *Qd Agric. J.* 100: 368-75.

_____. 1978. The development of the dentition of *Macropus giganteus* (Shaw). An attempt to interpret the marsupial dentition. *Aust. Mammal.* 2: 29-35.

Kirkpatrick, T.H., and P. Amos. 1977. Mammals and birds of the Millmerran Shire, south-east Queensland. *Qd J. Agric. Anim. Sci.* 34: 123-33.

Kirkpatrick, T.H., and P.M. Johnson. 1969. Studies of Macropodidae in Queensland. 7. Age estimation and reproduction in the agile wallaby (*Wallabia agilis* [Gould]). *Qd J. Agric. Anim. Sci.* 26: 691-98.

Kirkpatrick, T.H., and H.J. Lavery. 1979. Fauna surveys in Queensland. *Qd J. Agric. Anim. Sci.* 36: 181-88.

Kirkpatrick, T.H., and W.A. McDougall. 1971. The grey and the red kangaroo in Queensland. *Aust. Zool.* 16: 51-57.

Kirkpatrick, T.H., and J.S. McEvoy. 1966. Studies of Macropodidae in Queensland. 5. Effects of drought on reproduction in the grey kangaroo (*Macropus giganteus*). *Qd J. Agric. Anim. Sci.* 23: 439-42.

Kirkpatrick, T.H., and A.K. Searle. 1977. Mammals and birds of the Stanthorpe Shire, south-east Queensland. *Qd J. Agric. Anim. Sci.* 34: 109-21.

Kirkpatrick, T.H., and J.T. Woods. 1964. Comments on the proposed stabilization of *Macropus* Shaw, 1790. *Bull. Zool. Nomencl.* 21: 249-50.

Krefft, G. 1866. On the vertebrated animals of the lower Murray and Darling, their habits, economy and geographical distribution. *Trans. Philos. Soc. NSW* 1862–65, 1-33.

Lane, T. 1980. *The kangaroo in the decorative arts.* Melbourne: National Gallery of Victoria.

Lavery, H.J. 1982. Fauna. In *Queensland Year Book 1982*, 10-14. Brisbane: Australian Bureau of Statistics.

Lavery, H.J., ed. 1983. *Exploration north: A natural history of Queensland.* Melbourne: Currey O'Neil.

Lavery, H.J., and R.J. Grimes. 1974. Mammals and birds of the Ingham district, north Queensland. 1. Introduction and mammals. *Qd J. Agric. Anim. Sci.* 31: 383-90.

Lavery, H.J., and P.M. Johnson. 1968. Mammals and birds of the Townsville district, north Queensland. 1. Introduction and mammals. *Qd J. Agric. Anim. Sci.* 25: 29-37.

_____, and _____. 1974. Mammals and birds of the lower Burdekin River district, north Queensland. 1. Introduction and mammals. *Qd J. Agric. Anim. Sci.* 31: 97-104.

Leeper, G.W. 1970. *The Australian environment.* 4th ed. Melbourne: Melbourne University Press.

Le Souef, A.S. 1923. The Australian native animals: How they stand today and the cause of scarcity in certain species. *Aust. Zool.* 3: 108-11.

Livanes, T. 1975. The role of the kangaroo industry. In *Agriculture, forestry and wildlife: Conflict or co-existence?* ed. P.J. Jarman, 68-72. Armidale: University of New England.

Longman, H.A. 1922. South Queensland marsupials. *Mem. Qd Mus.* 7: 297-300.

_____. 1923. Is the kangaroo doomed? *Aust. Zool.* 3: 103-7.

_____. 1930. The marsupials of Queensland. *Mem. Qd Mus.* 10: 55-64.

Low, W.A., W.J. Muller, M.L. Dudzinski, and B.E. Low. 1981. Population fluctuation and range community use of red kangaroos in central Australia. *J. Appl. Ecol.* 18: 27-36.

Lumholtz, C. 1889. *Among cannibals: An account of four years' travels in Australia and of camp life with the Aborigines of Queensland.* London: John Murray.

Main, A.R., and M. Yadav. 1971. Conservation of macropods in reserves in Western Australia. *Biol. Conserv.* 3: 123-33.

Marlow, B.J. 1958. A survey of the marsupials of New South Wales. *CSIRO Wildl. Res.* 3: 71-114.

Martin, J.H.D. 1975. A list of mammals from Stradbroke Island. *Proc. R. Soc. Qd* 86: 73-76.

Martin, J.H.D., and Kirkpatrick, T.H. 1971. The mitotic chromosomes of a macropod hybrid. *Qd J. Agric. Anim. Sci.* 28: 287-91.

May, O.M., ed. 1982. *Queensland Year Book 1982.* Brisbane: Australian Bureau of Statistics.

Maynes, G.M. 1982. A new species of rock wallaby, *Petrogale persephone* (Marsupialia: Macropodidae) from Proserpine, central Queensland. *Aust. Mammal.* 5: 47-58.

McCann, J.C. 1975. Agriculture, forestry and wildlife in the Upper Clarence Region of NSW with particular references to macropods and the edge effect. In *Agriculture, forestry and wildlife: Conflict or co-existence?* ed. P.J. Jarman, 33-46. Armidale: University of New England.

McEvoy, J.S. 1970. Red-necked wallaby in Queensland. *Qd Agric. J.* 96: 114-16.

_____. 1979. The taxonomic status of the red Stradbroke wallaby. *Mammalia* 43: 581-83.

McEvoy, J.S., and T.H. Kirkpatrick. 1971. Mammals and birds of Booringa Shire, Queensland. *Qd J. Agric. Anim. Sci.* 28: 167-78.

McEvoy, J.S., K.R. McDonald, and A.K. Searle. 1979. Mammals, birds, reptiles and amphibians of the Kilcoy Shire, Queensland. *Qd J. Agric. Anim. Sci.* 36: 167-80.

Merchant, J.C. 1976. Breeding biology of the agile wallaby, *Macropus agilis* (Gould) (Marsupialia: Macropodidae) in captivity. *Aust. Wildl. Res.* 3: 93-103.

Moore, D.R. 1979. *Islanders and Aborigines at Cape York: An ethnographic reconstruction based on the 1848–1850 Rattlesnake journals of O.W. Brierley and information he obtained from Barbara Thompson.* Canberra: Australian Institute of Aboriginal Studies.

Mulvaney, D.J. 1966. The prehistory of the Australian Aborigine. *Sci. Amer.* 214: 84-93.

Mykytowycz, R. 1963. Occurrence of bot-fly larvae *Tracheomyia macropi* Froggatt (Diptera: Oestridae) in wild red kangaroos, *Megaleia rufa* (Desmarest). *Proc. Linn. Soc. NSW* 88: 307-12.

Newsome, A.E. 1965. The abundance of red kangaroos, *Megaleia rufa* (Desmarest), in central Australia. *Aust. J. Zool.* 13: 269-87.

_____. 1971. The ecology of red kangaroos. *Aust. Zool.* 16: 32-50.

Newsome, A.E., J.C. Merchant, B.L. Bolton, and M.L. Dudzinski. 1977. Sexual dimorphism in molar progression and eruption in the agile wallaby. *Aust. Wildl. Res.* 4: 1-5.

New South Wales Department of Mines. 1892. Annual report of Stock and Brands branch, 1889–92. Appendix F2. Sydney: Government Printer.

Noy-Meir, I. 1973. Desert ecosystmes: Environment and producers. *Ann. Rev. Ecology and System.* 4: 25-51.

Poole, W.E. 1973. A study of breeding in grey kangaroos *Macropus giganteus* and *Macropus fuliginosus* in central New South Wales. *Aust. J. Zool.* 21: 183-212.

_____. 1975. Reproduction in the two species of grey kangaroos *Macropus giganteus* and *Macropus fuliginosus.* Part two. Gestation, parturition, pouch life. *Aust. J. Zool.* 23: 333-54.

_____. 1979. The status of Australian Macropodidae. In *The status of endangered Australian wildlife,* ed. M.J. Tyler, 13-26. Adelaide: Royal Zoological Society of South Australia.

_____. 1980. Multivariate analysis of skull morphometrics from the two species of grey kangaroos *Macropus giganteus* and *Macropus fuliginosus. Aust. J. Zool.* 28: 591-606.

_____. 1982. *Macropus giganteus. Mammalian Species* 187: 1-8.

_____. 1983. Breeding in the grey kangaroo, *Macropus giganteus,* from widespread locations in eastern Australia. *Aust. Wildl. Res.* 10: 453-66.

Poole, W.E., S.M. Carpenter, and J.T. Wood. 1982. Growth of grey kangaroos and the reliability of age determination from body measurements. 1. The eastern grey kangaroo, *Macropus giganteus. Aust. Wildl. Res.* 9: 9-20.

Poole, W.E., and P.C. Catling. 1974. Reproduction in the two species of grey kangaroos *Macropus giganteus* and *Macropus fuliginosus.* Part one. Sexual maturity and oestrus. *Aust. J. Zool.* 22: 277-302.

Powell, J.G. 1973. Animal pests of the Herbert River district. *Cane Growers' Quart. Bull.* 36: 95-96.

Reading, F.W. 1947. Wallaby control. *Cane Growers' Quart. Bull.* 10: 170-72.

Ride, W.D.L. 1964. A review of Australian fossil marsupials. *J. R. Soc. W. Aust.* 47: 97-131.

_____. *1970. A guide to the native mammals of Australia.* Melbourne: Oxford University Press.

_____. 1971. On the fossil evidence of the evolution of the Macropodidae. *Aust. Zool.* 16: 6-16.

Robertson, G. 1981. Bridled nail-tailed wallaby *Onychogalea fraenata.* In *Kangaroos and other macropods of New South Wales,* ed. C. Haigh, 15-17. Sydney: New South Wales National Parks and Wildlife Service.

Roff, C. 1962. Kangaroo skins. *Qd Agric. J.* 88: 624.

Roff, C., and S. Jackson. 1971. The kangaroo industry in Queensland. Second supplement, 1966–1970. *Qd J. Agric. Anim. Sci.* 28: 159-65.

Roff, C., and T.H. Kirkpatrick. 1962. The kangaroo industry in Queensland. *Qd J. Agric. Sci.* 19: 385-401.

_____, and _____. 1966. The kangaroo industry in Queensland. First supplement, 1961–65. *Qd J. Agric. Anim. Sci.* 23: 467-73.

Roff, C., and L. Vaughan. 1977. The kangaroo industry in Queensland. Third supplement 1971–1975 and 1976. Unpub. information leaflet no. 3, Queensland National Parks and Wildlife Service, Brisbane.

Russell, E.M. 1969. Summer and winter observations of the behaviour of the euro *Macropus robustus* (Gould). *Aust. J. Zool.* 17: 655-64.

_____. 1974. Recent ecological studies on Australian marsupials. *Aust. Mammal.* 1: 189-211.

_____. 1974. The biology of kangaroos (Marsupialia-Macropodidae) *Mammal Rev.* 4: 1-59.

_____. 1979. The size and composition of groups in the red kangaroo *Macropus rufus. Aust. Wild. Res.* 6: 237-44.

Samuel, J.L. 1983. Jaw disease in macropod marsupials: Bacterial flora isolated from lesions and from the mouths of affected animals. *Vet. Microbiol.* 8: 373-87.

Sanson, G.D. 1978. The evolution and significance of mastication in the Macropodidae. *Aust. Mammal.* 2: 23-28.

Sattler, P.S., and R.J. Webster. 1984. The conservation status of brigalow (*Acacia harpophylla*) communities in Queensland. In: *The Brigalow Belt of Australia,* ed. A. Bailey, 149-60. Brisbane: R.Soc.Qd.

Scholz, B. 1980. The behaviour of the brush-tailed rock wallaby, *(Petrogale penicillata)*, in south-east Queensland. Unpub. report, Queensland Institute of Technology, Brisbane.

Sharman, G.B. 1959. Marsupial reproduction. In *Biogeography and ecology in Australia, monographiae biologicae 8,* ed. A. Keast, R.L. Crocker and C.S. Christian, 332-68. The Hague: W. Junk.

_____. 1961. The mitotic chromosomes of marsupials and their bearing on taxonomy and phylogeny. *Aust. J. Zool.* 9: 38-60.

_____. 1971. Management of kangaroos. *Aust. Zool.* 16: 73-82.

Sharman, G.B., J.H. Calaby, and W.E. Poole. 1967. Patterns of reproduction in female diprotodont marsupials. In *Comparative biology of reproduction in mammals: Symposium of the Zoological Society no. 15*, 205-32. London: Academic Press.

Sharman, G.B., C.E. Murtagh, P.M. Johnson, and C.M. Weaver. 1980. The chromosomes of a rat-kangaroo attributable to *Bettongia tropica* (Marsupialia: Macropodidae). *Aust. J. Zool.* 28: 59-63.

Shepherd, N.C. 1981. Predation of red kangaroos *Macropus rufus* by the dingo *Canis familiaris dingo* in northwestern New South Wales, Australia. *Aust. Wildl. Res.* 8: 255-62.

Short, J. 1982. Habitat requirements of the brush-tailed rock wallaby, *Petrogale penicillata*, in New South Wales. *Aust. Wildl. Res.* 9: 239-46.

Short, J., and G.C. Grigg. 1982. The abundance of kangaroos in suboptimal habitats: Wheat, intensive pastoral and mallee. *Aust. Wildl. Res.* 9: 221-27.

Smith, M.J., D.L. Hayman, and R.M. Hope. 1979. Observations on the chromosomes and reproductive systems of four macropodine interspecific hybrids (Marsupialia: Macropodidae). *Aust. J. Zool.* 27: 959-72.

Sparrowe, R.D., and H.M. Wight. 1975. Setting priorites for the Endangered Species Program. *Trans. N. Amer. Wildl. and Nat. Resources Conf.* 40: 142-56.

Speare, R., I. Beveridge, P.M. Johnson, and L.A. Corner. 1983. Parasites of the agile wallaby, *Macropus agilis* (Marsupialia). *Aust. Wildl. Res.* 10: 89-96.

Speare, R., P.M. Johnson, and A. Haffenden. 1982. Management of disease in captive macropods in north Queensland. In *The management of Australian mammals in captivity*, ed. D.D. Evans, 117-24. Healesville: Australian Mammal Society.

Spratt, D.M. 1972. Aspects of the life-history of *Dirofilaria roemeri* in naturally and experimentally infected kangaroos, wallaroos and wallabies. *Int. J. Parasit.* 2: 139-56.

Spratt, D.M., and G. Varughese. 1975. A taxonomic revision of filarioid nematodes from Australian marsupials. *Aust. J. Zool. Supplementary Series* 35: 1-99.

State Public Relations Bureau, Queensland. 1980. *Queensland Resources Atlas.* Second Edition. Brisbane: Premier's Department.

Stonehouse, B., and D. Gilmore, eds. 1977. *The Biology of Marsupials.* Baltimore: University Park Press.

Strahan, R., ed. 1980. Recommended common names of Australian mammals. Unpub. report, Australian Mammal Society, Sydney.

Strahan, R., ed. 1983. *The Australian Museum complete book of Australian mammals.* Sydney: Angus & Robertson.

Tate, G. H. H. 1948. Results of the Archbold expeditions. No. 59. Studies on the anatomy and phylogeny of the Macropodidae (Marsupialia). *Bull. Amer. Mus. Nat. Hist.* 91: 233-352.

———. 1952. Results of the Archbold expeditions. No. 66. Mammals of Cape York Peninsula, with notes on the occurrence of rainforest in Queensland. *Bull. Amer. Mus. Nat. Hist.* 98: 567-616.

Tate, R. 1879. The natural history of the country around the head of the Great Australian Bight. *Trans. & Proc. & Rep. Phil. Soc. Adelaide, S.A. for 1878–9,* 94-128.

Taylor, R. J. 1980. Distribution of feeding activity of the eastern grey kangaroo, *Macropus giganteus,* in coastal lowland of south-east Queensland. *Aust. Wildl. Res.* 7: 317-25.

———. 1982. Group size in the eastern grey kangaroo, *Macropus giganteus,* and the wallaroo, *Macropus robustus. Aust. Wildl. Res.* 9: 229-37.

———. 1983. The diet of the eastern grey kangaroo and wallaroo in areas of improved and native pasture in the New England Tablelands. *Aust. Wildl. Res.* 10: 203-11.

———. 1983. Association of social classes of the wallaroo, *Macropus robustus* (Marsupialia: Macropodidae). *Aust. Wildl. Res.* 10: 39-46.

— Thibodeau, F. R. 1983. Endangered species: Deciding which species to save. *Environ. Management* 7: 101-7.

Thomas, O. 1900. On a new kangaroo. *Proc. Zool. Soc. Lond.* 8: 112-13.

Tindale, N. B. 1959. Ecology of primitive Aboriginal man in Australia. In *Biogeography and ecology in Australia, monographiae biologicae 8,* ed. A. Keast, R. L. Crocker and C. S. Christian, 36-51. The Hague: W. Junk.

Tisdell, C. A. 1973. Kangaroos as an economic resource. Unpub. report, Economic Society of Australia and New Zealand (NSW branch), Sydney.

———. 1973. Kangaroos: The economic management of a common-property resource involving interdependence of production. Unpub. report, Sect. 24 (Economics), 45th ANZAAS Congress, Perth.

———. 1977. Wildlife: A national asset or pest to be managed? Unpub. research report no. 43 University of Newcastle, Newcastle.

Troughton, E. 1973. *Furred animals of Australia.* Sydney: Angus & Robertson.

Tyndale-Biscoe, H. 1973. *Life of Marsupials.* London: Edward Arnold.

Wakefield, N. A. 1967. Some taxonomic revision in the Australian marsupial genus *Bettongia* (Macropodidae) with description of a new species. *Vict. Nat.* 84: 8-22.

Walker, B. H. 1976. An assessment of the ecological basis of game ranching in southern African savannas. *Proc. Grassl. Soc. S. Afr.* 11: 125-30.

Waring, H. 1956. Marsupial studies in Western Australia. *Aust. J. Sci.* 18: 66-73.

Watson, J. A. L., C. Lendon, and B. S. Low. 1973. Termites in mulga lands. *Trop. Grassl.* 7: 121-26.

Whitley, G. P. 1970. *Early history of Australian zoology.* Sydney: Roy. Zool. Soc. NSW.

Wilson, G. 1959. Wallabies damaging cane in the Mulgrave area. *Cane Growers' Quart. Bull.* 23: 28.

Winter, J. W. 1970. How many roos can a roo-shooter shoot and still have roos to shoot. *Wildl. in Aust.* 7: 34-37.

———. 1981. Mammals of the Laura district. In *Early Man in North Queensland: Art and archaeology in the Laura area, terra australis 6,* ed. A. Rosenfeld, D. Horton and J. Winter, 45-49. Canberra: Australian National University Press.

Winter, J. W., F. C. Bell, L. I. Pahl, and R. G. Atherton. 1984. The specific habitats of selected northeastern Australian rainforest mammals. Unpub. World Wildlife Fund (Australia) report, Sydney.

Wood, J. T., W. E. Poole, and S. M. Carpenter. 1983. Validation of aging keys for eastern grey kangaroos, *Macropus giganteus. Aust. Wildl. Res.* 10: 213-17.

Wood Jones, F. 1924. *The mammals of South Australia. Part two. The bandicoots and the herbivorous marsupials.* Adelaide: Government Printer.

Woods, J. T. 1960. The genera *Proploopus* and *Hypsiprymnodon* and their position in the Macropodidae. *Mem. Qd Mus.* 13: 199-212.

Yourdan, E., and L. L. Constantine. 1979. *Structured design.* New York: Prentice Hall.

Ziegler, A. C. 1982. An ecological check-list of New Guinea recent mammals. In *Biogeography and ecology in Australia, monographiae biologicae 42,* ed. J. L. Gressitt, 863-94. The Hague: W. Junk.

Index